A HISTORY OF THE
38TH (WELSH)
AND 33RD
DIVISIONS

IN THE LAST FIVE WEEKS OF THE GREAT WAR

BY

MAJOR-GENERAL H. D. DEPREE

The Naval & Military Press Ltd

published in association with

FIREPOWER
The Royal Artillery Museum
Woolwich

Published by

The Naval & Military Press Ltd

Unit 10 Ridgewood Industrial Park,

Uckfield, East Sussex,

TN22 5QE England

Tel: +44 (0) 1825 749494

Fax: +44 (0) 1825 765701

www.naval-military-press.com

in association with

FIREPOWER
The Royal Artillery Museum, Woolwich

www.firepower.org.uk

Printed and bound by Antony Rowe Ltd, Eastbourne

A HISTORY OF THE 38TH (WELSH) AND 33RD DIVISIONS IN THE LAST FIVE WEEKS OF THE GREAT WAR

Maj Gen H. D. DePree

Bookseller: Naval and Military Press Ltd [*Publisher's blurb*]

Book Description: 2005 reprint of articles from the *Royal Artillery Journal*. 175 pages, with seven maps and 15 b/w plates The period covered by this account extends from the beginning of October 1918 and the Battle of the Beaurevoir Line to the Armistice, during which time the 38th Division was in V Corps (Lt Gen Shute) along with 17th, 21st and 33rd Divisions, in Gen Byng's Third Army. As the final advance proceeded the formation of the Corps for battle, movement and reliefs of divisions became almost a routine, apart for some special operation, and the divisions fought in pairs, the 33rd and 38th on the right and 17th and 21st on the left.

Thus this very much the story of the 33rd Division as well as the 38th. The latter was commanded by Maj-Gen T.A. Cubitt, the former by Maj-Gen R.J. Pinney. The author, a Gunner, commanded the 115th Brigade of the 38th Division throughout the period covered in this account and after the war became the Commandant of the Royal Military Academy, Woolwich, before retiring in 1931. The account is made up of a series of articles from the *RA Journal* (as the original pagination indicates), arranged in chapters, each dealing with one or more major battles - Beaurevoir, Cambrai, Selle, Sambre etc. The narrative is compiled from the war diaries and operation orders of the various formations concerned, and from the history of the 38th and 33rd Divisions and 33rd Divisional Artillery, supplemented by notes and experiences of officers who took part in the operations.

Unfortunately there is no contents list nor index to help the reader find his way around the narrative, though events are arranged in chronological order and chapters are headed so as to indicate the operations they describe. It is a very thorough and business-like account and makes a welcome expansion to the two divisional histories of which that of the 38th is a very short one while that of the 33rd consists in a large part of correspondence between commanders and of extracts from *The Times* and *Daily Mail*. This book has the added attraction in that it includes extracts from German regimental histories giving the enemy view of operations.

Afternote by RJMS 19 September 2012

Y Ddraig Goch September 1932, page 77 contains a letter from Maj-Gen DePree dated 28 August 1932 in which he writes:

> I have been writing a study of the daily doings of the 38th and 33rd Divisions during the last five weeks of the War for the *Royal Artillery Journal*. It is coming to an end with the last instalment in the issue of that *Journal* in October. The R.A. Institution propose publishing the whole seven chapters of about 160 pages in book form, paper bound, for 7/6, cloth bound, 5/-.
>
> They are only printing about 40 copies, but if there were any demand among the old Officers of the divisions for a copy, I am sure they would print more.

The regimental museum holds, I believe, at Mus. 1368 a copy of the first edition of this book which was given to Lieutenant-Colonel E.O. Skaife with a letter dated 1 March 1933.

Modern War. Troops digging in under a smoke barrage.

THE 38th (WELSH) DIVISION

IN THE LAST FIVE WEEKS OF THE GREAT WAR.

By Major-General H. D. DePree, c.b., c.m.g., d.s.o., *p.s.c.*

CHAPTER I.

A CERTAIN number of translations from the French have been published recently in the R.A. Journal, dealing with incidents in the Great War in which the French Army took part. It has been thought that it might be of interest to officers, especially to young officers who have joined since those stirring times, if some episodes in which the British Army took part could also be brought back to remembrance. It would seem to be desirable in any paper written for this Journal that these episodes should be described in a rather more professional way and looked at from a broader military point of view than is usually the case in the ordinary divisional or regimental histories. At the same time it is hoped that these studies can be made to serve a useful purpose; for dealing only with the action of small parts of the armies, they can go into much more detail than is possible in the official history, and might even to a certain extent collect material for it in advance. It is proposed in the following pages to give some description of the actions of the 38th Welsh Division under the command of Major-General T. Astley Cubitt, and of the 33rd Division, under Major-General Sir R. J. Pinney, which worked with it, from the time when having passed through the Hindenburg Line, in the last great offensive, they broke through the Masnieres—Beaurevoir line,—the last of the German positions deliberately prepared beforehand—and debouched into the open country beyond.

The subsequent fighting took place unhampered by any trenches except those which the Germans were able to dig as they fell back. The warfare was the most open that had been seen on the Western Front since the days of 1914, and it is a matter of opinion whether the struggles of really great armies whose flanks are difficult or impossible to turn can ever be of a more open nature than that witnessed at this time. What may be the answer to this question, and what effect the advance in mechanical science will have on it, can only be finally settled when it is put to the test in the next great war.

The narrative has been compiled from the war diaries and operation orders of the various formations concerned, and from the History of the 38th Division, written by Lt.-Col. J. E. Munby, the last G.S.O.1 of the Division immediately after the armistice, also from the History of the 33rd Division, and 33rd Divisional Artillery. Help has also been received from a number of officers who took part in the operations, and many of their notes and experiences have been embodied in it.

THE GENERAL SITUATION AT THE BEGINNING OF OCTOBER, 1918.

The story begins when the great British offensive of the autumn of 1918 had been going for close on two months. The offensive opened with the surprise attack of the Fourth Army under Sir Henry Rawlinson, on the 8th August, known as the battle of Amiens. It was continued by the Third Army under Sir Julian Byng on the river Ancre north of Albert on 21st August, in the battle of Bapaume, and from this time the advance progressed in continuous fighting, the Fourth Army on the right, and the First Army (Sir H. Horne) on the left joining in at the appropriate moment under Sir Douglas Haig's orders, the whole three British armies then driving forward in close combination till the resistance of the German armies collapsed at the armistice of 11th November.

The strategic plan which dominated these tremendous operations had been based on careful discussion between Marshal Foch and Field-Marshal Sir Douglas Haig, and had been settled at a conference on 23rd July. To quote the Commander-in-Chief's own words "It[1] was decided that after the disengagement of Amiens, if the nature of the success warranted it, that it should be more fully exploited before winter set in. It was subsequently arranged that attacks would be pressed in a converging direction towards Mezieres by the French and American armies, while at the same time the British armies, attacking towards the line St. Quentin—Cambrai, would strike directly at the vital communications running through Maubeuge to Hirson and Mezieres, by which alone the German

---

[1] Sir Douglas Haig's despatch, 21st December, 1918.

4

forces in Champagne could be maintained. (See Map I). As a secondary result of the advance of the British armies towards the all important railway centres about Maubeuge, the group of German armies in Flanders would find their communications threatened from the south, and any operations which it might be possible for the allies to undertake in that theatre at a later date would be powerfully assisted thereby. It was obviously of vital importance to the enemy to maintain intact his front opposite St. Quentin— Cambrai, and for this purpose he depended on the great fortified zone known as the Hindenburg Line."

"The brilliant success of the Amiens attack was the prelude to a great series of battles, in which, throughout three months of continuous fighting the British armies advanced without a check from one victory to another. The progress of this mighty conflict divides itself into certain stages, which themselves are grouped in two well defined phases :—

(a) During the first part of the struggle the enemy sought to defend himself in the belt of prepared positions and successive trench systems which extended from the spring-tide of the German advance, about Albert and Villers Bretonneux to the Hindenburg Line between St. Quentin and the Scarpe.

(b) Thereafter during the second period of the struggle our troops were operating in practically open country against an enemy who endeavoured to stand, on such semi-prepared or natural defensive positions as remained to him, for a period long enough to enable him to organize his retreat and avoid overwhelming disaster."

At the beginning of October this first phase was just coming to an end. The smashing of the Hindenburg Line had been begun in the opening days of September at its hinge just south of Arras, where it joined the famous switch, the Drocourt—Queant line. This great feat of arms known as the battle of the Scarpe was carried out by the left of the Third Army and the right of the First Army. The brilliant success gained here opened the way for further assaults on the Hindenburg Line in the neighbourhood of Havrincourt on September 12th. These and an attack by the Fourth and Third Armies on a seventeen mile front on September 18th, the whole known as the battle of Havrincourt and Epehy, brought the British armies within assaulting distance of the remainder of the Hindenburg Line, which from the village of Bantouzelle south to St. Quentin followed the line of the Scheldt or St. Quentin Canal, usually on its eastern bank.

The decision to attack this most formidable position was a very grave one for the British higher command. The losses of the British armies in the spring retirement, and in the sustained offensive of the autumn had been heavy. "Moreover, the political effects of an unsuccessful attack on a position so well known as the Hindenburg Line would be large, and would go far to revive the declining moral not only of the German army but of the German people." On the other hand the attacks of the Americans and French to the south and a proposed surprise attack near the Belgian coast depended to a peculiar degree upon the British attack in the centre. Sir Douglas Haig in the circumstances formed the opinion that the British attack was an essential part of the general scheme and that the moment was favourable. On a visit to England he had already reported on the 9th September that a change had taken place in the character of the war, and that a decision might be obtained in the very near future. He therefore decided to proceed with the attack which finally broke the Hindenburg Line, and which is known as the battle of Cambrai and the Hindenburg Line.

The battle of Cambrai, which on 5th October culminated in the capture of the remaining sectors of the Hindenburg Line, was commenced by the First and Third Armies on September 27th on the old battlefield of the previous autumn in the neighbourhood of Moeuvres and Flesquieres. The attack was completely successful and brought our troops on a broad front to the outskirts of Cambrai. On 29th September the Fourth Army after a prolonged and intense bombardment attacked the Hindenburg Line where it ran along the Scheldt Canal on a front of 12 miles northwards from St. Quentin, while the French First Army continued the line of attack to the south, and the right of the Third Army continued it to the north. On the right of the Fourth Army front the attack on the canal and Hindenburg Line to the south of Bellicourt was completely successful, but the attack of the II American Corps which formed part of that Army across the tunnel north of Bellicourt met with a qualified success till the situation was cleared up by the Australian Corps which was supporting the Americans. Still further to the left the Third Army after severe fighting reached the Hindenburg Line on the canal between Vend-huille and Marcoing. The situation now was that the Hindenburg Line had been pierced or turned everywhere except on the right of the Third Army between Vendhuille and Marcoing. It is here that it is proposed to take up the doings on the right of the Third Army in greater detail.

THE POSITION OF THE 38TH DIVISION IN THE ADVANCE.

As already stated the Third Army began the great advance on the Ancre on August 21st, and from that moment the 38th Division fought on the right of that Army, either in the front line or in close support. It formed part of V Corps (Lieut.-General C. D. Shute) which consisted of four divisions :—

17th Division	Maj.-Genl. P. R. Robertson
21st Division	Maj.-Genl. D. G. M. Campbell
33rd Division	Maj.-Genl. Sir R. J. Pinney
38th Division	Maj.-Genl. T. A. Cubitt.

Gradually the formation of the corps for battle and movement and the reliefs of divisions became almost a routine, except for some special operation such as the passage of the Scheldt Canal. The divisions fought in pairs, the 33rd and 38th on the right and the 17th and 21st on the left. One or other of each pair carried out the initial attack in each battle and went to as great a depth as it could without unduly exhausting itself, and on the final objective the second of the pair "leap-frogged" and carried on the advance, while the original attacker followed up in close support, and went up again into the front line when the second in its turn required a rest.

The artillery of both divisions of a pair supported the leading division throughout, under the orders of the C.R.A. of that division. The guns of the 38th Division were therefore continuously in action or moving forward into action throughout nearly three months, except for one period of 72 hours. Occasionally for some special operation army brigades of field artillery were added. In spite of broken roads and railways and long distances from railhead stupendous amounts of ammunition were fired, and every yard of the ground was covered with a creeping barrage to as great a depth as the artillery could reach after each prepared attack.

The machine guns of both divisions also assisted the leading division by firing a machine gun barrage in the original attack, and a portion of the guns of the leading division then went forward with its infantry, in close support, when the zone of barrages had been left behind. A few tanks supported each attack, but they were very few as by this time a comparatively small number remained, and the majority of those that were left were with the Fourth Army.

The 38th Division crossed the Ancre and made the initial attack of V Corps on August 21st taking Thiepval and Pozieres in the first two days. It also made the final attack on the edge of the Forest of Mormal on November 4th. Between those two dates its course lay right across the battlefields of The Somme in 1916 and Le Cateau in 1914, and many names made famous by those two battles occur again.

By September 28th, as already stated, the Fourth and Third Armies were up against the Hindenburg Line, and the 38th Division which was in support of the leading divisions of V Corps was moved into old trenches near the ruined villages of Sorel-le-Grand and Heudicourt. It remained here, ready to move at 2 hours notice, till 3rd October, when the success of the Fourth Army enabled it to be moved in a south easterly direction.

THE EVENTS LEADING UP TO THE ATTACK OF THE THIRD ARMY ON THE MASNIERES—BEAUREVOIR LINE.

The fighting on 29th September brought the right of the Third Army into contact with the Hindenburg Line on the Scheldt Canal. Its right rested at Ossus (S.19.central)[1] from which point V Corps held the line northward with the 33rd Division on its right, the 21st Division on its left, and the 17th and 38th Divisions in support; the latter standing ready to go through the gap made by the Fourth Army. Reconnaissance showed that all the bridges had been blown up, that the trenches on the far bank were strongly held, and all

---

[1] See Map. II. The method used for fixing points on a squared map was different during the war to that used now. It has been used in this paper, and is explained at the foot of Map II.

attempts by patrols to cross were made impossible by heavy machine gun fire. Attempts were made to repair the bridges, and form a cork floating bridge, but work was much hampered by snipers on the east bank sometimes not more than 30 yards away.

As stated above the 29th September was also the day on which the Fourth Army began its attack on the Hindenburg Line. The general plan for the attack was that on the left of the Fourth Army the II American Corps should attack the Hindenburg Line across the Bellicourt Canal Tunnel, and having taken it should turn north and south to clear that line, thus facilitating the passage of the canal to the north by the Third Army. The Australian Corps were then to leap-frog and go on to take the Masnieres—Beaurevoir line. As it turned out the II American Corps and III Corps, who held a small front between the Americans and the Third Army made no progress on the 29th. Large numbers of American troops disappeared into the mazes of the Hindenburg system, but the Germans still held the outposts of the Line. The Australians therefore, instead of leap-frogging and going forward, were constrained to spend the next few days in heavy fighting to capture the deep defences of the Line. The work was complicated by the fact that there might be parties of Americans holding out here and there, which induced reluctance as regards putting down barrages, and its accomplishment was one of the finest feats of arms in the war. It was not till October 1st that the 3rd Australian Division succeeded in capturing the village of Bony over the middle of the tunnel, and the main Hindenburg Line.

On the night of September 30th the XIII Corps relieved[1] III Corps on the left of the Fourth Army, and on the night of October 1st the 50th Division of that Corps relieved the 3rd Australian Division in front of Gouy and Le Catelet. It was on the progress of the 50th Division therefore, that the advance of the Third Army across the canal now depended.

The attack of the Fourth Army was resumed on October 3rd, and Gouy and Le Catelet[2] were cleared by the 50th Division while further to the south the continuation of the Masnieres—Beaurevoir line was taken as far north as Prospect Hill which lies a mile

---

[1] The Story of the Fourth Army in the Battles of the Hundred Days.

[2] Le Catelet and Gouy are large twin villages about 3,000 yards E.S.E. of Vendhuille. (Map II).

Section of a trench which formed part of the main Hindenburg Line near BONY.

north west of Beaurevoir.[1] The attack was continued on the 4th October and the 50th Division captured La Pannerie South, and Hargival Farm lying to the south west of it on the canal. It established its line through those places and along the northern slopes of Prospect Hill pending the arrival of the 38th Division which was already on the move to take over from it.

As previously stated[2] the 38th Division had been held ready near Sorel-le-Grand since September 28th prepared for three different lines of action, that is either to relieve the American troops and continue their northward advance, or to relieve the troops of XIII Corps at Vendhuille, or to assist in a frontal attack against the Hindenburg Line. The first course was the one which really formed part of the general plan, the others being alternatives, and it was carried out in spirit, though the troops actually relieved were the 50th Division, not the Americans, owing to the check which the latter had sustained.

3rd October.

As soon as the attack of the 50th Division on Gouy and Le Catelet on October 3rd was seen to be going well, the Third Army ordered V Corps to move the 38th Division to the neighbourhood of Bony, which lies in the Hindenburg Line above the canal tunnel (2,500 yards south west of Le Catelet). This necessitated a flank march across the enemy's front over ground parts of which the enemy could see, and the whole of which was under continual shell-fire and infested by gas.

4th October.

The move was carried out in two bounds and during the second on October 4th the 115th Brigade (Brig.-Genl. H. D. De Pree) with the 151st Field Company, R.E., and "A" Company, Machine Gun Battalion, reached Bony. During this march the signs of the previous day's fighting were very apparent. The American dead in great numbers were being laid out in long lines for burial, and on all sides were disabled British tanks which had been destroyed by artillery fire, or had been caught in a mine field. That night the 115th Brigade starting from Bony relieved the 50th

---

[1] Beaurevoir lies about 3,200 yards south of Villers Outreaux.
[2] "History of the 38th Welsh Division".

Division on the high ground north of Le Catelet about La Pannerie South, facing north. The relief was a difficult one, for the situation was complicated and the troops had difficulty in finding their way. It will be seen that the move was carried out from the south, while the general front of the British Armies faced east, and the enemy were both to the north and east.

5th October.

The Great Hindenburg Line had thus been turned so far as V Corps was concerned, and on the morning of October 5th patrols of the 33rd Division were able to cross the canal in the neighbourhood of Honnecourt, and were soon followed by the leading troops. It was found that the enemy was beginning to withdraw slowly to the Masnieres—Beaurevoir line, and the 33rd Division occupied the Hindenburg Line from Richmond Quarry northwards while the 21st Division occupied it on their left. At the same time the 38th Division were ordered to swing eastwards and advance on Aubencheul, Villers Outreaux and Mortho Wood. The 124th Field Company, R.E., and the Glamorgan Pioneers of the 38th Division were at once employed to bridge the canal at Ossus and they worked with such a will that the whole of the divisional artillery, which had been supporting the 33rd Division, the 33rd Divisional Artillery and the 34th Army Brigade, R.F.A., were got across and into action on the far side, ready to support the advance of the 38th Division.

In order to carry out its instructions the 38th Division ordered[1] up the 113th Brigade (Brig.-Genl. H. E. apRhys Pryce) on the left of the 115th Brigade, and directed it on Mortho Wood whilst the 115th Brigade was directed on Villers Outreaux. At the same time the 114th Brigade (Brig.-Genl. T. Rose Price) was ordered into the Hindenburg Line east of Ossus.

The 115th Brigade had taken over from the 50th Division the previous night on a two battalion front with the 10th S. Wales Borderers on the right and the 17th Royal Welsh Fusiliers on the left. The brigade had been facing north, and now had to advance eastward. It did so with these two battalions in front supported by the 2nd Royal Welsh Fusiliers. The two battalions

---

[1] 38th Division Order, No. 237.

first exploited to the north (towards La Pannerie North and Basket Wood) by means of strong battle patrols, and then wheeled towards the east. The 10th South Wales Borderers on the right advanced with "C" and "D" companies in front and "B" and "D" in support. Little opposition was encountered till a point 300 yards south east of Aubencheul was reached. Here the enemy used artillery and machine guns freely, so a halt was made, and the ground gained was consolidated. The 17th Royal Welsh Fusiliers on the left advanced in the same way to a position with its leading troops immediately south of Aubencheul, and consolidated there.

The 113th Brigade moved through Bony with the 14th Royal Welsh Fusiliers as advanced-guard supported by the 13th Royal Welsh Fusiliers. The Le Catelet—Nauroy trench line in S.12 was occupied without opposition, but an advance from this was met by very heavy fire from Mortho Wood. Both battalions therefore took up a position in this line with the 13th Royal Welsh Fusiliers on the left and the 16th Royal Welsh Fusiliers in support near Basket Wood. During the night therefore the 38th Division held a line from the Railway in S.30.b., west of Aubencheul to Bonabus Farm, S.11.b., where it was in touch with the 21st Division. The 33rd Division had thus been squeezed out, and the front line of V Corps was held by 38th and 21st Divisions.

6th October.

Active patrolling was carried out during the night,[1] and as a result the 17th Royal Welsh Fusiliers occupied Aubencheul, inflicting considerable casualties on the enemy. The 10th South Wales Borderers were therefore able to push forward again in the morning and sent two platoons into the sunken road south east of Aubeucheul and the quarry east of the village. The battalion was now in touch with the 50th Division on the right and 17th Royal Welsh Fusiliers on the left; and patrolling showed that the Masnieres—Beaurevoir line was very strongly held and wired, and attempts to penetrate it failed. The 2nd Royal Welsh Fusiliers moved at 8.30 a.m. from Le Catelet to trenches south of Basket Wood. On the 113th Brigade front patrols of the 14th Royal Welsh Fusiliers still found Mortho Wood strongly held, and were unable to force their way through it.

---

[1] War Diary, 10th South Wales Borderers.

During the night of the 5th/6th the 38th Divisional Artillery (Brig.-Genl. T. E. Topping, a distinguished Territorial Army officer) moved up to the support of the Division, crossing by the bridge made by the divisional engineers and pioneers at Ossus. The approach to the bridge was congested, and the scene at the crossing was a most animated one, all sorts of troops vieing with each other to cross as quickly as possible. The artillery brigades moved, the 122nd Brigade, R.F.A., to positions south of Basket Wood and the 121st Brigade to positions both south and north of it, with wagon lines about 2000 yards west of the guns, and 1000 yards east of the canal. The 33rd Divisional Artillery, consisting of the 156th and 162nd Brigades, R.F.A., the 34th Army Brigade and the 13th Brigade, R.G.A., were also placed under General Topping's orders. Reports of the exact location of our front line were hard to obtain, but the artillery at once commenced harassing fire on the Masnieres—Beaurevoir line.

By the morning of October 6th it was evident that the enemy intended to make a stand in the above line. At 11.30 a.m. therefore V Corps issued a preliminary order for a concerted attack on it on October 8th in conjunction with the corps on either flank, in the event of the line not having been gained before then.[1] The task allotted to the 38th Division was to pierce the line in two places, between the mill in T.20 and the sugar factory in T.14 and also at the salient in T.7.d., with a view to enveloping Villers Outreaux. The 21st Division was to pierce it further north with Angles Chateau, T.2.b., as its first objective. The more extended objectives of the two divisions were to be Malincourt and Walincourt respectively. Six tanks were to be allotted to each front line division.

The Attack of the 38th Division on the Masnieres—Beaurevoir Line.

7th October.

Active patrolling was carried out during the night of 6th/7th and as a result the 10th South Wales Borderers on the right reported "the enemy's position as being strongly held by machine guns and fortified by all means used in modern warfare, the barbed

---

[1] V Corps G 375.

Wire in the Masnieres—Beaurevoir System.

wire being very conspicuous in its numerous belts, and of a thickness not hitherto encountered in such a quantity". The 17th Royal Welsh Fusiliers sent in very similar reports. The line had been deliberately prepared as a part of the Hindenburg system, and was enormously strong, consisting of concrete shelters or dug outs fifty or a hundred yards apart with very strong wire in front of them. The trench had not been dug except hastily in places where it was actually required.

The Royal Munster Fusiliers of the 50th Division attacked Villers Farm at dawn but failed to take it.

On the front of the 113th Brigade the 14th Royal Welsh Fusiliers at last managed to push patrols through Mortho Wood and established posts in the sunken road on the east side of it. No other movements took place during the early part of the day, but preparations for the attack next day were energetically pushed forward.

The divisional commander had attended a conference at V Corps H.Q. at 19.15 hours on 6th October on the forthcoming operations, and at 05.15 on 7th October a warning order was issued by 38th Division. This was amplified at a conference which the divisional commander held at 115th Brigade H.Q. in the afternoon after he had seen the corps commander. This was attended by infantry brigadiers, the C.R.A., and the machine gun battalion commander. The divisional commander had previously also attended a conference of the neighbouring corps (XIII) at 10.00 hours. The final divisional order[1] was issued at 22.40 hours in confirmation of the conference. The objectives of the brigades were given as follows :—

115th Brigade. The main road from Marliches Farm along the north east edge of Villers Outreaux to the light railway in T.3.d.

113th Brigade. The sunken road in T.3.

114th Brigade. The high ground east of Malincourt U.1. to the south edge of Mill Wood O.31 to N.30., and to exploit the success further to the east.

The final objective of the 66th Division which was to attack on the right was given as Serain (3500 yards south east of Malincourt),

---

[1] 38th (Welsh) Division Order, No. 239.

and of the 21st Division on the left as Mill Wood and Walincourt. The area beyond the 66th Division objective was to be exploited by cavalry.

The forming up places for brigades were given, and the plan of the 115th Brigade was modified from that given in V Corps order G.375, in that its right battalion was ordered to form up in the part of the Masnieres Beaurevoir line which had already been taken by the 50th Division, so as to turn this line. The 114th Brigade was to form up on the objective of the first attack when that had been taken.

All the attacks were to be made under a creeping barrage, moving generally at the rate of 100 yards in 5 minutes. The action of the machine guns was to be as follows: 2 Coys., 33rd M.G. Bn., and "C" Coy., 38th M.G. Bn., to assist in the barrage for the initial attack. "A" and "B" Coys., 38th M.G. Bn., to accompany 115th and 113th Brigades to the first objective to support the attack of the 114th Brigade. "C" and "D" Coys. to accompany 114th Brigade to assist it in consolidating.

As regards tanks :—

(a) 2 tanks were to assist in mopping up the fortified area T.2.c. and d.

(b) 2 tanks to enter Villers Outreaux at daybreak.

(c) 4 tanks including (a) to accompany the reserve battalion, 114th Brigade, to mop up Malincourt Wood and village.

(d) 2 tanks to join (b) after dawn.

The villages were not to be attacked by leading battalions, but to be mopped up by battalions in brigade reserve, in co-operation with tanks.

The actual orders issued by the divisional artillery and the 115th and 113th Brigades on receipt of the above are given in Appendix I. Supplementary orders of V Corps[1] in continuation of their G.375 giving zero hours, and further instructions were issued in the course of the afternoon. These laid down that the zero for the first attack was to be 01.00 on 8th October, and the zero for the second attack (starting from the eastern side of Villers Outreaux) was to be 05.15.

---

[1] G 510/7.

The zero hour for the Fourth Army and the remainder of the Third Army was fixed for 04.30. The infantry brigade commanders held conferences with their subordinates about 16.00 hours on the conclusion of the divisional conference. It was therefore late before the units got their final orders. The divisional artillery spent the day in doing what they could to cut the enemy's wire, but it was an altogether impossible task to deal with such a mass of wire in a single day. Moreover the corps heavy artillery had been unable to get forward in time, and was therefore unable to do much. Individual batteries were able to help to some extent. For instance the officer commanding C/122 Battery which was supporting the 17th Royal Welsh Fusiliers was asked by Lieut.-Colonel R. L. Beasley the officer commanding the battalion to do what he could to cut wire at the place they proposed to attack. He managed to cut two narrow lanes in the visible wire, but could not manage the second line as it was hidden behind a slight rise. It is improbable that more than this was accomplished on the front of any of the attacking battalions, and the division was faced with a very difficult if not impossible task if the enemy held his ground, and kept alert through the night. The best chance of success would have been to attack with the assistance of tanks to overcome the wire, but the attack was ordered for 1 a.m., and in those days tanks were unable to operate by night. It was therefore necessary to attack without them and hope that the enemy might be caught napping.

As will be seen from the orders of the 115th Brigade[1] the plan for that brigade was for the 10th South Wales Borderers on the right to form up in T.26.b. and T.20.d. to the east of the Masnieres—Beaurevoir line, which in that neighbourhood was in the possession of the 50th Division, and the 17th Royal Welsh Fusiliers to form up in T.13.b. facing north east. They were to advance at 01.00 hours each with its own separate barrage, one on each side of Villers Outreaux. The village itself was to be left till dawn, when three companies of the 2nd Royal Welsh Fusiliers were to advance in co-operation with four tanks, and were to mop it up.

---

[1] See Appendix I.

8th October.

There was no difficulty as regards the assembly of the 17th Royal Welsh Fusiliers as they were not required to go outside the ground which they were holding; but it was very different with the 10th South Wales Borderers. It was necessary for them to be pulled out of the line and side-step to the right. After the divisional conference at 115th Brigade H.Q., Major C. A. Bowen commanding 10th South Wales Borderers was summoned there for a conference of the battalion commanders of the brigade at 4 p.m. There he received his instructions and was told to bring his battalion out of the line at dark, and to pick up guides from the 50th Division at a certain point to lead him to his assembly place. As it turned out these guides never arrived, but Major Bowen, acting on his instructions, on his return to his unit had at once sent men of his own during the short amount of daylight that remained to reconnoitre the assembly position. These men when the time came led the battalion to the assembly position, in T.2.o.b. The battalion was delayed in its march by getting mixed up in a relief of the 50th Division and only arrived just before zero hour. Major Bowen was informed by a staff officer that there was no wire; but whether the Beaurevoir line was not in possession of the 50th Division as far north as was thought, or whether the 10th South Wales Borderers had failed to reach the place intended is not clear, and the fact remains that when it advanced to the attack it found very strong wire in front of it covered by machine guns.

It is very difficult to find out what actually occurred in the darkness at the junction of the two armies. The 1st K.O.Y.L.I. of the 50th Division also attacked, at 01.00 hours, presumably on the right of the 10th South Wales Borderers, with Villers Farm as its objective, and this was captured at 02.45. But in spite of this the 10th South Wales Borderers was unable to get forward till dawn. A possible explanation is that a pocket of the enemy were left in the Beaurevoir line on the left of the 1st K.O.Y.L.I., and held up the 10th South Wales Borderers for a time.

The 17th Royal Welsh Fusiliers on the left of the 115th Brigade advanced in the most gallant manner at zero (01.00 hours) to the storm of the Masnieres—Beaurevoir line which lay immediately in front of it. But unfortunately the enemy was on the alert and

One of many anti-tank and machine gun posts on the ridge in front of BEAUREVOIR.

the attack was repulsed with heavy loss. It was quite easy to follow the course of the attack next day. One company fought its way through the wire and its commander, Captain J. H. Lewis, lay dead just behind the last strand of wire at the head of many of his men. At another place a few brave men had fought their way right through the wire but had been killed just before they reached the trench. At another place a German who had dug himself a little pit in the wire lay dead in it surrounded by six or eight of our men, whom he had shot or bombed before he was killed himself. But these gallant efforts were of no avail and the survivors fell back sullenly to their starting off place and faced the enemy. There they were reorganized by their officers for a further attack. The battalion during the course of the day, mostly in this attack, lost 10 officers and 120 men, which meant the greater part of the officers and nearly half the men that went into battle.[1]

The 113th Brigade also assembled for the attack during the night. The 14th Royal Welsh Fusiliers which had led the advance on 5th October and had been in the line ever since remained in reserve. The 16th Royal Welsh Fusiliers on the right formed up west of the north and south road in S.12.b. and d. and then pushed up as near as possible to the road in T.7.central. The 13th Royal Welsh Fusiliers assembled just east of the western trench in T.1.c. The battalions advanced to the attack at 01.00 as ordered the 16th Royal Welsh Fusiliers with "A" and "B" companies in front and "C" and "D" in support, the 13th Royal Welsh Fusiliers with "A", "B" and "C" companies in front and "D" company in reserve. Strong wire and vigorous machine gun fire were met with in the centre of the attack from pockets of enemy in T.1.c., and the attack was held up. The 13th Royal Welsh Fusiliers[2] on the left thanks to the initiative of Captain Wynne Edwards, who during a personal reconnaissance the day before had found two gaps in the enemy's wire, got through in one spot.

Further to the left on the front of the 21st Division no success is reported in the divisional war diary till 09.10 hours, when the 1st objective is reported captured, but a breach must have been

[1] At this time battalions left a very large "battle surplus" in camp, and only took into the fight about 300 men.

[2] Divisional History.

made in the enemy's line at zero, as a battalion commander of
that division informed the writer, that he had noticed during
the day that the German wire did not stretch across a road leading
through the German line in his area. He had therefore quietly
formed his battalion in fours on the road, and had successfully
doubled them through the gap at zero. This probably accounts
for the fact that at 04.27 Angles Chateau was reported to the 13th
Royal Welsh Fusiliers as being in our hands.

Broadly speaking however the fact remains that no advance
was made during darkness on the V Corps front and the attacks
made at 01.00 had been repulsed with severe loss. It would seem
therefore that the decision to attack without tanks in the middle
of night ahead of the neighbouring corps was an unfortunate one.
The almost universal lesson of the war had been that partial and
isolated attacks had seldom been successful and had always been
costly. In this case the fact of very strong uncut wire was an additional reason for deferring the attack till tanks could co-operate.
If any difference were to be made in the hour of the attack of
V Corps as compared with neighbouring formations it would seem-
ingly have been better to defer it till the attack of the Fourth Army
which was already in possession of the Beaurevoir line had had time
to make its effect felt. The trouble caused by the early attack
of V Corps did not end here,[1] as it drew a heavy retaliation of
artillery fire, which came down on the 198th and South African
Brigades of the Fourth Army, which were assembling immediately
on its right, and inflicted severe casualties on them.

Although the attack had failed for the moment, there was
no reason to believe that the check would be a lasting one. The
great attack of the Fourth and Third Armies was to be launched
at 04.30 hours, and at that time the few tanks which had been
allotted to the division were to join in. When the time came
these gave the required impetus in the centre, on the front of the
17th Royal Welsh Fusiliers, which led on to success.

It was quite easy to see what happened from the combined
headquarters of the 115th and 113th Brigades, which had been
established close together for purposes of intercommunication[2] on

---

[1] Story of the Fourth Army.
[2] For the same reason the H.Q. of the 122nd Brigade R.F.A. (Lt.-Col. R. C. Williams)
which was affiliated to the 115th Brigade for the first operation was also established close by.

the hill south west of La Pannerie South in S.28.d. in a concrete
German observation and signal station. It was a very strong
place, a retrenchment of the Hindenburg Line, and though it had
been subject to a severe bombardment of the British heavy artillery
at the end of September and the beginning of October, the concrete shelters had not suffered at all.   The H.Q. of the 115th
Brigade had been established there on October 5th, here the extent
to which the enemy had suffered was very apparent, and it was clear
that he had had a bad time during his retreat.   Dead men and
horses and broken down vehicles were all over the place.   The
Prussian Guard had evidently been used for the defence of this
part of the line as many of them were identified.

From this place a fine view could be obtained over both the
British and German fronts, and it looked straight up to the village
of Villers Outreaux, which was the main object of the first attack.
The first attack at 01.00 was a splendid sight, with the hundreds of
flashes of the British guns firing as hard as they could in every
hollow on the one side, and the flashes of the bursting shells and
the innumerable coloured lights which the Germans sent up on the
other.   The main attack in the half light of dawn at 04.30 was an
even grander sight, with the great barrage opening on either flank as
far as the eye could reach.   The Fourth Army were putting down a
smoke barrage, and the bursting of the shells filled with phos-
phorous showed up like fireworks against the great rolling clouds
of white smoke.   At this moment three of the four tanks allotted
to the 115th Brigade appeared between Aubencheul and Villers
Outreaux, and at once went into the wire and began working up
and down the trenches and along the northern edge of Villers
Outreaux.   It was easy to see their 6 pdr. guns spitting fire at the
German machine guns in the half light.   Their arrival had an
immediate effect.   The 2nd Royal Welsh Fusiliers had been
detailed in orders to send one company to mop up the Beaurevoir
line immediately it had been taken by the 17th Royal Welsh
Fusiliers, and to hold the other three companies in readiness to
co-operate with the tanks in mopping up Villers Outreaux.   Lieut.-
Col. C. C. Norman, commanding the 2nd Royal Welsh Fusiliers,
seeing that the front line had not been taken by the 17th Royal
Welsh Fusiliers at once issued fresh orders to his battalion to

5

advance with the tanks. He formed up "A" and "B" companies for the attack, and ordered "B" company[1] to move with the tanks and break through the enemy's trench line at all costs. "B" company under Captain Kirby succeeded in breaking through first and was quickly followed by "C" company. The 17th Royal Welsh Fusiliers led by Lieut.-Col. Beasley in person formed on their left and advanced also.[2] Their attack was materially assisted by the enterprise of Major A. D. C. Clarke, commanding C/122nd Battery, who as already stated had done good work cutting wire on October 7th, and who while awaiting the order to move his battery forward had come up into the front line and brought a telephone with him. From here he not only reported the situation, but directed the fire of his battery into the enemy's trench and thus materially assisted the advance of "B" company, 2nd Royal Welsh Fusiliers.[3] This

---

[1] History of the 38th Division.

[2] Brigadier C. C. Norman gives the following account of the incident from his own point of view :—

"2nd Royal Welsh Fusiliers arrived according to plan in front of the village just as dawn was breaking, expecting to find 10th South Wales Borderers and 17th Royal Welsh Fusiliers on the flanks of Villers Outreaux and tanks waiting to help them mop it up. Instead they were met by a hail of machine gun fire, they gradually learnt that the night attack had completely failed and they could see no signs of the promised tanks. The prospect was gloomy indeed. It looked as though we must wait for hours if not for days, hiding behind cover and waiting for a regular attack to be staged. Then suddenly the tanks appeared—two of them. Their approach hadn't been noticed—there was even a lull in the machine gun firing at the moment of their arrival. 2nd Royal Welsh Fusiliers were fortunately well concentrated; it was easy to get orders to company commanders. It seemed worth while to have a try, anyhow, to get through with the help of the tanks at the S.W. corner of the village, where, if a company could maintain itself amongst the buildings there, it would be easy to pass the other companies through and turn the line. It all came off. The result was really dramatic 'C' Company (I think) on reaching the south edge of the village found Germans streaming back across the open. Beasley came up on the left and in almost less time than it takes to write, the job was done. I could hardly believe my eyes".

[3] It will be interesting to give here the narrative by Major Clarke of the doings of his battery as combined with Brigadier Norman's account; it gives a close and graphic picture of a modern battle.
"On the evening of 6th October it was decided to place one battery (C/122) at the disposal of the battalion commander of the left battalion which held a front with its right on the Aubencheul—Villers Outreaux road

and its left some six hundred yards further north. A suitable position giving a range to the enemy front line of about 1800 yards was selected and occupied, communication was established with the battalion commander and a suitable O.P. reconnoitred and linked up with the battery. C/122 was requested to take on wire cutting as energetically as possible during the only available day (October 7th) before the attack.

Though an O.P. was established in the outpost line from which excellent observation was obtainable on the wire, and though the range was a most useful one for wire cutting, it was impossible in so short a time to make any great impression on the wire especially in view of the fact that 106 fuzes were then very much in demand and rather difficult to obtain at short notice. At the end of the day several gaps had been cut and the location of these submitted to the battalion commander. As, however, his plans had been considerably altered during the day, necessitating some change of direction, the gaps cut were not of much value. (It will be remembered that Lt.-Col. Beasley stated that the battery was unable through lack of observation to cut gaps in the support line wire). But from dusk to 10.30 p.m. when patrols were going out, the guns of the battery were switched on to the new front to be attacked in an attempt to do some damage to the wire, but any observation was quite out of the question.

At 01.00 on the 8th the attack was launched under cover of a barrage. The divisional artillery had been warned that, if the attack proved a success, an advance would be made, and the area of the new battery positions had been pointed out; teams were to be brought up to the gun positions by dawn and every preparation made for closely following up the enemy. During the progress of the attack, owing to the pitch darkness of the night, and to the fact that communications generally had failed, it was impossible to gather what the situation was, but when shortly before dawn orders were received to stand fast it became obvious that the expected progress had not been made.

Soon afterwards O.C. C/122 was requested by O.C. 122 Brigade, R.F.A. to proceed to the line and endeavour to get in touch with the situation. Taking with him two telephonists, and tracking the wire as they went, the B.C. made straight for the O.P. which he had used the previous day, the battalion and company H.Q. of the battalion he had covered being also along his route prior to the attack. The telephone line was badly cut up by shell fire, especially so as the O.P. was approached, and though the distance traversed was scarcely a mile much time was spent in repairing the numerous breaks.

On arrival in the O.P. it was found that no progress had been made by the battalion, if anything a slight withdrawal had been made since the previous day. During wire-cutting operations on that day the artillery O.P. had been established in the outpost line some 150 yards north of Aubencheul, the main front line with company H.Q. was disposed along a sunken road 150 yards in rear of the outpost line, and the supporting company was entrenched about 200 yards in rear of the sunken road. On his arrival on the morning of the battle, the B.C. found the support company "non est", having been absorbed during the course of the battle, the outpost line appeared to have been withdrawn to the sunken road, while such of the troops as were not casualties were endeavouring to reorganize in a shallow fold of the ground about 300 yards short of the sunken road.

It was apparent that they had been enveloped and heavily punished by annihilating fire from the enemy's artillery, while casualties from hostile machine guns had been numerous, and though very gallant efforts had been made to get forward without success, it was apparent that such officers and men as remained had been very badly shaken by the ordeal through which they had passed. By this time the hostile artillery fire had slackened but a murderous machine gun fire was being maintained over the whole area.

As observation over the required area was difficult to obtain from anywhere else owing to the unsuitability of the ground, the B.C. decided to endeavour to reach and make use of the O.P. he had used on the previous day, and though to escape machine gun fire it was necessary to crawl the last 100 yards on his stomach, the place was eventually reached and an excellent view of the whole situation obtained, a certain amount of cover from machine gun fire being obtained from a narrow trench dug on the previous day.

It at once became evident that the enemy considered himself master of the situation. Along the entire length of the trench he was exposing himself continuously, while machine guns could be observed firing from many places. Having established communication with his battery, the B.C. at once directed the fire of his guns on the whole trench. Having been wire-cutting the previous day approximately on the same sector, this was easily and quickly accomplished and some excellent shooting followed (as was afterwards found with good results). Special attention was paid to two concrete block-houses sited fairly close together, from which machine gun fire was being directed and the two guns of one section were severally registered on these two points. Having distributed his own guns along this trench and ordered a suitable rate of fire to cope with the situation, the B.C. next got into communication with two artillery brigade H.Q's and reported the situation fully. As a result of this a heavy "crash" was put down along the full extent of the trench, and a withering fire maintained.

Within a short time after this a white flag was observed being waved on a long stick from behind one of the concrete block-houses referred to above; thinking this to be only one of many ruses adopted by the enemy, no notice was taken of this beyond continued observation and reporting to brigade, in fact a greater volume of fire was directed against the spot whenever the flag appeared, it being considered highly improbable that any inmates were really desirous of giving themselves up, after making so firm a stand with so much success. However, as the waving of the flag continued in spite of the volume of our fire, while hostile machine gun fire had practically ceased, the infantry were informed, and a strong patrol was sent out to investigate the situation, protection from any attempts at bad faith being insured by the maintenance of artillery fire until our men were within such a distance of the block houses as to cause our fire to be a danger. On the arrival of the patrol no less than about 90 prisoners came out from the two block-houses and gave themselves up.

The defence of the sector at once collapsed, troops were at once pushed forward and rapid progress made. The right flank of the division which had been held up by the failure of its left flank to get forward was able to continue the advance".—While undoubtedly there were several factors which caused the enemy's resistence suddenly to collapse, there can be no doubt that the prompt, timely and effective action of Major Clarke and his telephonists contributed materially towards it. His brigade commander Lt.-Col. R. C. Williams writes of him, that he, a temporary officer, was the best battery commander, regular or temporary, who served under his orders during the war.

company advanced straight forward, while "C" company turned to the right and cleared the way for the advance of the rest of the battalion. The initiative and energy of the battalion commanders on the spot in taking advantage of the advance of the tanks immediately put a new complexion on the situation. The enemy began surrendering or running away in all directions and their main line of defence was soon in British hands. "B" company of the 2nd Royal Welsh Fusiliers worked round east of the village and "A" company round the west, and all the companies co-operated with the tanks in mopping up the village. Methodical progress was then made by both battalions and the tanks to their final objective.

Assisted by the attack of the Fourth Army and the success in front of Villers Outreaux the 10th South Wales Borderers to the south got forward also. They had been left in considerable confusion by the events of the night, but they were reorganized into groups by the officers, and such parties as could be collected were led forward to the objective in S.16 where they dug themselves in under Major Monteith, the remainder being brought forward later in the day. The advance was not effected without considerable opposition,[1] but the objective of the 115th Brigade on either side

---

[1] During the course of the attack of the 10th South Wales Borderers, C.S.M. J. H. Williams, D.C.M., M.M., gained the Victoria Cross for a conspicuous act of bravery. It may be worth quoting the citation of the reward to show the nature of the fighting.

"During the attack on Villers Outreaux, when observing that his company was suffering heavy casualties from an enemy machine gun, he ordered a Lewis gunner to engage it, and went forward under heavy fire to the flank of the enemy post, which he rushed single handed, capturing 15 of the enemy. These prisoners realising C.S.M. Williams was alone turned on him and one of them gripped his rifle. He succeeded in breaking away and bayoneting five enemy, whereupon the remainder again surrendered. His gallant action and total disregard of personal danger was the means of enabling not only his own company but also those on the flanks to advance".—His arrangement of fire to cover the assault was admirable and in accordance with the best methods of minor tactics, but the gallantry of the assaulting party had to compensate for its smallness!

of the eastern end of Villers Outreaux was gained during the course
of the morning.

As already stated the original attack of the 113th Brigade was
little more successful than that of the 115th Brigade. The 16th
Royal Welsh Fusiliers on the right lost 1 officer and 34 other ranks
killed, 4 other ranks missing, 7 officers and 112 other ranks wounded,
and made no real progress. It was not till daybreak that they and
the 13th Royal Welsh Fusiliers on the left were able to get forward
with the help of tanks. At this time the two battalions of the
114th Brigade who should have passed through on the final objective
got mixed up in the fight. In fact the war diary of the 16th Royal
Welsh Fusiliers reports that they leap-frogged at 04.00 hours.
There can be little doubt that the intervention of these two fresh
battalions gave an impetus to the attack on this part of the front
in the same way that the 2nd Royal Welsh Fusiliers did on the
front of the 115th Brigade. The supporting battalion of the 113th
Brigade, the 14th Royal Welsh Fusiliers, also became engaged, and
the whole line moved forward fighting heavily.

It will be as well now to trace the action of the 114th Brigade.[1]
Its battalions had occupied trenches in the Hindenburg Line in
S.27 and 21 during the 7th October, and they moved up to a staging
area in the Catelet—Nauroy line, west of Aubencheul by midnight,
the 13th Welsh on the right, 14th Welsh in the centre and 15th
Welsh on the left. At 02.00 hours they again moved forward
to try and reach assembly positions, which were fixed on the
assumption that the attack of the 115th and 113th Brigades would
be successful.

The assembly positions were to be as follows :—

    13th Welsh on the right the road in T.16.b.
    15th Welsh on the left the road in T.3.central.
    14th Welsh in support the road in T.2.d.

The first two were the final objectives of the two leading
brigades. A field artillery barrage, strengthened by heavy artillery
and machine guns behind it, was to fall at 08.00, and it was to
advance at 08.20 at 100 yards in 4 minutes. Meanwhile in order to
fire it the whole of the artillery of the 33rd and 38th Divisions and
the machine guns of the 38th Division, after firing the barrage

---

[1] 114th Infantry Brigade, "Narrative of operations near Villers Outreaux".

for the first attacks, were to move forward. The battalions were ordered to be in the assembly positions at 1½ hours before the above zero, but owing to the check to the 115th and 113th Brigades it was many hours later before they reached them.

When the situation of the two leading brigades became known to the 38th Division, the attack of the 114th Brigade was put off three and a half hours till 11.30., at which time it was now arranged that the barrage was to fall, the batteries moving forward in time to fire it at that hour.

At 08.00 114th Infantry Brigade headquarters found it had only been possible to stop the 13th Welsh on the right from advancing. The 14th and 15th Welsh on the left had become involved in the operations of the 113th Brigade and were heavily engaged with hostile machine guns and posts in the neighbourhood of Mortho Wood, in the Beaurevoir line itself, in Angelus Orchard and in the field works in T.2.c. The 14th Royal Welsh Fusiliers of the 113th Brigade as their share of the combined attack of the battalions of the two brigades cleared the Wood and the Angelus Orchard, working with a section of tanks. The two tanks operating with the 14th Welsh[1] were both knocked out. The 14th Welsh had a severe fight in the trenches in T.2.c. and d., and the 15th Welsh who had succeeded in fighting their way up to the Villers Outreaux—

---

[1] Personal narrative of Lt.-Col. G. Brooke, Commanding 14th Welsh.

"On moving forward from the staging area, after having received reports that 113th Brigade had attained all objectives (the brigade moving in columns of fours, 50 yards between platoons), we came under machine gun fire when at about T.7.a. 0.4. from machine guns in the wood about T.7.a. 3.5. I ordered the leading platoons to clear the wood, which they failed to do as the wood was heavily wired. I then went forward with an orderly to personally reconnoitre and found impossibly strong wire all along and just inside the wood. I remember saying to myself, 'I wish to goodness I had a couple of tanks'. None had been mentioned in orders, and I never expected any, but at that moment I heard a noise and turned round and there they were. I've never had a wish gratified so promptly, or appreciated it more. I hailed the tanks and they soon made short work of the wire and machine guns, thus enabling us to continue our advance. I saw both these tanks knocked out a little later, one quite close to me. They were hit by a Boche field gun, in a well sited and hidden forward position, which gun we got when we advanced. It was under a tree in some bushes and quite invisible from the front, and so placed that any tank coming over the ridge was 'easy meat' for it".

Ardissart Farm (N.26) road only got forward from there when "A" company of the battalion succeeded in rushing Angles Chateau from which a heavy cross fire was coming.

The 13th Royal Welsh Fusiliers met with strong belts of wire and opposition in T.1.c. and in the sunken road in T.2.a. and d. it was held up by heavy small arms fire from Villers Outreaux and from Angles Chateau on the other side. A 77$^{m/m}$ battery firing from T.9.a. over open sights caused delay and loss. But opposition was overcome by 11.00 hours, and the first objective reached in time to allow the 114th Brigade to launch its further attack at the appointed hour.

The 13th Welsh which had been ordered to reach its assembly position by the south side of Villers Outreaux moved off at 04.15 from the Nauroy line in file and halted in the sunken road in T.19.b., having received instructions not to cross the Beaurevoir line before 05.15, so as not to get mixed up in the earlier attacks. No information could be obtained of the 10th South Wales Borderers, and there was some hostile shelling and machine gun fire. So the adjutant, Captain H. L. Jones, went forward with a runner to reconnoitre, and a report was sent back to Brigade H.Q. which had moved up to S.24.a. About 06.30 orders were received for it to move back to its original position, to the great disappointment of every one; but it was necessary as the battalion was being uselessly exposed to fire fortunately without casualties. At 08.00 Captain Jones returned with the information that the attack on Villers Farm had been successful but without news of the 10th South Wales Borderers. As a result of this information the battalion was ordered to advance at 09.30 in artillery formation with scouts in front by way of the valley in T.25 and 21 to the assembly position in T.16.b. Considerable hostile shelling was experienced and several casualties sustained before this was reached.

To turn to the doings of the other arms. The divisional machine gun battalion in addition to firing the original barrages had been actively assisting the advance. Lieut. E. A. Evans by his skilful handling of his own and captured machine guns materially helped the advance of the extreme left of the division, and also did good work by pointing out to the infantry gaps in the wire made by the tanks.

Air photograph showing VILLERS-OUTREAUX and ARDISSART FARM.

"A" company did some useful covering fire on both sides of Villers Outreaux, and part of it assisted in mopping up in the village.

The artillery was only just up in time for the 11.30 attack.[1] Up till 10 a.m. the situation had been so obscure that the guns could not be allowed to go forward; but by 11.30 eleven of the sixteen batteries were in action near Aubencheul and Villers Outreaux and the remaining five came into action there ten minutes later.[2]

[3]At 11.50 the 114th Brigade attacked as ordered preceded by

---

[1] History of the 38th Division.

[2] The personal narrative of Lt.-Col. R. C. Williams, commanding the 122nd Brigade, R.F.A., is of interest in showing what he had to do and how his batteries got forward. "October 7th was a terribly strenuous day for me. A warning order had come out late the night before on the subject of a big attack to take place on the night of October 7th/8th. I went out in the morning to select positions to be advanced into after the first phase of the attack and from which to fire the second phase.
I got back to my H.Q. at 2 p.m. to find that I had to proceed at once to a conference at 38th Divisional Artillery H.Q. I did not get away from the conference till about 8 p.m., when I proceeded direct to my batteries and gave out instructions verbally for a barrage at 1 a.m. next morning. I got back to my H.Q. on top of my high hill E. of Vendhuille at 10 p.m. I arranged for two of my batteries to move at 4.30 and two at 5.30 a.m., after the (presumed) success of the first phase at 1 a.m.
. . . . I of course cancelled these moves on the failure of the 1 a.m. operation. In spite of the failure of this everything went very well later in the morning, and in preparation for the 2nd phase at 11.30 a.m. I moved the batteries forward 2,000 to 3,000 yards in a bee line to positions 1,000 yards S.E. of Aubencheul, with the H.Q. 700 to 1,400 yards west of the batteries, the wagon lines still remaining 1,000 yards east of the canal and 5,000 yards behind. Two of the batteries fired the prearranged barrage from the beginning but the other two started late. Owing to some doubt as to the exact position of our front line I was compelled at one stage of the proceedings to stop my batteries and those of the 156th Brigade, R.F.A., which were working under me, from firing the first part of the barrage. (Note.—This is possibly in connection with an incident reported by Lt.-Col. Beasley, commanding 17th Royal Welsh Fusiliers, that his battalion was being shelled by our own artillery). In open warfare accurate information of the exact position of our front line is most important and necessitates the employment of artillery officers' patrols to keep in touch with the situation and maintain telephonic communication with their artillery brigade".

[3] "Narrative of operations near Villers Outreaux"; 114th Brigade.

a creeping barrage. Two sections of "D" company, 38th M.G. Bn., two Stokes mortars of 114th L.T.M. Battery and one section of 124th Field Company, R.E., were attached to each of the 13th and 15th Welsh for consolidation. Stokes mortars and ammunition were moved up by pack mules to Malincourt, whence the mortars were man-handled forward.

The 13th Welsh advanced south of Malincourt village on a 500 yards frontage. Considerable hostile shell fire was experienced but the advance was well carried out and the objective reached at 13.00 hours.

The 15th Welsh advanced on a 500 yards frontage north of Malincourt. There was some hostile shell fire but the battalion was chiefly worried by machine guns in Mill Wood, which was not attacked by the next brigade on the left. One of them was silenced by Lewis guns, light trench mortars and machine gun fire.

The 14th Welsh captured Malincourt with little opposition moving rather later than the 13th and 15th Welsh.

The brigade was established as follows to resist a possible counter-attack :—

13th Welsh from the Quarry in U.1.c. to the house and enclosure in T.6.b., inclusive, with 1 company in support in the orchard in T.6.c. Of the 8 machine guns that were attached to the battalion only 2 reached the objective owing to casualties, and these were established on the high ground in U.7.a.central. 2 of the missing guns were got up later and joined the other two, providing fire across the front and to the right flank.

15th Welsh from Deheries to Malincourt Mill inclusive, to N.30.c.0.0. 2 light trench mortars N.36.a.7.2. 6 machine guns N.35.a.9.3

14th Welsh T.6.b.3.1. to N.36.d.0.2. 1 company in T.6.a. in support.

Two sections C company, 38th M.G. Bn., consolidated at T.11.central and two sections at N.35.c.central.

The brigade had been ordered to push forward later if possible to the high ground to the south east of Mill Wood. In view however of 33rd Division having to pass through the 38th Division at dawn on 9th October, and the probable uncertainty of obtaining accurate information of our dispositions after a further advance, the orders were cancelled, and the leading troops were withdrawn west of the Deheries road before morning.

The artillery was again moved forward, and some of the batteries came into action east of Malincourt, 9000 yards from the position they had occupied at the beginning of the action. The 114th Brigade continued to hold the position given above till the 33rd Division passed through next morning; while the 113th Brigade remained in support and the 115th Brigade went into billets in Villers Outreaux. This was the first time the troops had seen or entered a habitable house since they left rest billets on the 4th August.

The division captured 7 officers and 373 other ranks, 20 guns (including 1 eight inch howitzer) and many machine guns. The casualties were 69 officers and 1221 other ranks. All the wounded were cleared by the field ambulance by next morning.

As the narrative will now be concerned with the 33rd Division who carried on the advance, this will be a convenient place to take a glance at the opposing German troops.

THE GERMANS OPPOSITE THE VTH CORPS.

The Vth Corps forming the right of the Third Army was opposed during the latter part of the war by the 2nd German Army, which had been commanded for one and a half years by General der Kavallerie Von der Marwitz, who had commanded a cavalry corps in 1914. He gave up command on the 23rd September, 1918, and this was soon discovered by the British Intelligence staff; but for a considerable time the name of his successor was not known. In the end it was found out that he had exchanged with General Von Carlowitz who was commanding the 5th German Army opposite Verdun. General Von Carlowitz remained in command of the 2nd German Army till the end of the war.

In the German Army, as in the British, the armies and corps remained fairly permanently in the line, while the divisions were relieved at frequent intervals, as they grew tired. Opposite the Vth Corps were the LIVth Corps (General Von Larisch), known during stationary warfare as the "Busigny Group", and the IVth Reserve Corps (General Von Conta). The vicissitudes of the retirement brought different formations opposite to one another at different times, but one or other of these corps were always to be found in the line of advance of our Vth Corps.

By the time of which we are speaking the strain on the German armies had been very heavy, and for a proper understanding of the operations it is necessary to remember that the German soldier in the latter half of 1918 was a very different man to what he had been up to the time when his great offensive of the spring of 1918 had been brought to a halt.

Sir Douglas Haig speaking of the results of the battle of Bapaume about the beginning of September[1] says " the disorganization which had been caused by our attacks on the 8th and 21st August had increased under the pressure of our advance, and had been accompanied by a steady deterioration in the moral of his troops. Garrisons left as rear-guards to hold up our advance at important points had surrendered as soon as they found themselves threatened with isolation". The Commander-in-Chief was one of the first to notice this deterioration, but as a matter of fact it had begun earlier. When once the German soldier had been brought to a halt after the spring offensive, he never dug himself in again as he had been accustomed to do. Whether this was from discouragement or from over self confidence it is difficult to say; but it was one of the causes which resulted in his being put out of France, with relatively far less effort and loss than would have been necessary some months earlier.

A measure of his comparative value as a soldier at this time can be obtained from the doings of the 38th Division, without going any further. At the beginning of the great advance the division starting from the opposite side of the Ancre in two days fighting captured alone the two great strongholds of Thiepval and Pozieres. The capture of these same places in 1916, during the battle of the Somme, had required the efforts of many divisions spread over several weeks of the most desperate fighting.

Formerly British troops breaking into a German position on a small front found themselves cut off; now they were more likely to cause the German troops behind whose flanks they had arrived to surrender. As the advance went on the deterioration increased, but this does not mean to say that there were not many brave

---

[1] Sir Douglas Haig's despatch, 21st December, 1918, para. 25.

men left who were prepared to work their machine guns to the last, and to sell their lives dearly; but the unyielding spirit under all circumstances among the great mass of the men had gone.

Our intelligence summaries at this time frequently contained the orders of German formations dealing with lack of discipline in the ranks. For instance an extract from an order of the 51st Infantry regiment, 11th Division, dated 21st September, 1918, reads as follows: "The number of cases in which men have disregarded their oath of allegiance has considerably increased of late. Since the beginning of the year 104 cases (12 during August and so far 32 during September) of absence without leave, disobedience of orders and insubordination have been reported to the division".

By the beginning of October 183 battalions, equal to 20 divisions, had been disbanded since the beginning of the year owing to losses. The army and divisional heavy batteries had been reduced from 4 to 3 pieces, and even the third piece of the 21$^{c/m}$ batteries was withdrawn shortly afterwards.

As the above quoted despatch of Sir Douglas Haig states "the urgent needs of the moment, the wide extent of front attacked, and consequent uncertainty as to where the next blow would fall, and the extent of his losses had forced the enemy to throw in his reserves piecemeal as they arrived on the battle front. On many occasions in the course of the fighting elements of the same German division had been identified on widely separated parts of the battle front". As the fighting progressed there were no fresh divisions at all to relieve those exhausted in the line, and frequent identifications were made of divisions that had been taken out of the line for the shortest possible rest and pushed in again. For instance the 30th Division which had only been resting since 16th October near Englefontaine (see Map 1), came back into the line and counter-attacked on 21st October near Le Cateau. Again three other divisions which had been in the line well into October, were put in again on the front with which we are dealing by 19th October. In any comparison therefore of the fighting here described with that earlier in the war it is necessary to take these facts into consideration.

GERMAN ACCOUNTS OF THE FIGHTING.   30TH INFANTRY DIVISION.

Many histories of German units have been published of recent years, of which two or three are concerned with the fighting on the front of V Corps. Among these is a description of the doings of Infantry Regiment No. 93 about Villers Outreaux on October 8th. This merely consists of a rather sketchy description of confused fighting, and companies being surrounded or headquarters being captured, also of the losses inflicted on the retiring Germans by the British aircraft. There is however a description of the battle from the point of view of Infantry Regiment No. 105 in its regimental history, which gives a clear and connected account of events, and which it may be of interest to quote fully. This regiment was holding a part of the Masnieres—Beaurevoir line opposite the extreme left of the 38th Division and to the north of it. The events recorded are therefore concerned with the 38th Division and the 21st Division, the other attacking division of V Corps.

The description reads as follows :—

"After a quiet night hostile infantry advanced during the morning of 7th October in small columns, into the low ground north of Montecouvez (N.31). Stronger detachments of the enemy came under fire of the German artillery and were dispersed. Hostile fire on the position held by the regiment increased to a heavy bombardment by the hostile artillery with aeroplane observation which included the German principal line of resistance, and the supporting points of the position in various farms. The back areas and avenues of approach to the position came under dispersed fire. Strong enemy concentrations were observed at Mortho Wood, and about 9 p.m. the sound of tanks was reported from the region of Bonne Enfance Farm (M.30), which pointed to approaching hostile attack. The regimental staff went to its battle-headquarters at Walincourt while the transport of the regiment was moved back to Caudry. At midnight 7th/8th, a heavy bombardment took place against the neighbouring sectors on the right and left of the regiment.[1] The sector held by the 105th infantry regiment apart from its left flank was hardly bombarded at all. At this moment news was received from the 30th infantry division that it would be relieved on the night of the 9th/10th October and be used as attacking troops; the 105th infantry regiment was to be relieved this night and to come into position at Deheries. Events however, prevented this order from being carried out for at 5 a.m. the British attack which was only expected to commence after the artillery bombardment, fell on both the neighbouring sectors. The hostile attack penetrated the German position on the left held by the

---

[1] The original attack of V Corps.

99th infantry regiment. Touch with the 105th infantry regiment to the south was therefore lost by the 99th, and the left flank of the 105th in order to prevent itself being turned had to be thrown back towards the S.E. until it got into touch with the 99th infantry regiment at Ardissart Farm. In order to secure the flank here two light machine gun groups of the III/105 were put in. Major Petri of the 99th infantry regiment with three companies made a counter-attack from the S.E. against the chateau[1] and park west of Malincourt which had been lost. The 9th and 12th companies of the 105th regiment moved to support from the north to Haut Farm (N.27). At 6.30 the chateau was re-taken by the 99th infantry regiment. The hostile artillery bombardment now fell with all its fury on the whole sector of the 30th Infantry Division, and also on that sector of the 105th infantry regiment which up to now had not been bombarded. Heavy hostile attacks[2] were now renewed on the right flank of the sector held by the 99th regiment and on the chateau and park which had just been captured. The British succeeded in again breaking through here, and swinging to the north were able to get behind the front line battalion of the 105th. Once more the left flank of II/105 had to be bent back, until at Ardissart Farm it got into touch with the reserve battalion of the 99th regiment. The British also broke in on the right of the sector held by the 105th regiment, which was held by the 143rd regiment, crossed the main line of resistance and rolled up the position from the south. Consequently the right flank of the I/105 had to thrown back in a N.E. direction until it got into touch with the reserve battalion of the 143rd. In order to avoid the danger of the sector being turned, portions of the 1st and 2nd battalions of the 105th were drawn back to the reserve line, which now became the main line of resistance. In order to protect the flank on the left of the 3rd company 105th this had also to be withdrawn to the reserve line. On the other hand I/105 were able to repulse strong hostile flanking attacks against Hurtebise[3] Farm, but were unable to recapture the old main line of resistance. A large portion of II/105 who had not received the order to retire to the reserve line defended themselves in the old line with rifles, machine guns and hand grenades against all British attacks in anticipation of a German counter-attack. The battalion commander of II/105 only succeeded in evacuating his battle-headquarters with a portion of the staff the remainder falling into the hands of the British.

At 8.15 a.m. orders were received by the 105th regiment to hold the line Esnes—Malincourt regardless of losses. A reserve battalion of the 143rd regiment was put into a supporting line behind the sectors of the 143rd and 105th regiments with orders to hold this position at all costs, and to collect and hold up any of its retreating detachments in this line. The position held by the 105th regiment as well as those by the regiments on each flank were still under heavy hostile artillery fire. The enemy was

---

[1] Angles Chateau. (T.2).

[2] By the 113th and 114th Infantry Brigades.

[3] North of Ardissart Farm.

now bombarding the whole sector, with shells which gave off a thick white smoke. These thick clouds rendered visibility difficult, and entirely did away with light-signal communication. On the other hand this smoke turned out to be an advantage to us, in that under its protection the higher command ordered the Hurtebise Farm to be evacuated and the position here drawn further back. Soon after this the farm was occupied by the enemy.

The front line of the 105th regiment now ran from the wood $1\frac{1}{2}$ kilometres west of Walincourt to just east of Hurtebise Farm, bending back in a N.E. direction to the junction with the 143rd regiment. On the left touch had been lost with the 99th and the order to gain touch with it on the left at Haut Farm could not be carried out, as Haut Farm had already been occupied by the enemy. About 10.45 a.m., a report was received from the 99th infantry regiment that owing to severe pressure on the flank from Villers Outreaux they had had to fall back. By putting in the 9th and 12th Companies of the 105th regiment on the left of the regimental sector, efforts were again made to get touch with the 99th regiment, but it was not found possible to fill up the gap. At 11.35 the adjutant of II/105 reported that the British had advanced as far as the western edge of the Sargrenon valley.[1] I/105 was still holding the strip of wood east of Hurtebise Farm, but the left flank of the position was seriously threatened by hostile flanking machine gun fire from the S.E. and S. Orders were now received from the regiment to withdraw all parties of the regiment west of the Sargrenon valley to the heights west of Walincourt, and these were then put into the line there on the left of the 11th company of the 105th. Haut Farm which was strongly held by the enemy, now came under the fire of the German artillery, who in some cases were firing direct.

About 3 p.m. hostile concentrations and tanks were observed two kilometres west of Walincourt and were fired on with effect. Apparently these were preparations for an attack against the position held by 105th regiment. The attack did not materialize, at it was apparently nipped in the bud by the German destructive fire. In the evening orders were received from the 30th Division that the regiments of the division were to retire during the night of the 8th/9th to a position running north and south through the western edge of Montigny, as the front of the Second Army was being drawn further back. This withdrawal was carried out under cover of darkness without interference.

---

[1] Attack of the 114th Infantry Brigade on the second British objective. The Sargrenon Brook runs half a mile west of Malincourt.

APPENDIX I.

38TH DIVL. ARTY. OPERATION ORDER NO. 106.
7th Oct. 1918.

Ref. 57.c S.E. $\Big\}$ 1/20,000
57.b S.W.

1. Reference 38th D.A.O.O. No. 105, plan of attack of 38th Division is as follows:—

    (a) 115th Infantry Brigade is to capture VILLERS OUTREAUX. The village will not be attacked frontally. One battalion is to move round it from the south and one from the north.

    (b) 113th Infantry Brigade will advance east from MORTHO WOOD and join up with 115th Infantry Brigade on final objective.

    (c) Subsequently 114th Infantry Brigade is to pass through and envelope MALINCOURT (one battalion passing north and one south of the village, the third mopping up the village itself later.

2. Divisional Boundaries are:—

    Southern.   T.20.b.0.5.—T.16.c.0.0.—T.17.a.0.0.—T.18.a.0.0.— U.7.c.0.9.—U.2.c.0.0.—U.3.a.0.0.

    Northern.   T.1.b.3.0.—N.33.c.0.0.—N.34.central—N.30.c.0.0. —O.2.c.0.0.

    Inter Brigade Boundary.   T.7.d.3.2.—T.5.d.5.6.—cross roads O.32.b.

3. The above attacks will be supported by 4 separate barrages details of which are given below.

4. (a) *Attack of Right Battalion, 115th Infantry Brigade.*
    Infantry forming-up line T.27.a.0.5.—T.20.d.6.5.
    Final Objective Road T.16.b.6.2.—T.10.c.5.4.
    Supporting Artillery 156th Brigade, R.F.A.
    Opening line of barrage T.21.d.1.0.—T.21a.4.4.
    Final line T.11.c.3.0.—T.10.central.

6

Barrage opens at zero, remains on opening line till +15, then lifts forward 100 yards in 5 minutes to final line.

The barrage will halt for an additional 10 minutes (i.e., 15 minutes in all) on the following lines :—

(1) 300 yards beyond sunken road running through T.21.central.

(2) 300 yards beyond line of trenches in T.16.a.

(b) *Attack of the Left Battalion 115th Infantry Brigade.*

Infantry forming-up line north east of AUBENCHEUL and 200 yards behind the opening barrage line.

Final Objective Road T.9.b.2.7.—T.10.c.5.4.

Supporting artillery 122nd Brigade, R.F.A.

Opening line of barrage T.14.c.5.2.—T.13.b.3.8.—T.7.d.3.2.

Southern boundary of barrage T.14.c.5.2.—T.9.b.9.1.— T.10.central.

Northern boundary of barrage T.7.d.3.2.—T.10.a.0.7.

Final line T.10.central—T.10.a.0.7.

Barrage opens at zero and lifts forward at +5 at rate of 100 yards in 5 minutes to final line.

Barrage will halt for an additional 10 minutes (i.e., 15 minutes in all) on the following lines :—

(1) T.14.c.8.5.—T.7.d.7.0.—T.7.d.7.3.

(2) T.9.c.5.0.—T.9.a.0.0.

(c) *Attack of 113th Infantry Brigade.*

Infantry forming-up line T.1.central—T.7.central.

Final Objective Road T.3.d.3.0.—N.33.c.8.0. with patrols to quarry in T.3.b. and high ground in T.3.d.

Supporting artillery 121st Brigade, R.F.A., on right half, 162nd Brigade, R.F.A., on left half.

Opening line of barrage T.7.d.3.2.—T.1.d.3.8.

Final line of barrage T.10.a.0.6.—N.34.c.0.7.

Barrage will open at zero and lift at +5 at rate of 100 yards in 5 minutes to final line.

Barrage will halt for 10 minutes (i.e., 15 minutes in all) on the following lines :—

(1) T.8.c.4.5.—T.2.a.3.4.

(2) Grid line dividing squares T.2., T.8. from T.3., T.9.

(d) *Attack by 114th Infantry Brigade.*

Infantry forming up line—Final objective of 115th and 113th Infantry Brigades.

Supporting artillery 156th, 122nd, 121st and 162nd Brigades. R.F.A.

Barrage will be divided into two portions corresponding to the line of advance of the two battalions.

Southern Barrage. 156th Brigade on right, 122nd Brigade on left.

Opening line T.17.a.7.3.—T.10.central.

Final line U.2.c.0.2.—O.31.c.0.0.

Northern Barrage. 121st Brigade on right, 162nd Brigade on left.

Opening line T.4.d.2.7.—N.34.c.1.4.

Final line O.31.c.0.6.—O.25.c.0.5.

Both barrages will open at zero and lift at +20 at the rate of 100 yards in 4 minutes to final line. There will be no halts.

5. (a) In barrages (a), (b) and (c) each brigade should detail one 18 pdr. battery to cover each half of the brigade lane and superimpose the third 18 pdr. battery over the whole lane, keeping its fire 100 yards in front of the other two.

(b) Fire of 4·5″ howitzers will be 300 yards in front of rear 18 pdrs. In barrage (d) all batteries of each brigade should cover the whole brigade lane, so that if owing to the move forward a battery arrives late there will be no gap in barrage.

6. During barrage (a) 156th Brigade will detail one 18 pdr. battery to open at zero on the brickfield, T.21.a., remain there until arrival of creeping barrage and then step forward up the road on south east edge of VILLERS OUTREAUX until arrival at final line.

7. (a) During barrage (d) a box barrage will be placed on MALINCOURT and the area east of it. Each brigade will detail one section 18 pdrs. for this task.

(b) Area to be covered:—T.11.a.4.9.—T.4.b.4.0.—T.5.d.9.7.—T.5.b.5.6.

(c) Barrage will open at 08.00 and search and sweep the whole area till 08.45. At 08.45 the barrage will step forward from the west to the east edge of the area.

(d) On arrival there fire will be switched onto DEHERIES, N.36.d., and remain there until arrival of creeping barrage, fire will then cease.

8. 156th Brigade will arrange if ammunition is available to place a smoke screen from T.17.a.7.3.—T.10.central from the time the brigade gets into action in its new positions until 08.00.

9. Rates of fire will be dependent on the ammunition situation.

10. Brigades provided the tactical situation permits, will move forward independently to positions as detailed in para. 4 of 38th D.A.O.O. No. 105 on completion of barrage for attack by 115th and 113th Infantry Brigades.

11. Brigades will arrange to connect their new headquarters with the advanced R.A. report centre at S.24.a.2.8.

12. (a) 121st Brigade will be in liaison with 113th Infantry Brigade.
    122nd Brigade will be in liaison first with 115th Infantry Brigade and subsequently with 114th Infantry Brigade.

    (b) 156th Brigade will detail one battery to be in close liaison with the right battalion, 115th Infantry Brigade.

13. 13th and 22nd Brigades, R.G.A. (five 6″ howitzer batteries and three 60 pdr. batteries) are co-operating in the operation.

14. D.T.M.O. will arrange a programme for six mobile 6″ trench mortars in accordance with instructions already received.

15. There will be no fire at any time outside the Divisional Boundaries.

16. (a) Zero hour for the attack of 115th and 113th Infantry Brigades is 01.00, 8th October.

    (b) Zero hour for the attack of 114th Infantry Brigade is 08.00, 8th October.

17. Artillery Brigades to acknowledge.

Issued 22.35.

(signed) J. E. MARSTON,
Major, R.A.,
Brigade Major, 38th Divisional Artillery.

115th Infantry Brigade B.M. 1406.

10th South Wales Borderers.
17th Royal Welsh Fusiliers.
2nd Royal Welsh Fusiliers.
115th L.T.M. Battery.
151st Field Company, R.E.

1. The 38th Division is attacking at 01.00 to-morrow morning with 113th Brigade and 115th Brigade.

The objective of 115th Brigade the road MARLICHES FARM through T.10 central to light railway T.3.d.3.3.

The objective of 113th Brigade is road from T.3.d.3.3. to road junction T.3.a.8.9.

2. At 1 a.m. also 1st Battalion K.O.Y.L.I. of 50th Division are attacking northwards on VILLERS FARM from forming up places in T.20.d.

3. The attack of 115th Brigade will be carried out by 10th South Wales Borderers on the right and 17th Royal Welsh Fusiliers on the left. 2nd Royal Welsh Fusiliers will mop up part of the BEAUREVOIR LINE and VILLERS OUTREAUX as stated below.

4. Action of battalions will be as follows :—

10th South Wales Borderers.

Forming up place. Facing north east in bottom of valley in T.26.b. and T.20.d.

Battalion will advance to final objective with halts of ten minutes at :—

(a) Sunken road in T.21.a. and d.

(b) Trench in T.16.a., c. and d.

Advance will be covered by creeping barrage which will open at ZERO on approximate line T.21.d.8.0. to T.21.a.4.5. where it will stand for 15 minutes when it will move forward to beyond final objective at 100 yards in 5 minutes with two 10 minute halts in front of the positions mentioned above.

17th Royal Welsh Fusiliers.

Forming up point. Facing north east with leading wave approximately T.13.b.3.3. to T.13.b.0.8.

Battalion will advance to final objective by the north side of VILLERS OUTREAUX with one halt of 10 minutes on road in T.8.b. and d.

Advance will be covered by creeping barrage which will open at ZERO on the wire and trench from about T.14.d.0.8.—T.7.d.0.8. It will stand for 10 minutes on the front trench to enable the troops to get through the wire. It will advance to beyond final objective at 100 yards in 5 minutes with halts of 10 minutes on the above trench and 100 yards beyond the road in T.8.b. and c.

2nd Royal Welsh Fusiliers.

Will detail one company to follow in rear of 17th Royal Welsh Fusiliers and mop up BEAUREVOIR LINE from the south of the right flank of attack of 17th Royal Welsh Fusiliers. Remaining three companies will operate at dawn with 4 tanks to mop up VILLERS OUTREAUX. The tanks will rendezvous on the south west outskirts of VILLERS OUTREAUX at dawn. Details of the co-operation between the tanks and infantry will be arranged between O.C., 2nd Royal Welsh Fusiliers and O.C. Tank Detachment.

5. (a) The compass bearing of each attack will be worked out by battalions, and platoons will be kept well concentrated and led by officers provided with compasses. The outlets from VILLERS OUTREAUX will be picketed by the attacking battalions as they pass them.

(b) The O.C., 10th South Wales Borderers will take steps to safeguard his right and right rear.

(c) The two battalions will effect a junction north east of the village, the dividing line between them being the road through T.10.central inclusive to 10th South Wales Borderers.

6. Two companies of 33rd Battalion, M.G. Corps, and C company, 38th Battalion, M.G. Corps will co-operate with the artillery in the creeping barrage.

7. Two guns of 115th L.T.M. Battery now with 10th South Wales Borderers will accompany that battalion in the advance for use in consolidation. Two guns of 115th L.T.M. Battery with 17th Royal Welsh Fusiliers will co-operate in the opening barrage and from ZERO +30 minutes will be at the disposal of 2nd Royal Welsh

Fusiliers for mopping up work. The officer in charge of these two guns will get into touch with O.C., 2nd Royal Welsh Fusiliers to receive orders.

8. "A" company, 38th M.G. battalion will follow in rear of 16th South Wales Borderers in their advance and on reaching the final objective will take up positions :—

    (a) To support the advance of 114th Brigade through 115th and 113th Brigade at 08.00 tomorrow.

    (b) To assist against any counter-attack on our final objectives by direct fire.

    (c) To protect the rear of the two front battalions from attack from VILLERS OUTREAUX.

9. Instruction for action of 151st Field Company, R.E., in consolidation have been issued separately.

10. 114th Brigade will assemble in rear of the final objective of 115th and 113th Brigades before dawn and advance at 08.00 under a barrage to the objective U.1.b—road T.6.b.central to SALINCOURT FARM—south west edge of MILL WOOD with advanced troops at cross roads O.32.b.2.3. and high ground O.25.central.

11. First moves of battalion headquarters will be :—
    10th South Wales Borderers T.19.b.3.8.
    17th Royal Welsh Fusiliers S.12.d.8.3.

12. An advanced report centre will be established at S.24.a.5.0. from 24.00 tonight and 115th Brigade headquarters will move to this place at 06.00 tomorrow. An officer of brigade headquarters will also be at VAUXHALL QUARRY from 21.00 tonight, to which place as well as to advanced report centre, 10th South Wales Borderers will send information.

13. Brigade units, "A" company, M.G. Battalion, and 115th L.T.M. Battery to ACKNOWLEDDGE.

                (signed) A. J. WRIGHT,
19.00   Captain,
7.10.18.   Brigade Major, 115th Infantry Brigade.

    Copies to 38th Division, 38th Division R.A., 113th and 114th Brigades, 151st Field Company, R.E., Tank Officer, and 131st Field Ambulance.

Secret.   Copy No.

113TH INFANTRY BRIGADE ORDER NO. 258.

Ref. S.M. 578.B. S.W. 1/20,000.   7th October, 1918.

1. Vth Corps and corps on both flanks will attack tonight at 01.00
38th Division will attack with 115th Brigade on the right and
113th Brigade on the left, 114th Brigade in reserve at first, eventually passing through 113th and 115th Brigades after they have
reached their objectives.

   21st Division is on the left. 1st objective ANGLES CHATEAU and
high ground in neighbourhood, pushing on later in three bounds
to SELVIGNY.

2. 113th Brigade's objective will be spur in T.3., from T.3.d.9.5.
to N.33.d.4.0., with support line along or near road between
T.3.d.3.3. to T.3.a.8.9. Liaison posts to be established with flank
Battalions at last two map references, 16th Royal Welsh Fusiliers
with two sections, 13th Royal Welsh Fusiliers with one platoon.
The brigade's attack will be carried out as under :—

   16th Royal Welsh Fusiliers on right, 13th Royal Welsh Fusiliers on the left, 14th Royal Welsh Fusiliers in reserve.
   16th Royal Welsh Fusiliers' right boundary, junction of
   trench and road T.8.c.2.8., cross roads in T.8.b.—T.3.d.3.3.
   Brigade's left boundary as already detailed. Inter battalion
   boundary will be T.2.c.0.0. to T.3.b.5.5.

3. Attack will be carried out under an artillery barrage, rate
5 minutes per 100 yards, with halts of 10 minutes on trench north
and south through ANGELUS ORCHARD, and just beyond road in
T.2.d. and T.8.b. Barrage commences on a north and south line
T.7.d.4.2. to T.1.d.4.8.

4. B company, M.G. battalion from general line of sunken road
in S.6.b. and d. will fire an indirect barrage on conclusion of
which it will move to T.2.b., and finally to spur in T.3.b. and d.

   113th L.T.M. Battery will move to neighbourhood of T.7.b.9.3.

   6″ T.M. Mobile Section to neighbourhood of T.1.b.9.3.

123rd Field Company, R.E., will make strong points in T.8.a. and in T.2.b. and T.3.b. employing one section on each.

Strong points in T.8.a. and T.2.b. will be garrisoned by 14th Royal Welsh Fusiliers, that in T.3.b. by 13th Royal Welsh Fusiliers.

5. At dawn 2 tanks will come down the MONTECOUVEZ—VILLERS OUTREAUX road, and can be called on to deal with any points that require mopping up. 4 tanks detailed for 114th Infantry Brigade will be in T.2.c. at dawn. These may be called on if necessary, but must not be delayed.

6. Assembly positions will be as follows :—

16th Royal Welsh Fusiliers will form up west of north and south road in S.12.b. and d. They will then push up as near north and south road in T.7.central as possible, and be ready to move from that line at ZERO.

13th Royal Welsh Fusiliers will assemble just east of the western trench in T.1.c.

14th Royal Welsh Fusiliers. Three companies will be on the line of the north and south road in S.12.b. and d. One company in sunken road in S.6.d.

7. O.C., 123rd Field Company, R.E., will attach two sections to 13th Royal Welsh Fusiliers, one to 16th Royal Welsh Fusiliers.

The sections will move forward as follows :—

One section in rear of 14th Royal Welsh Fusiliers right com-companies, and two sections in rear of 14th Royal Welsh Fusiliers left companies.

113th L.T.M. Battery will move in rear of 14th Royal Welsh Fusiliers.

Each battalion will have attached to it for locating and examining headquarter dug outs three tunnellers.

8. *Mopping up*. 16th and 13th Royal Welsh Fusiliers will be responsible for mopping up from sunken road in T.8.b. and T.2.d. forward to objective.

14th Royal Welsh Fusiliers will be responsible for mopping up west of above road.

ACKNOWLEDGE by quickest means of communication.

9.   Advanced brigade report centre will be at S.12.c.1.8.   Visual and wireless station at S.18.c.1.8.   Battalions to establish visual station at S.6.d.8.6. approximately.

——— Captain,
Brigade Major, 113th Infantry Brigade.

Issued through signals at 22.00.
In confirmation of verbal orders at 18.00.

CAMBRIN

FOSSE 8

LENS

ORCHIES

DROCOURT

DOUAI

ST. POL

ARRAS

R. SCARPE

MONCHY

HENIN

HAMLINCOURT

AYETTE

BULLECOURT

HEBURTERNE

QUÉANT

MOEUVRES

CAMB.

FLESQUIRES

BAPAUME

HAVRINCOURT

MARCOING

MASNIER

GOUZECOURT

THIEPVAL

HIGH WOOD

HEUDICOURT

BANTOUZEL

POZIERES

BAZENTIN

VILLERS GUISLAIN

HONNECOUR

VILL

ALBERT

MAMETZ

FRICOURT

SAILLY SAILLISEL

EPEHY

ILE CATE

BEN

MORLANCOURT

St Pierre Vaast Wood

VENDHUILLE

BOUCHAVESNES

ROISEL

SUZANNE

CLERY

PERONNE

BONY

BELLICO

AMIENS

R. SOMME

VILLERS-BRETONNEUX

CANAL

ST QU

HINDEN LINE

MILES 10   5   0

KILOMETRES 10   0   10

[To face page 374.

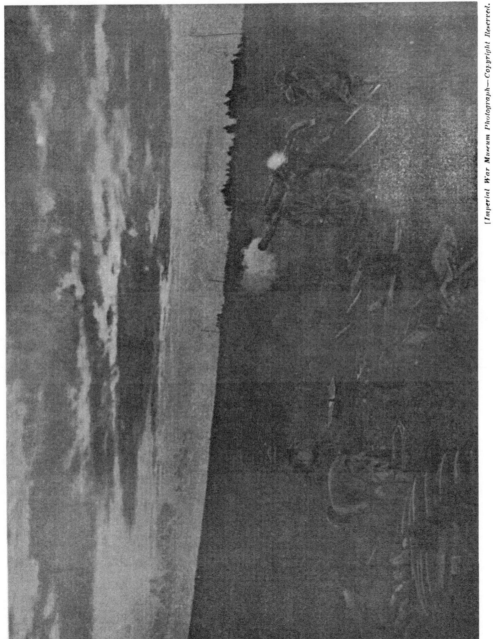

DAWN—OCTOBER 1918.

THE 38th (WELSH) DIVISION
IN THE LAST FIVE WEEKS OF THE GREAT WAR.

By Major-General H. D. DePree, c.b., c.m.g., d.s.o., *p.s.c.*

CHAPTER II.

The Pursuit to the Selle River.

AT 18.00 hours on 8th October V Corps[1] gave orders for the enemy to be followed up with the greatest vigour, and for the 33rd and 17th Divisions to move forward so as to pass through the advanced troops of the 38th and 21st Divisions respectively at 05.20 on October 9th and continue the advance, the 33rd Division on Clary exploiting towards Bertry, and the 17th Division on Caullery exploiting towards Montigny. As soon as the front of the 38th and 21st Divisions was covered by the advance of the other two divisions the two former were to be reformed as rapidly as possible on a one-brigade front and advance in support of the two leading divisions, regulating their advance by the latters' progress. All energies were to be concentrated on getting the field artillery supplied with ammunition during the night, so that the guns could keep well forward in close support of the infantry. On the right the XIII Corps of the Fourth Army were given from Busigny Station to Maretz as their first objective, and Honnechy—Maurois as their second. The IV Corps on the left of V Corps were also to advance abreast of them.

The leading brigade of the 33rd Division was the 19th Infantry Brigade (Brig.-Genl. C. Mayne). [2]They remained in the Hindenburg Line until the evening of 8th October, when the 33rd Division ordered them forward to the Le Catelet—Nauroy line[3] preparatory to a continuation of the advance. Accordingly the Cameronians on the right and the 5th Scottish Rifles on the left were moved to this line of trenches immediately west of Aubencheul. The 1st

---

[1] V Corps G 458.
[2] Narrative of operations 5th—10th October, 1918. 19th Infantry Brigade.
[3] See Map No. 2.

Queen's were moved to a position just south of Basket Wood, and Brigade H.Q. moved to La Terriere. At 6 p.m. the divisional commander, Major-Genl. Sir R. Pinney, arrived at brigade H.Q. and gave verbal orders for the 19th Brigade to continue the advance, passing through the advanced troops of the 38th Division on the Serain—Walincourt road at dawn.

For the purposes of this operation the following troops were affiliated to the 19th Infantry Brigade :—

> "E" Squadron, North Irish Horse (V Corps Cyclist Battalion).
>
> 94th Brigade, R.F.A.
>
> 121st Brigade, R.F.A. } 38th Division.
> 122nd Brigade, R.F.A.
>
> 156th Brigade, R.F.A., 33rd Division (actually placed under orders of the brigade).
>
> "C" Company, 33rd Battalion, M.G. Corps.

Orders were accordingly issued for the brigade to march at 02.00 hours on 9th October via Aubencheul, Villers Outreaux and Malincourt. On arrival at Malincourt the brigade was to advance in battle formation, 1st Queen's on the right with the Clary—Maretz road, exclusive of the villages, as their objective, and the 5th Scottish Rifles on the left with Clary village as their objective. The 5th Scottish Rifles were in addition allotted the task of exploiting the success in the direction of Bertry. The Cameronians were to remain in brigade reserve at Malincourt Quarry. Brigade H.Q. was established in the eastern outskirts of Villers-Outreaux. The following troops were allotted to each of the attacking battalions :—

1 Section, "C" Company, 33rd Battalion, M.G. Corps.

1 Troop, "E" Squadron, North Irish Horse.

The 81st Brigade, 66th Division, and the 51st Brigade, 17th Division, were operating on the right and left of the brigade respectively.

9th October.

The night march was successfully carried out as far as the western outskirts of Malincourt. Here the road had been mined by the enemy and the delay mine exploded about an hour before

3

the brigade passed this point. It was impossible to get transport
through and Lewis guns were unloaded. A delay of three quarters
of an hour was caused, but the line of the Walincourt—Serain
road was nevertheless crossed at 05.20 as ordered.

The 1st Queen's[1] on the right advanced with "C" and "A"
companies in the front line, "B" company in support of "A",
and Battalion H.Q. following "C". [2]The 5th Scottish Rifles
advanced with "A", "C" and "B" companies in front and "D"
in reserve. A few of our own shells fell in the jumping off place
of "A" company of the 1st Queen's killing 2 and wounding 6 men.
There was no enemy shelling but his machine guns were active
during the advance on the front of the 1st Queen's, especially from
the direction of Elincourt. "C" company on the right however
pushed on and forced him to evacuate these positions by outflanking him. When the 1st Queen's reached the hollow 1000
yards north of Elincourt a dense fog descended and it was impossible to see more than 100 yards. The battalion pushed on however
and at 08.00 the fog lifted disclosing "C" company advancing
within 200 yards of the objective (the Maretz—Clary road) with
Battalion H.Q. 300 yards in rear. "A" and "B" companies had
slightly lost direction and were advancing near Hurtevent Farm
1 mile west of Clary. By 08.45 the whole battalion was on the
objective, its left in touch with the 5th Scottish Rifles, but its right
flank in the air. This latter battalion had met with no opposition
and the three mile advance to Clary was rapidly carried out. At
Clary and to the east of it the enemy attempted to make a stand.

About this time a 77$^{m/m}$ battery of three guns came into action
against the 5th Scottish Rifles, firing over open sights, from near
the little copse 300 yards east of the southern extremity of Clary.
"A" company of the Queen's got a Lewis gun into action against
their southern flank, while the 5th Scottish Rifles worked round
on their other flank with the result that all three guns with their
detachments and teams were captured.

Clary was captured and cleared of the enemy by 09.30 and
many civilians were liberated in the village. Brigade H.Q. were
moved to Deheries and from thence to Hurtevent Farm. The

---

[1] Report on operations 9th October, 1st Queen's.
[2] War Diary, 5th Scottish Rifles.

battalion in reserve, the Cameronians, was moved to Deheries and thence to Iris Farm.

A delay of three hours now occurred in Clary. The officer commanding 5th Scottish Rifles apparently did not realize that he was to push on towards Bertry with all speed, as he informed the officer commanding 121st Brigade, R.F.A., when the latter went into the village to arrange for another advance, that his orders were to take Clary and to go no further. Brigade H.Q. were not in close enough proximity to rectify the mistake at once, probably owing to the rapidity of the advance, the fog, and possibly the tendency of the headquarters of formations to remain too far in rear for a moving battle, a practice necessitated by the general conditions and heavy shelling of stationary warfare. Whatever the cause may have been three hours were lost which might have been of great importance in a pursuit.

[1]It will be advantageous now to give some account of the action of the supporting artillery. The 156th Brigade, R.F.A., was detailed to act in close support of the advance of the 19th Infantry Brigade, and at zero, 05.20 hours, fired to cover the infantry as far as O.32.central (between Elincourt and Bois du Gard).

When the check at Clary occurred two guns of A/156 and three of B/156 together with some advanced sections of the 162nd Brigade, R.F.A., which had followed close on the heels of the infantry, came into action immediately on the western outskirts of the village and successfully engaged the enemy machine guns over open sights. Shortly afterwards the infantry established themselves on the eastern outskirts of Clary, whereupon two of the advanced guns of B/156 were pushed through the village and again came into action, shooting over open sights with very good effect at a range of 800 yards. A single gun of B/156 was also brought into action at O.17.b.4.7. against hostile machine guns at O.12.d.0.0. which were holding up troops of the 17th Division on the left.

In the meantime the rest of the field artillery working with the 33rd Division had been advancing rapidly, and by 10.00 hours all four brigades, R.F.A., were in action west and south of Clary, supporting with their fire the advance of the 19th Infantry Brigade

---

[1] Supplementary report on operations of 33rd Division on 9th October, 1918. "History of the 33rd Divisional Artillery."

and the British cavalry operating in the neighbourhood. They had been ordered by the C.R.A., 33rd Division, to keep in touch with the infantry, and follow as quickly as possible. At 10.30 B/162 came into action firing over open sights at hostile machine guns in the Bois-de-Gattigny (P.25). This enabled the cavalry to move round and envelop the wood. About the same time C/121 shelled with good effect the scrub in O.6.d. and P.7.a. (east of Montigny). Several batteries also engaged a concentration of the enemy in O.24.b. (east of Clary) and inflicted casualties.

The personal narratives of the officers commanding the two brigades of the 38th Divisional Artillery operating on this day give a very good idea of the course of the fight and also of the experiences of an artillery brigade commander in a moving battle of this nature. Lieut.-Col. R. C. Williams, commanding 122nd Brigade, R.F.A., writes :—

"The day of October 9th was very strenuous. A continual stream of orders and telephone messages kept coming through during the night to my headquarters on the eastern outskirts of Villers Outreaux, 1000 yards from my batteries. From some time during the night I had come under orders of the C.R.A., 33rd Division (Brig.-Genl. G. H. W. Nicholson). As a result of orders received during the middle of the night I moved my batteries forward at 05.30 to positions 1,800 to 2,000 yards west of Clary, with headquarters at Hurtevent Farm (O 21.d.) and wagon lines within 2,500 yards of the furthest battery. From the positions occupied south of Malincourt during the early part of the morning, very little firing was carried out owing to uncertainty as to the position of our infantry. From the second positions west of Clary we fired a bit. Owing to the rapidity of the advance the ammunition supply was very difficult, and it was best not to fire away more ammunition than was actually necessary.

Our infantry kept pushing on all day and during the afternoon I advanced my batteries through Clary and came into action again 700 yards west of Bertry, south of the Clary—Bertry road, headquarters 2,000 yards east south east of Bertry in a factory outhouse. My batteries did not fire from these positions, as it was not clear how far our infantry had got. Not much opposition had been encountered all day.

The first advance of the day was 6,800 yards as the crow flies and the second 4,500 yards. Three different sets of positions were occupied by the batteries, while my own headquarters occupied four different locations.''

Lieut.-Col. G. P. MacClellan, commanding the 121st Brigade, R.F.A., describes the day's operations as follows :—

"Late at night on the 8th October, when the brigade was in bivouac near Aubencheul, I received orders to report to the C.R.A., 33rd Division in that village at (I think) 05.00 next morning.

Next morning there was a thick fog, and I had some difficulty in finding him. When I did find him he told me that information was meagre, but that I was under the orders of Brig.-Genl. Mayne, 19th Infantry Brigade, 33rd Division.

I found Brig.-Genl. Mayne on the eastern outskirts of Villers Outreaux; he told me that his brigade was advancing on a two battalion front, and that he wanted me to support, in any way that I was able, his left battalion, the 5th Scottish Rifles, which was directed on Clary, and which had already started. He could tell me nothing of the situation in front, and we could see nothing, as the fog was still very thick. I had already ordered the 121st Brigade into position of readiness near Villers Outreaux, and rode on with my adjutant and a small staff to try and catch up with the 5th Scottish Rifles. In spite of hard riding into the fog we could not find them, but a straggler stated that they had gone on. On this I sent an officer to direct the brigade to a position in observation west of Malincourt, and went on towards Clary. Very shortly after this the fog lifted, and having received more reports that the infantry were still going ahead, I ordered the brigade into positions in N 36.d, west of Deheries, but before they were occupied sent another order to the batteries to come on towards Clary with all speed.

I caught up the 5th Scottish Rifles just before they arrived at Clary (I cannot say for certain whether this was before or after I had sent the last order to move on that village, but think it must have been before), and went into the village to find out the situation. The enemy were still holding the ridge east of it, and the O.C. Scottish Rifles (I think that he was Lieut.-Col. Spens) told me that his orders were to get Clary, and that he was going no further. This made it useless to bring guns into the village, and the brigade, which arrived very shortly after this, was brought into action behind the ridge about 1,500 yards west of it. Batteries were just under cover, with voice control, or very short telephone lines, from O.P.'s in front. Any further advance at the moment involved loss of command, and loss of view. From their positions all the batteries were able to shell parties of the enemy which could be seen retiring towards Bertry, at ranges of 2,500—3,500 yards. Very shortly after the brigade arrived Lieut.-Col. B. A. B. Butler, commanding a R.F.A. brigade, came up with one section of 18-prs. of his brigade. The 122nd Brigade, R.F.A., arrived some time afterwards.

After a delay of two or three hours the enemy's rearguard, which was hanging on to the ridge east of the village, was attacked by the infantry, assisted by some cavalry, who had come in from our right. When this advance was decided on I sent forward C Battery (Major A. H. Peskett), for close support work. This battery did very well, coming into action against enemy located in a cornfield at a range of about 1,000 yards. These were holding up the advance of the battalion on our left, belonging to another division, and they left when they were shelled.

Major Peskett had been clamouring to be allowed to go on into Clary long before I allowed him to do so, and I now sent him on again in the direction of Bertry, on which the infantry were now advancing, and brought forward the rest of the brigade by batteries. The position occupied was just north west of Bertry, and from it the retiring enemy was shelled again. Batteries were in practically open positions, with O.P's close by; in one case the O.P. was a tree almost alongside the guns. Ranges were about 3,500—4,000 yards, and firing was indirect, as the view was restricted by trees, etc. This was the position at night. Cavalry were operating ahead of us, and the brigade Interpreter and myself, on a reconnaissance into Bertry at about 16.00, found only two wounded Germans in a cellar, and the local inhabitants collected in the school."

[1]The action of Cavalry has been mentioned. These were part of the Cavalry Corps which was working under the orders of the Fourth Army. Their role was to keep in close touch with the advancing infantry and to take advantage of any success to carry out the following tasks :—

(a) To move in the general direction of Le Cateau, securing the railway junctions at that place and Busigny.

(b) To operate against the flank and rear of the enemy opposing the Third and First Armies, working in close conjunction with those armies.

(c) To cut the enemy's communications about Valenciennes.

In pursuance of these objects the Cavalry Corps pushed forward the 3rd Cavalry Division (Major-Genl. A. E. W. Harman), which moved forward early on the morning of the 9th October with the straight Maretz—Le Cateau road as the axis of its advance, having the 6th Cavalry Brigade (Brig.-Genl. B. G. E. Paterson) to the south of it and the Canadian Cavalry Brigade (Brig.-Genl. B. G. R. W. Paterson) to the north, with the 7th Cavalry Brigade (Brig.-Genl. B. G. A. Burt) in reserve. The objective of its left brigade was the ridge west of Le Cateau astride the Le Cateau—Cambrai road, and the spurs covering the crossing of the Selle River at Montay and Neuvilly. Consequently the left Cavalry Brigade was at first operating on the right of the 19th Infantry Brigade about Clary, and later in front of it in the neighbourhood of Le Cateau.

---

[1] War Diary 3rd Cavalry Division.
,,   ,,   Canadian Cavalry Brigade.

Between 10.00 and 11.00 hours, in the course of their advance, the Canadian Cavalry Brigade found the 19th Infantry Brigade held up by machine gun fire from the line western edge of Gattigny Wood—Clary. A squadron of the Fort Garry Horse was sent forward against the western edge of Gattigny Wood, covered on its left flank by Lord Strathcona's Horse who were ordered to seize the small wood in O.23.d. and the high ground east of Clary. The whole advance was covered by one battery of Royal Canadian Horse Artillery. This was the attack in which B/162 also co-operated by firing into Gattigny Wood. By 11.10 the Fort Garry Horse had captured the western edge of the Wood. This squadron advanced through the position held by the 1st Queen's at 10.45 and the prisoners that resulted were collected by "C" company of that battalion. At the same time the leading squadron of Strathcona's Horse established itself on the high ground north east of Clary in O.18. But the enemy still held the part of the wood next the Maretz—Maurois road, and only abandoned it on the infantry attacking. In this operation the cavalry took 230 prisoners, 1 5'9" howitzer, 2 field guns, and 30 or 40 machine guns.

On the 5th Scottish Rifles continuing the advance east of Clary, a large number of enemy machine guns opened fire from the high ground south of the Clary—Bertry road. As Montigny and part of Gattigny Wood were still in the enemy's possession the envelopment of these machine guns was a difficult matter. The advance, however, of the British cavalry to the south where the 3rd Cavalry Division were pushing forward vigorously in the neighbourhood of Honnechy, outflanked them from that direction, and in conjunction with this movement the 5th Scottish Rifles at 13.50 seized the high ground and with it many of the machine guns.

At this time orders were received by the 19th Infantry Brigade over the telephone from the 33rd Division to continue the advance beyond Bertry on the line Troisvilles—Neuvilly, to cross the Selle River and to establish a line on the high ground east of it. The Cameronians were ordered to carry out this operation and the 1st Queen's to move forward and support it.

Meanwhile the Canadian Cavalry Brigade continued its advance and captured Maurois with 40 prisoners, and took 42 more between Bertry and Clary. Pressing on in spite of opposition, with the help of their horse artillery, they took Reumont and Troisvilles capturing 1 officer and 29 other ranks. By dark they held a line from the high ground 500 yards south west of Montay through Rambourlieux Farm along the road to Troisvilles. To cover the exposed right flank of this line from the direction of Le Cateau one regiment less one squadron was moved up Pont des Quatres Vaux. Patrols pushed on and entered Neuvilly and Montay.

On the right of the Canadians the 7th Cavalry Brigade which had been moved forward was assembled north of Reumont with one squadron advanced to Q.1.c. in touch on the left with the Canadians and on their right with the 6th Cavalry Brigade which had a line of posts north east and south east of Reumont and Honnechy.

[1]Under cover of this exceedingly energetic advance of the cavalry the 19th Infantry Brigade reached Bertry without opposition. Some casualties were incurred by the Cameronians from shell fire to the north and east of the village where the enemy put down a barrage. Over 1500 civilians were liberated here who received the troops with a most enthusiastic welcome.

The enemy attempted to make a stand at Troisvilles holding the ridge in J.34. This ridge was captured after stiff fighting. The battalion pushed forward to the outskirts of Troisvilles where the left flank was held up by small arm fire from a strong point. This post, which was afterwards found to be held by twenty to thirty men with a machine gun, was attacked by two riflemen of the battalion (Hillhouse and Peel) on their own initiative. They rushed the post with the bayonet taking two unwounded prisoners.

The whole line then advanced inflicting heavy loss on the retreating enemy. As it was then getting dark orders were issued by the brigade to halt for the night, and a line was established east and north east of Troisvilles. The 1st Queen's were moved up to a support position on the eastern outskirts of Bertry. During this advance they moved in battle formation, and were held up by fire from P.3.c. for a time. This caused them to lose touch with the

---

[1] Narrative of operations 5th—10th October, 1918. 19th Infantry Brigade.
War Diary 1st Battalion Scottish Rifles (Cameronians).
,,   ,,   1st Queen's.

Cameronians, but the officer commanding rode forward on a bicycle and regained touch.

About 18.00 hours the enemy launched a counter-attack from Audencourt, but were repulsed by the Cameronians and one company of the 1st Queen's who were moved up to support their left flank, which was in the air. While these events were in progress the villages of Inchy and Caudry were seen to be burning. During the evening the Cameronians sent out patrols in conjunction with the cavalry, and three platoons patrolled forward into Neuvilly and reached the river. Here they came under heavy fire and Captain Baker who was in command of the infantry was killed. The N.C.O. who assumed command was forced to fall back owing to casualties and increasing opposition; but valuable information was gained.

The battalion had advanced over 15 miles across country in the course of the day, and the manner in which at the end it rose superior to fatigue and drove the enemy from successive strong positions was worthy of the best traditions of the British Army. The officer commanding (Lieut.-Col. The Hon. H. Ritchie), who had only returned to duty the day before, was wounded again.

As regards the artillery, the batteries moved forward to positions near Bertry about 15.00 hours. The 156th Brigade, R.F.A., fired about 500 rounds between that time and 17.00. At 16.30 hours an aeroplane dropped a message to say that the enemy were retreating in J.26 and 27 north west of Troisvilles, and this area was engaged by all four brigades R.F.A., and when darkness fell all their batteries were in action between Bertry and Clary.

The histories of the two German infantry regiments previously quoted throw an interesting and valuable light on the fighting of the 9th October. The 93rd Infantry Regiment of the 8th Division found the troops which held up the advance of the 19th Infantry Brigade at Clary and were engaged in the fighting with the Canadian Cavalry Brigade east of that place.

Throughout the fighting the regiment appears to have been in constant danger of being outflanked from the south, and the narrative affords striking testimony to the great value of the thrusting and enveloping tactics of the cavalry on this day.

The following is a translation of the history of the events of this day :—

"During the night 8/9th October, the regiment was withdrawn to the heights east of Clary. They entrenched at dawn with their right in touch with the 99th Infantry Regiment on the Clary—Bertry road and on the left with the 72nd Infantry Regiment in Gattigny Wood. At 11 a.m. the enemy attacked with large forces. At Honnechy, which was held by the division on our left, the enemy broke through and rolled up our left flank. English cavalry suddenly broke through from Gattigny Wood and managed to get behind our two battalions working along a sunken road. A certain amount of panic ensued, the left flank which was wavering received considerable losses from an English machine gun; a certain number of men were taken prisoners. Owing to the energy of the 1st and 2nd Battalion Headquarters, especially the bold handling by Lt. Dieckmann, it was found possible to make the troops hold their ground, to drive back the British by a counter-attack and to again release certain prisoners. The breaking through of the enemy at Honnechy made the retirement of the regiment to Troisvilles and Montay a necessity. Owing to the exposed flank, portions of the regiment were obliged during their slow retirement to halt continually and form front to the south and south west, in order to prevent the 99th Infantry Regiment being outflanked by the enemy. Thus portions of the 93rd Infantry Regiment were constantly in danger of being cut off themselves. Troisvilles was held until 5.30 p.m., several attacks being beaten off. It was only after the enemy penetrated in force and from all sides into the village that a rapid retreat was begun.

While subsequently a portion of the regiment with parts of the 72nd Infantry Regiment were holding up a powerful cavalry charge from the south, other portions of the 93rd, in touch with the 99th, were retiring fighting on Neuvilly. They had to halt and fight several times in order to cover the retreat of our artillery, which was closely supporting the infantry by direct fire on the enemy's cavalry and infantry.

Portions of the 93rd Regiment were holding, when night fell, the bridges of Neuvilly, and repulsed a rapid attack of the enemy here. The enemy assembled during the night at Montay. Units were reorganized and the Hermann Stellung on the high bank of the Selle occupied.

In spite of the strenuous nature of the previous week the 93rd Regiment had in the last 48 hours accomplished something superhuman. Although two days without food in constant touch with an attacking enemy on roads which were harassed by numerous hostile aeroplanes with bombs and machine guns, it had held its positions, and only evacuated them when they had been turned by the enemy or on receipt of orders to do so. To hold these positions everyone including headquarters with their runners and signallers had to fight in the line. Thus the 8th and 9th October, 1918, in spite of casualties and loss by prisoners, were days not without honour for the regiment, the same regiment which on 26th August, 1914, attacked victoriously in the same area, now retired past the grave of its former commander in Clary, under totally altered fighting conditions before an enemy superior in numbers and materiel." [1]

The 105th Infantry Regiment, a Saxon unit, whose narrative of the fighting of 8th October has already been given, held successive positions just to the north of the line of advance of the 19th Infantry Brigade. They formed part of the 30th Division and had on their left the 99th Infantry Regiment, who in their turn had on their left the 93rd Infantry Regiment whose narrative has just been quoted

In the case of the 105th Infantry Regiment also the effects of the advance of the cavalry and 19th Infantry Brigade are to be traced. It will be seen that this advance affected not only the 8th German Division, which was attacked, but also the whole of the 30th Division on its right.

The narrative of this regiment runs as follows :—

"In the early morning of October 9th, the 105th Infantry Regiment had occupied their new position on the western side of Montigny, the I/105 on the right and the III/105 on the left, in the front line. The regimental battle headquarters were on the eastern side of Montigny, and on the right flank they were in touch with the 143rd Infantry Regiment, but their left flank was open, owing to the 99th Infantry Regiment having retreated too far, but touch was obtained later on in the morning by the 99th advancing into line again. The retreat of the regiment was covered by two officers patrols which had remained behind in the old position, while behind them, as support and rearguard companies the II/105 held Walincourt. Towards 4 a.m., the British advanced in strength on Walincourt and pressed the weak protective detachment back, and they withdrew slowly towards Montigny. On the way eastwards from Selvigny they fell in with a field battery of the 84th Field Artillery Regiment of the 30th Division, and an anti-tank gun in position, which had not received the order to withdraw. They covered the retreat on Montigny, and towards 7.15 a.m. they were again in touch with their own regiment.

At 10 a.m. followed strong frontal attacks on Montigny from the enemy. These were completely repulsed by artillery and machine-gun fire. The British dug themselves in at some 800 metres distance, and to the west of the original position of the 105th Regiment. Soon the regiments in Montigny came under heavy enemy fire from guns which had been brought up, which fire soon became a drum fire. At the same time strong enemy attacks were made on the division on the left of the 30th Infantry Division,

---

[1] On the night 10/11th October the regiment was relieved in the Hermann Stellung and marched to Poix du Nord, where it remained in rest till 15th October, when it moved forward to Bousies and from 18th October onwards was engaged in fighting along the Englefontaine—Le Cateau road till it was finally relieved in this area on October 27th.

whose front was driven further back. In order not to be outflanked the 99th Infantry Regiment had to follow the retreat of the troops on their left.[1] Consequently the 105th Infantry Regiment also bent their left flank sharply round towards the east. The position of the III/105th consequently came under heavy flanking fire from the direction of Clary. As the division on the left, and the 99th Regiment,[2] which had withdrawn with them, retreated still further, and the enemy were on the point of outflanking Montigny, the III/105th were next withdrawn, while the I/105th took up a rallying position on the heights east of Montigny. The regimental staff of the 105th Infantry Regiment moved its headquarters to the Trouquoi Farm behind the road from Troisvilles to Audencourt, and the I/105th having carried out their task were withdrawn to the regiment's position on the Bertry—Caudry embankment of the railway, held on the right by the III/105th and on the left by I/105. This line was only to be held until the evening, as the position of the 2nd Army on the western ridge of the heights between the Selle brook and the embankment on the railway from Solesmes to Le Cateau, was to be pulled back into the Hermann Stellung.[3]

Exactly at 5.45 p.m., it was observed that the division on the left was in full retreat owing to an enemy attack and was evacuating Troisvilles, and that the enemy already held the heights north of Bertry. On account of the pressure being put on their left wing the 30th Infantry Division had also to further withdraw, chiefly because hostile detachments had taken them in the rear, and were already in possession of the road from Troisvilles to Audencourt. The regimental staff had to retreat hastily to avoid being captured by the British, who were now pouring out of Troisvilles. The 30th Infantry Division were therefore immediately sent back from their former position to the railway embankment Solesmes—Le Cateau. The 105th Regiment went back through Beaumont, Inchy and Neuvilly, and occupied the Hermann Stellung S.E. of Neuvilly, on and to the west of the railway embankment Solesmes—Le Cateau. In the new position certain entrances to dug-outs and other preparations had been begun, and it had been organized into a main line of resistance and a foreground, the latter being strengthened by outposts. The former ran along the railway embankment Solesmes—Le Cateau, and the latter extended to the Selle brook. The position was held by the 105th Infantry Regiment with I/105 on the right and III/105 on the left.

The enemy fire had ceased, as the enemy infantry took over the railway embankment Caudry—Bertry; evidently the enemy artillery were changing their position. So the night of October 9th/10th was peaceful.''

---

[1] This refers to the thrust further to the south by the cavalry and the 19th Infantry Brigade.

[2] The 99th Infantry Regiment belonged to the 30th Division.

[3] This probably means that the railway embankment between Bertry and Caudry was only to be held as a rearguard position, till the Hermann Stellung on the east bank of the Selle River could be occupied.

The moves of the two supporting infantry brigades of the 33rd Division were as follows.   At 09.00 the Division issued orders for the 98th Infantry Brigade (Brig.-Genl. J. D. Heriot-Maitland) to march at 11.00 on Clary and the 100th Infantry Brigade (Brig.-Genl. A. W. F. Baird) on Deheries.   At 11.15 when the 19th Infantry Brigade was ordered to press forward and cross the Selle north of Le Cateau the 98th Infantry Brigade was ordered to march on Troisvilles, but in view of the check at Clary it was subsequently halted just west of that place, and remained there.   The head-quarters of both these infantry brigades and of all the artillery brigades collected at Hurtevent Farm for the night, and that of the 100th Infantry Brigade went to Deheries.   The positions of the troops were not altered throughout the night.

In the 38th Division the 114th Infantry Brigade was ordered to Bertry, but as that place was still under shell fire, it was moved to Clary.   The units of the 113th Infantry Brigade billeted in Malincourt, and the 115th Infantry Brigade remained in and around Villers Outreaux.

At this time the railhead of the 38th Division was at Fins and the Divisional Train in the neighbourhood of Epehy several miles west of the St. Quentin Canal.   The train was therefore very hard put to it to feed the troops, especially the artillery east of Clary. The 330th Company, A.S.C., had to deliver to the wagon lines under fire and was not finished till 11 p.m., having left its refilling point at 8 a.m.   It then had to return to Aubencheul, where it arrived next morning, having performed a march of 40 miles in the 24 hours.

10th October.

At 21.45 hours on 9th October the 33rd Division issued orders[1] for the 98th Infantry Brigade to advance through the outposts of the 19th Infantry Brigade at 05.20 next morning, preceded by patrols, with the object of seizing the crossing of the Selle and establishing itself on the high ground in K.16. and K.10. north of Montay.   The 100th Infantry Brigade were to march at 05.00 and support the 98th, but not to close up nearer than 2,000 yards behind the rear troops of the 98th Brigade without orders from Divisional Headquarters.   Information was given that the 66th

---

[1] 33rd Division Order No. 362.

Division on the right was also advancing with a view to capturing Le Cateau.

As soon as the 98th Brigade had passed through, the 19th Brigade was to be reformed, ready to move forward at one hour's notice.

[1]The 98th Infantry Brigade advanced as ordered early on the morning of 10th October with the 2nd Argyll and Sutherland Highlanders leading, the 4th King's Liverpool Regiment in support and the 1st Middlesex in reserve. The brigade headquarters closed at Hurtevent Farm and opened at Troisvilles at 05.00.

[2]The 2nd Argyll and Sutherland Highlanders leaving Clary at 04.00 marched through Bertry to P.3.d. and formed in artillery formation astride the Bertry—Troisvilles road, with "A" company on the right, "B" company on the left, "D" company right support and "C' company left support. They moved off in this formation across country, and passed through the outposts at 05.20. Considerable numbers of cavalry were out in front, but no definite information as to the whereabouts of the enemy could be obtained. One squadron of the 5th Corps Cyclists was detailed to assist, and one section of the Divisional mounted troops was attached to the battalion for purposes of liaison. The advance proceeded satisfactorily without difficulty until the Le Cateau—Cambrai road was reached when the enemy put down a barrage on the line K.26. central—Rambourlieux Farm. The battalion pushed on in spite of it and reached the line K.21.central. to K.14.c.0.0.

As the barrage was now heavy and no troops of the 66th Division on the right and 17th Division on the left could be seen anywhere, it was decided to halt till their arrival. About 08.00 troops of the 66th Division were seen to come over the slope of the hill in K.26, moving forward rapidly and in good order. As soon as these troops arrived on the right of the battalion "A" company and "D" company (which had moved up during the halt to form a defensive flank on the right) and elements of "B" company pushed forward. "C" company and the remainder of "B" remained in support where they were. At the same time troops of the 17th Division were seen advancing well from Inchy.

---

[1] War Diary, 98th Infantry Brigade.

[2] Account of operations 9th—12th October. 2nd Argyll and Sutherland Highlanders.

As soon as the advance was recommenced, the whole line came under intense fire from rifles and machine guns and from field guns firing over open sights from across the river. Very heavy casualties were incurred and eventually the advance was held up with scattered elements in K.14.b and K.15.central (close down to the Selle River). The enemy shelling continued intense throughout the morning and early afternoon, and the position of our troops remained unaltered, the divisions on the right and left being checked also. All the leading troops were now on the forward slope with practically no cover.

The 7th Cavalry Brigade also advanced in the early morning with the object of passing through the Canadian Cavalry Brigade at 06.00. The 6th Inniskilling Dragoons sent one squadron to Le Cateau and Montay, and the 7th Dragoon Guards sent one squadron to Neuvilly. The brigade moved to the area between Rambourlieux Farm and the Inchy—Le Cateau road. An officers patrol of the 17th Lancers was sent to reconnoitre the Selle valley north west of Neuvilly. All these advanced detachments reported meeting with heavy fire and that the line of the Selle River was strongly held. At 09.30 the brigade was withdrawn 1000 yards to avoid shell fire, leaving out two observation posts. In this short time it had lost 9 officers wounded, 11 other ranks killed, and 73 other ranks wounded, 51 horses killed, 59 wounded and 21 missing. The infantry who held this front subsequently found that a sunken road in front of Rambourlieux Farm was left full of dead horses and cavalry equipment. In the evening the Cavalry Corps was withdrawn from in front of the Fourth and Third Armies, as it became apparent that the situation was now unsuitable for cavalry.

"K" Battery, R.H.A., was supporting the 7th Cavalry Brigade and came into action against hostile guns firing in the open north of Neuvilly. The 122nd Brigade, R.F.A., also supported the 7th Cavalry Brigade. Its commanding officer, Lieut.-Col. R. C. Williams, had moved forward at a very early hour in the pitch darkness. At 05.00 he pushed on ahead himself with one of his majors (A. D. C. Clarke) and some orderlies to reconnoitre and gain touch with the situation, the batteries following at 05.30 to a prearranged rendezvous. They found themselves a long way ahead of any other artillery, and at one time they were in front of the infantry. All the morning they worked with the 7th Cavalry Brigade, until the latter was withdrawn.

Lieut.-Col. Williams brought his brigade into action with the three 18 pdr. batteries north of the Inchy—Le Cateau road, 3,000 yards west north west of Le Cateau, and the howitzer battery 600 yards south of the road with O.P's on the high ground to the east of the batteries. This howitzer battery must have occupied very much the same position as the batteries of the XXVIIth Brigade, the left brigade of the 5th Division, which held the right of the British Line at the Battle of Le Cateau. The brigade H.Q. occupied two different positions during the morning and finished up sharing "B" Battery H.Q. on the Le Cateau—Inchy road. The batteries were under battery control firing by direct observation till the 5 p.m. operation.

All indications hitherto had pointed to a rapid withdrawal of the enemy, but on the railway line and high ground east of the Selle, the resistance now seemed very determined, and the batteries had rather a bad time. About mid-day the B.C's at their O.P's saw infantry and guns retiring north east in large numbers. The range was long, so "C" Battery was ordered forward 1000 yards. [1]It had to cross a ridge in full view of the enemy and as the leading section surmounted the crest it came under heavy shell fire and almost at once the firing battery wagon of No 1 sub-section became a casualty, the wheel driver and his horses being killed by a shell. When 200 yards down the forward slope the hand wheeler of No. 1 gun stumbled and fell while at the gallop, bringing the whole team to a standstill in full view of the enemy and under heavy shell fire. Quickly grasping the situation, with great coolness, the section commander, 2nd Lieut. J. C. Parsons, dismounted all but the lead driver and with great rapidity succeeded in extricating the fallen horse and getting the gun into action with the least possible delay. While the enemy's artillery was attracted by this stationary target the centre and left sections cleared the crest at the gallop, and led with great gallantry by Major A. D. C. Clarke, got into action only a few hundred yards from the enemy's infantry. The battery did splendid work against columns of hostile troops

---

[1] "History of the 38th Division."

and transport retiring up and over the high ground near Forest. It maintained itself in this position all day in the face of heavy fire. It is interesting to note that in order to avoid loss the B.C. ordered "Limber Supply". The gun teams and firing battery wagons were removed to a flank, the firing battery wagons returning to the guns and replacing the gun limbers later, during a temporary lull in the shelling. The supply of ammunition during the remaining hours of daylight was a task of some difficulty, which resulted in many additional casualties.

The History of the 33rd Divisional Artillery gives an interesting picture of the advance over the ground held by the 5th Division in 1914 :—

"Seven o'clock on the morning of the 10th saw all batteries on the move again, supporting an advance of the 98th Infantry Brigade assisted by cavalry, upon the bridge heads east of the river Selle between Neuvilly and Montay. This was a great day for the guns, and indeed for all the troops concerned, for the advance was carried out in true drill book style. Cavalry patrols in front, infantry following on, batteries first in "battery column" and then manœuvring into line, the whole countryside around Troisvilles presented the amazing spectacle of vast masses af troops moving steadily forward as though on an Aldershot field day. The 156th Brigade lay on the right of the 162nd, and together the two brigades manœuvred up to the crest of the hill which commanded the crossing of the Selle. By 8.0 a.m. the infantry were within 800 yards of the river, where they halted till such time as the divisions on the right and left had come up into line, and by the same hour the batteries had pushed through Troisvilles to a point midway between that village and Le Cateau, from which positions they vigorously shelled hostile batteries and machine guns.

In addition to the delay on the flanks, the enemy on the immediate front was showing signs of increased resistance. Several hostile field batteries had come up and were firing over open sights at our infantry, while our own batteries as they neared the crest of the hill came under heavy shell fire. With ammunition wagons detached, however, the guns pressed on under severe fire and reached the crest whence, over open sights, they were able to assist the infantry in no small measure, and throughout the day continued to engage hostile troops and movement of every description.

At the same time the German batteries rendered our positions very uncomfortable with 77 m.m. and long-range fire, while the teams which went back to Troisvilles to water found the village congested with cavalry, artillery and infantry pack-horses, all of whom suffered severe casualties through being spotted by an enemy aeroplane which called down a shell-storm upon the entire village."

4

Lieut.-Col. G. P. MacClellan describes the doing of the 121st Brigade, R.F.A., in the following words :—

"The next morning, the 10th, the brigade was ordered into position in K 31, east and south east of Troisvilles. Peskett and I, with the O.O. went ahead to reconnoitre. The latter was sent back to lead B.C's to a rendezvous, but he made a muddle, and they did not arrive for a very long time; and we had the mortification of seeing the A.G. come up, followed by the rest of the force, and all the best places which we had earmarked for ourselves were occupied by others. The artillery was mostly in a valley south east of Troisvilles, and south of the Le Cateau—Cambrai road, but one battery of the 122nd Brigade, commanded by Major A. D. C. Clarke, D.S.O., M.C., was north of the road, and quite 1,500 yards in advance of any other battery. The battery position itself was under cover, but the approach to it was over some hundreds of yards of absolutely open ground, for which reason I had earlier decided against it; Major Clarke's battery, however, remained there for days without undue loss, and did most effective work from it.

Having failed to get the best positions, as mentioned above, the 121st Brigade came into action at the bottom of the valley, with batteries, of necessity, nearly in line, with big intervals between them, and with brigade H.Q. about 100 yards behind the line, in a bell-tent. O.P's were on the high ground west of Le Cateau, one being in the cemetery made by the Germans for the British killed at the battle in 1914."

But the sad fact remains that all this movement and improvised action was of little avail once the Germans really turned to bay, and held their ground with machine guns and artillery in force.

[1]About 15.00 orders were received by the 2nd Argyll and Sutherland Highlanders to resume the attack at 17.00 in conjunction with the 66th and 17th Divisions. They were to make the attack with the 4th King's in close support, ready to push through if the 2nd Argyll and Sutherland Highlanders should be checked.

Owing to casualties and sniping on the forward slope, it was very difficult to obtain communication with the companies and issue orders. Eventually "C" company was ordered to attack on the left and "B" company on the right, with instructions to carry forward with them in their advance all the men of "A" and "D" companies whom they could find lying out on the ground that had been crossed in the morning. It will be remembered that "A" and "D" companies had led the original advance.

---

[1] Account of operations 9th—12th October. 2nd Argyll and Sutherland Highlanders.

At zero the attack proceeded under a barrage as arranged. The enemy placed a very heavy barrage on our advancing troops, but they pushed forward with great determination and gallantry and "B" and "C" companies crossed the river, "C" in K.9.c. and "B" in K.15.b. At least two platoons of the 17th Division on the left crossed also in conjunction with "C" company. On the right the 66th Division entered Montay but failed to cross the river.

A few bridges were found which were heavily wired, but they were cleared and made use of. Many men waded and swam across the river.

"B" and "C" companies continued to make satisfactory progress, and "B" established a post at K.16.a.central when held up by machine gun fire, with another post immediately behind on the road in K.16.a. These posts were slightly wired during the course of the night. "C" company on the left, though not in touch with "B" company, made similar progress, until it was suddenly discovered that the 17th Division had gone back and the enemy were working round their left from the village of Neuvilly. "C" company therefore withdrew with difficulty to K.14.central and the road in K.14.b.

The 4th King's were ordered to reinforce the two companies of the 2nd Argyll and Sutherland Highlanders, which were now very weak, by two companies, to form a defensive flank on the left facing Neuvilly with the other two companies, and gain touch with the 50th Infantry Brigade on the left which had failed to capture Neuvilly.

Owing to the darkness the 4th King's men did not reach their positions till dawn, and only after some confused fighting.

The day's operations as they appeared to the 105th Infantry Regiment on the German side are given below. Its position evidently lay to the north of the part of the front attacked by the 2nd Argyll and Sutherland Highlanders, so that the details of the fighting are not so interesting, but the reference to the re-organization of the regiment is worthy of notice :—

"At 9.0 a.m. on the 10th October, the first enemy patrols were seen on the heights west of the Selle brook and driven off by artillery fire. Already in the afternoon the enemy artillery were ranging on the railroad from Solesmes to Le Cateau and the roads leading to it. From 6 till 8 in the evening there was a heavy drum fire on the position on the heights

east of the railroad, on Amerval, and on the cross-roads 500 metres south of
Amerval. Still there was no attack on the position of the 30th Infantry
Division. On the other hand there was news from the 8th Division,
which had been put in on the left of the 30th Division, of a strong attack
from the enemy against Neuvilly, from the direction of Inchy, which was
easily repulsed the enemy sustaining heavy casualties from this attack.

The battalions which had been so weakened by the attack on October
9th, were each formed into two companies and known as I/105, out of the
1, 2, 3 and 4 companies/105; III/105 out of the 9, 10, 11 and 12/105.
Four companies of cyclists[1] from Amerval were placed at the disposal of the
30th Infantry Division as a reserve.

In the evening an enemy attack over the Selle brook was repulsed by
fire; patrols during the night found the foreground free from the enemy,
as far as the Selle brook, but it was ascertained that the enemy were
entrenched on the western band of the brook, especially towards the mill
south of Neuvilly."

CHAPTER III.

THE ATTACKS ON THE SELLE POSITION.

11th October.

The position on the morning of the 11th was as follows :—
60 men consisting of the remains of "B" company, 2nd Argyll and
Sutherland Highlanders and elements of "A" and "D" companies
with a few stray men of the 4th King's were in two posts across the
river in K.16.central. "C" company was in K.14.central, and "D"
company in K.21.b. and K.15.c. One company of the 4th King's
had managed to push forward before dawn and had established
itself across the river in K.9.c and west of the river in K.8.d.

During the course of the morning it was ascertained that the
66th Division had taken Montay and touch was established on the
western bank of the river.

Throughout the day "B" company, 2nd Argyll and Sutherland
Highlanders were exposed to extremely severe machine gun fire
and sniping from the high railway embankment which was strongly
held by the enemy and looked straight down into our posts.
About 18.30 the enemy counter-attacked "B" company and the
forward post was evacuated, the line of the road in K.16.c. being
held instead. A further platoon from "D" company was sent

---

[1] The 2nd Army was given a cyclist Brigade of six battalions of picked troops up to
full strength to assist in covering the withdrawal. This was distributed along the army
front.

Richmond Valley

Selle River.

Line of railway

Level Crossing

THE SELLE RIVER.   Just north of LE CATEAU.

From "The Story of the Fourth Army" by kind permission of General Sir Archibald Montgomery-Massingberd, K.C.B., etc.

across the river to reinforce "B" company and was placed in position to cover their right flank between the road and the river.

During the operations of these two days in the exposed ground close in front of the enemy's position the 2nd Argyll and Sutherland Highlanders lost 9 officers and 192 other ranks killed, wounded, and missing, a very high proportion of the number that went into battle. The attack of the battalion, which could hardly be expected to be completely successful if the enemy held such a good position in strength, still gained a footing across the river. The gallantry and determination with which the attack was pressed home after the long day of lying out on the exposed slopes, and the tenacity with which the ground gained was held were beyond praise.

[1]On 10th October Third Army had issued orders to V Corps to continue its operations to establish bridge-heads across the Selle on the high ground in K.17, K.11, and K.5. IV Corps and other corps on their left were to continue their advance to the Selle, and when it was reached the high ground from K.4 to the north was to be secured to safeguard the crossings. Patrols from the Corps Cavalry were to be pushed forward to keep touch with the enemy, but no further advance by the main bodies was to be carried out east of that line.

[2]At 13.55 XIII Corps 'phoned to V Corps to say that they could not attack next day owing to lack of ammunition. At 23.30 V Corps heard by telephone from Third Army that Fourth Army did not intend to do anything further at the moment, as resistance was stiffening. Any attack by V Corps would therefore be unsupported on its right.

The third Army issued no further orders on 11th October, but V and IV Corps arranged to continue their attack early on the morning of the 12th October. V Corps accordingly issued their G.588 at 18.35 ordering the 33rd and 17th Divisions to establish themselves on the high ground K.17. to K.3. to cover the construction of bridges. The zero hour was to be at 05.00. 66th Division were instructed by XIII Corps to throw forward their

---

[1] Third Army. Narrative of operations 1st October to 11th November, 1918.
[2] War Diary, V Corps.

left on to the spur K.17.—K.23. to protect the right of the 33rd Division, after it had established itself on the high ground in K.17. Pending the arrival of the 66th Division, 33rd Division was to be responsible for its own right flank.

The 33rd Division in their turn issued orders at 19.30.[1] The C.R.E. of the division was to throw 12 bridges over the river between K.16.c.5.0. and K.9.c.2.0. to enable the 100th Infantry Brigade to cross to the attack. Of these bridges at least two were to be capable of taking pack transport. The following troops were ordered to assemble in J.30., under the C.R.E., at 17.30 to construct the bridges :—

> 11th and 212th Field Companies, R.E.
> 1 company, 18th Middlesex (Pioneers).
> 2 companies from the reserve battalion, 100th Infantry Brigade.

The 100th Infantry Brigade were to carry out the attack on a two battalion front. The attacking battalions were to pass over the bridges and assemble on the north east side ready to advance at zero (05.00 hours).

12th October.

11 footbridges (9 fit for pack animals) were reported as ready by 02.00, only two casualties being incurred during their construction. The approaches to the bridges were improved and marked with tapes by the pioneers. [2]The whole operation was covered by the two companies of the 2nd Worcesters, the reserve battalion of the 100th Infantry Brigade. Prisoners subsequently stated that they were aware that bridge construction was going on, but beyond reporting the matter nothing seems to have been done to interfere with our operations, which were being conducted within close range (600 yards) of the enemy's posts along the railway. This little incident throws much light on the state of the German Army at this period. It could never have occurred earlier in the war.

The move to the assembly positions involved for the two attacking battalions a night march of three miles from Troisvilles

---

[1] 33rd Division Order, No. 363.
[2] Report on operations of 100th Infantry Brigade, October 12th, 1918.

on a very dark night, the passage over the newly constructed bridges, and assembly in battle formation within a few hundred yards of the enemy. The timings worked out satisfactorily. The 16th King's Royal Rifle Corps guided by Captain Collins, Gordon Highlanders, attached to the 100th Infantry Brigade Staff, were reported in their assembly position on the left by 04.25.; the Glasgow Highlanders on the right guided by Captain Walker, General Staff, 33rd Division, by 04.50. The latter were unfortunately caught in an artillery barrage on their way up and suffered about 40 casualties.

The general plan of attack was for the two battalions first to rush the line of the railway, which was believed to be strongly held and wired, and then to push up the spur between the ravines in K.16.d. and K.9.d. to the final objective. The Glasgow Highlanders were to throw back a defensive flank from the road junction in K.17.b. towards Richemont Mill. The two companies of the 2nd Worcesters which had formed covering parties for the bridge construction were to push up to the line of the railway embankment and consolidate it.

Headquarters were established as follows :—

> 16th King's Royal Rifle Corps in ravine in K.14.d. to move to Quarry in K.9.d. as soon as the attack had succeeded.
>
> Glasgow Highlanders in the chateau in K.22.c. to move to the ravine in K.16.d.
>
> 2nd Worcesters in K.26.b.
>
> Brigade headquarters in Rambourlieux Farm in K.19.b.

No creeping barrage could be provided for the attack owing to shortage of ammunition. The available ammunition was to be retained for protective barrages to cover consolidation and meet counter attacks. A preliminary bombardment of the enemy's position along the railway was also impracticable owing to the short notice and the fact that the 2nd Argyll and Sutherland Highlanders were holding posts close up to the railway from which they could not be withdrawn during daylight. An artillery officer makes the following caustic remarks on the operations :—

"The arrangements for this attack were faulty there being no prearranged barrage, and the batteries being expected to support the infantry by observed fire. At this time of year on the river Selle, one can see nothing till about 10 a.m. Personally, I had my batteries doing a little map-shooting all the time till the mist cleared—during the same period some energetic brigade and battery commanders probably slept soundly."

This difficulty in using observed fire in support of a big attack will probably occur on most occasions, as such attacks generally take place at dawn, when the usual mist is greatly thickened by the smoke and dust of a heavy bombardment.

As it was obvious that the railway cutting and the spur above it in K.22.b. would be of great tactical importance, and as no co-operation in the form of an attack was to be obtained from the 66th Division on the right, a company of the 33rd M.G. Battalion was specially detailed to engage these points from zero onwards. Two sections of another company were detailed to give covering fire from the high ground west of the Selle, and the other two sections of this company were detailed to give immediate support to the attacking battalions, and to assist in the consolidation of the objective.

Two Stokes Mortars of the 100th Trench Mortar Battery were placed in the Orchard in K.22.a. to fire on the railway embankment immediately to the right of the Glasgow Highlanders advance from zero onwards.

[1]The two attacking battalions formed up along the road in K.16 and 9, the Glasgow Highlanders on the right with two companies in front and two in support, each on a two platoon frontage. The 16th King's Royal Rifle Corps were in similar formation, "A" company with "C" company in support on the right, and "D" company with "B" in support on the left.

During the forming up the enemy who had noticed the bridging operations and were very much on the alert opened a hot fire on the Glasgow Highlanders, but did comparatively little damage owing to their being in dead ground.

At zero both battalions advanced rapidly, the light being just sufficiently good. The advance was met by a heavy fire but in spite of it the 16th King's Royal Rifle Corps made headway, and though no reports were received at battalion headquarters from

---

[1] War Diary, Glasgow Highlanders, 16th King's Royal Rifle Corps and 100th Infantry Brigade.

company commanders, returning wounded reported that the attack was proceeding satisfactorily. At 08.00 "C" company reported that they were in position on the high ground in K.10., with their right in the air, as the 9th Highland Light Infantry (the Glasgow Highlanders) were held up, but were making progress towards the railway. "D" company were reported to be without officers owing to casualties, but they were said to be on their objective. In their advance over the railway the 16th King's Royal Rifle Corps took 30 or 40 prisoners.

The Glasgow Highlanders were not so successful. When they moved a barrage fell on them, and a nest of machine guns on the railway opened an enfilading fire. They were unable to surmount a belt of wire running along about 60 yards from the railway, and the leading companies decided to withdraw to the road. At 06.00 it was found that the 16th King's Royal Rifle Corps had reached the railway. This eased the situation and gave the battalion a chance of gaining ground on the left. It was therefore decided to advance again and take the machine guns from the left. This was done and the machine guns with about 40 prisoners were captured. (A nice piece of " 'soft spot' tactics".) A further advance was then attempted, but heavy machine gun fire from along the railway in K.22.b., and from some practice trenches on the hill-side made this impossible. Two of the machine guns temporarily attached to the battalion were posted on the railway to protect the right flank, and a captured machine gun was used to cover the right rear of the battalion. As an advance straight to the front was found impossible, it was decided to work up a small depression south of the ravine in K.16.a. and b., and attack from that direction. A small party reached K.16.b.9.9., but on arriving there it was found that the King's Royal Rifle Corps were falling back. This small party therefore withdrew to the railway.

At 09.00 Colonel Pardoe commanding the 16th King's Royal Rifle Corps was sufficiently satisfied with the position on his own front to feel that he could move his headquarters to the Quarry in K.9.d. As the party left the ravine in K.14.d. a heavy barrage was put down on the whole battalion area, but especially severely on the ravine, the bridges across the Selle, and the line of the railway. In conjunction with this barrage a successful counter-attack was launched by the enemy from the north on the left flank of "A" and "C" companies. This was made possible by the fact that the right of the 17th Division had made little progress about Neuvilly.

Battalion headquarters consequently arrived at the Quarry to find it occupied in force by the enemy. A Lewis gun was brought up by the headquarters which prevented the enemy crossing the railway at that point. Colonel Pardoe was badly wounded here, and a runner was sent back to report the situation to Major Willis who had been left at the report centre in ravine K.14.d. Meanwhile the adjutant and intelligence officer with the Lewis gun held on and tried to find out the situation in front. The barrages and machine gun fire at this time were very heavy and the headquarters eventually fell back to the road about K.15.a.1.0., where the report came in that the leading troops had been driven in from the final objective and had taken up a position on the railway. By noon the battalion, under continued pressure from the left, had withdrawn disorganized to the road through K.14.b. and 15.c., and the headquarters to the old place in the ravine. Reorganization was begun at once.

The barrage which came down on the 16th King's Royal Rifle Corps at 09.20 fell on the Glasgow Highlanders on the railway also. It lasted for one and a half hours and caused a number of casualties. It then lifted onto the valley behind. During the barrage the enemy worked round the right of the battalion in twos and threes and crossed the railway at K.22.b.4.5. They were engaged with rifle and machine gun fire, but they managed to get on, and shortly afterwards they opened machine gun fire along the railway from emplacements in the cutting.

At 10.20 it was found that the King's Royal Rifle Corps' flank had also been turned and the Glasgow Highlanders to prevent themselves from being surrounded fell back to the road in K.16., where they maintained themselves east of the river in spite of the heavy losses they had suffered, and the fact that both their flanks were in the air.

At 10.00 the officer commanding 1st Middlesex, of the 98th Infantry Brigade, arrived at the headquarters of the 100th Brigade to place himself under its orders. He was directed to establish himself at the headquarters of the 16th King's Royal Rifle Corps and to prepare to carry out a fresh attack, with a view to driving the enemy back from the railway. This attack was not carried out, as by the time the leading companies had arrived the situation on the left had made it temporarily impracticable.

At 12.20 the brigadier was informed by the divisional commander that at 14.00 a further effort was to be made by the 17th Division to clear the ground in front of the right battalion of that division, to enable it to reach the railway line, and that at 17.00 a further general attack was to be made by that division, with which the 100th Brigade was to co-operate, to reach the objectives originally laid down.

The gist of the above was at once explained verbally by telephone to all battalion commanders, and they were directed to reorganize their units at once, with a view to renewing the attack. The 1st Middlesex was to be on the left of the new attack. As it was obvious that the line of the railway embankment was again strongly held, it was arranged to shell it as thoroughly as possible with all available artillery till 5 p.m. The attack was to open with five minutes intense artillery bombardment, and was then to be supported with a creeping barrage. From 14.00 hours onwards the enemy's artillery fire slackened somewhat, but heavy sniping with rifles and machine guns made all movement round and in front of battalion headquarters very difficult. At 15.45 instructions were received from the division postponing the attack from 17.00 to 17.30. At 16.00 telephonic instructions were received cancelling the attack, owing to the situation of the 17th Division having been rendered unfavourable, its left battalion which had hitherto maintained itself on its objective having been driven in.

The 100th Brigade was therefore ordered to consolidate its position on the Selle River with posts on the eastern bank to cover the bridges.

The brigade took between 60 and 70 prisoners.

The strength on going into action and casualties were as follows :—

	Strength on going into action.		Casualties.	
	Officers	Other ranks	Officers	Other ranks
2nd Worcesters	15	299	4	46
16th King's Royal Rifle Corps ...	13	372	4	143
Glasgow Highlanders	19	312	8	160

The fighting of the day is described in the History of the 105th Infantry Regiment in the following words :—

"The 11th of October and the night of the 11th/12th, apart from artillery fire from time to time, were quiet, then on the 12th October at 6 a.m., there was a terrific and sudden drum fire over the whole German position. Shortly after a strong enemy attack against the left wing of the 105th Infantry Regiment and the right wing of the 205th Infantry Regiment developed. (The enemy advanced to the attack between the two regiments, up a hollow which gave them cover). He succeeded in penetrating to, and establishing himself on the Montay—Amerval road, and in the eastern corner of the cutting in the position occupied by the 205th Regiment. III/105 then prepared to counter-attack; this followed at 10 a.m., after heavy artillery fire as a preparation and was entirely successful.[1] III/105, supported by I/105, one cyclist company (Jag. 14) and part of 205th regiment, attacking from a north-westerly direction, succeeded in driving the English out of the position they occupied in the main line of resistance and in doing so took several prisoners and released some who had been taken prisoner. The last enemy posts were driven back across the Selle brook by officers patrols by the evening of October 12th, and the German position was again in our own hands."

As stated in the History of the 105th Regiment the River Selle position formed the southern part of the Lys—Hermann Stellung, a line of defences projected but not prepared by the Germans. Some valuable light is thrown on this point and on the intentions of the German High Command by two orders captured later, at the end of October.

The first is an order, dated 18th October, by the 18th Reserve Infantry Brigade which states "The tactical situation makes it absolutely necessary to push on more quickly the consolidation of Hermann Stellung into a permanent line of defence. It is not overlooked, however, that the present condition of the troops

---

[1] This was evidently the barrage and counter-attack which drove the 16th King's Royal Rifle Corps back from the position they had taken.

renders the task of stimulating their zeal in erecting defensive works all the more difficult".

The other is an order, dated 19th October, by General Von Larisch, commanding LIV Corps, opposed to V Corps (British), which runs as follows:—"The Army Group will accept decisive battle on the Lys—Hermann line. This must be held at any price. To be notified to all commanders down to regimental commanders".

Given that the enemy intended to hold his ground, and it was now quite evident to the British higher command that he did so, there was no reason to hope that another attack like that of October 12th launched without proper artillery support would be any more successful than that had been.

Consequently there was nothing to be done except to sit down and wait till all the means required to mount a full-dress attack could be brought up. It may be questioned whether even the attack of 12th October was justified, after the information gained by the reconnaissance in force of the 10th October.

While the operations just described were in progress the 38th Division had been closed up to Troisvilles and Bertry with a view to relieving the 33rd Division in the line on the night of 12th/13th October, but owing to the outcome of the fighting on the 12th this relief was postponed till the night of 13th/14th.

This will be a suitable place to trace the movements of the brigades of the 38th Division, and to give some account of the conditions prevailing behind the front line.

After the battle of 8th October, at the end of which the 114th Infantry Brigade was the leading brigade of the 38th Division, this brigade was ordered to move to billets at Bertry on 9th October, but as that place was under shell fire its destination was changed to Clary. There it remained refitting, resting and training till 12th October. On that day the brigade commander and officers commanding units proceeded to the headquarters of the 100th Infantry Brigade for reconnaissance of a relief, and the units started for Troisvilles, but the G.S.O.1, 38th Division, ordered them to return to Clary to their original billets, on the postponement of the relief.

The 113th Infantry Brigade after the battle remained in Malincourt on the 10th and 11th, and on the 12th moved to Bertry, where it relieved the 19th Infantry Brigade, as supporting brigade of the 33rd Division. The move was made across country, and artillery formations were practised on the way.

The 115th Infantry Brigade remained around Villers Outreaux on 9th October and moved to Clary and Bertry on the 11th. The 17th Royal Welsh Fusiliers and 10th South Wales Borderers were accommodated in Clary and the 2nd Royal Welsh Fusiliers and machine guns in Bertry. On 12th October the whole brigade moved to Troisvilles in anticipation of relieving the 100th Infantry Brigade in the line. Officers and N.C.O's from each battalion were as usual sent up into the line to reconnoitre the positions they were to hold and the lines of approach to them.

A remarkable feature of these days was the joy and excitement of the civil population who had defied the German orders for evacuation, and had now been liberated after four years enemy occupation. They everywhere received the troops with the greatest enthusiasm. Tricolour flags were soon conspicuous and speeches of welcome from village Maires were frequent. The inhabitants quickly learned to raise white flags on the houses occupied by them, and our troops did their best to spare these from fire or damage. The Germans had used the Church at Clary as a hospital, and on leaving had placed a dozen 5·9″ shells in position to blow it up. These were removed by the divisional engineers of the 38th Division and stacked outside, and when Lieut.-Col A. G. Lyttelton commanding the 38th Machine Gun Battalion arrived, he found the Curé and his underling sweeping out a great deal of German litter, the place full of soldiery, and a very gallant battalion commander playing the Hallelujah Chorus on the organ with his adjutant blowing it.

A very curious incident happened on the British entry into Bertry. In this village was found a British cavalryman who had been kept in hiding by an old woman of the village in a cupboard in her cottage, all among the German soldiers billeted in it, ever since the retirement from Mons in 1914. When our troops got into the village this man was arrested as a suspicious character. At that moment an officer of the Cavalry Corps Staff (Major Drake, 11th

Hussars) happened to drive by in a motor car. The man called out to him that he knew him, and sure enough the officer recognized him as having been in his troop. They had all been cut off near this place, and the officer and one man had got away and made their way back to Boulogne, while this man had lurked about for four years, and by an extraordinary coincidence his troop officer was one of the first people he saw when the British came in in 1918.[1]

The treatment which the inhabitants had received had depended a good deal on the officer who happened to be commandant of the place. The Germans had commandeered all the corn and there were no animals of any sort about. About a fortnight before the British entry, the inhabitants had received an order to bring in all their chickens, but instead they killed them and buried them, and ever since they had been living on chicken pies. The Germans themselves were very badly off, and they used to complain to the inhabitants that they were comparatively better off than themselves, as they got food from the American Commission which distributed rations to the inhabitants in the occupied areas.

There is an interesting entry in the War Diary of the Adjutant and Quartermaster General's Staff, 38th Division, which states that the staff gave a free tea and cinema show to the children of Bertry on the 19th October.

No mention has been made of the doings of the Royal Air Force, but their activity had been great throughout, and by this time a marked superiority had been established over the enemy air-force whose bombing during the earlier part of the year had been most severe on the troops just behind the line and in the back areas. Although not strictly within the period embraced by this narrative, it may be of interest to give an account of the doings on three days of fine weather as seen by the troops on a single brigade front in the middle of September, when the 38th

---

[1] This incident was taken from a private letter of the writer's, but since writing the above he has found that it is described at length in Captain Spear's book "Liaison," Appendix XXIII.

This patrol of the XIth Hussars was cut off after the battle of Le Cateau, and besides Trooper Fowler another man belonging to it Corporal Hall was also befriended and concealed by another peasant family in Bertry. After some time he was betrayed by a woman of the village and shot by the Germans, while the family were maltreated and imprisoned. After the Armistice the women who were chiefly instrumental in protecting these soldiers received a small grant from the War Office, and subscriptions were raised for them by the officers of the XIth Hussars and by the *Daily Telegraph*. They came to England and were received by the King.

Division was in the line west of the St. Quentin Canal, and when air activity was specially great.

On the first day of which we are speaking the Germans suddenly put down a fierce bombardment on our front trenches, which after a quarter of an hour advanced over the support and reserve lines. It looked as if a big attack might take place, but the enemy only sent over an attack on a front of 400 or 500 yards. Our men behaved very well, put up their heads at once as soon as the barrage lifted and beat off the attack. Soon after this a German plane came over quite low, not more than 200 or 300 feet up, and began to look and see what had happened. Our guns and machine guns fired at it, but it came back two or three times. At last the machine guns hit it, and it turned and came down in a hollow just behind the German line, where our aeroplanes located it. That night the enemy came over bombing and the troops saw two of their big bombing planes brought down. The searchlights concentrated on them, and in a few seconds the tracer bullets were seen rushing into them out of the darkness from our fighting planes. One plane burst into a great ball of fire and fell like a stone, and when it hit the ground all the bombs and petrol burst into a great red blaze. The other must have been hit in the part where it carried its light signals, because it carried on for miles slanting lower and lower towards the German lines, spitting out red, white and green lights and rockets all the way. At last it also came down in flames.

The next day seven of our planes were seen to catch a German, and he very soon came slanting down in flames. Altogether three bombing planes and two others were brought down close round the neighbourhood this day. It might have been hoped that after these losses this part of the line might have had a quiet night, but the bombing that night was some of the heaviest experienced in the war. Literally hundreds of bombs were dropped, and gas shelling kept people awake all night. One more German plane was brought down in the searchlights. It fell like a great ball of fire spitting out coloured lights. It was a brilliant moonlight night and the spectacle a very fine one. Although the effect was not immediate, this kind of thing oft repeated on a great length of front gradually established British air superiority, of which the troops began to reap the benefit by the time the River Selle was reached.

13th October.

In the evening the 115th Infantry Brigade relieved the 100th Infantry Brigade in the line. The units left their billets at Troisvilles at 16.45. The 2nd Royal Welsh Fusiliers were on the right, "C" and "D" companies in front line, "A" and "B" in support. The 10th South Wales Borderers on the left had "A" and "D" in front with "B" and "C" in support and reserve. The dividing line between battalions was the junction of the hedge and stream at K.15.d.8.7.—the hedge at K.20.b.8.4. and the road junction at K.25.a.6.0. The leading companies held the bridgeheads across the river where they existed. Both battalions had their headquarters at Rambourlieux Farm. The 17th Royal Welsh Fusiliers, in brigade reserve remained in Troisvilles.

The 100th Infantry Brigade after relief marched to billets for the night in Troisvilles, and next day moved back to Clary.

14th, 15th, 16th and 17th October.

No change took place in the general situation on these days. Battalions in the front line sent out strong fighting patrols at night, which inflicted casualties on the enemy and brought back information of the enemy's disposition on the railway. One of these patrols, of the 10th South Wales Borderers, on 18th October endeavoured to occupy and hold the quarry in K.15.b. They succeeded in capturing it and killing the garrison with bombs; but after posts had been established, the place was found to be too liable to be cut off, and was evacuated. The battalions relieved their front line companies on the night of the 16th with their supporting companies.

The splendid old Rambourlieux Farm with its fine farm buildings standing high up on the forward slope, where the two battalion headquarters had been established, was subjected to almost continuous bombardment with all natures of light and medium shells.

The four brigades of field artillery covering the divisional front at this time were firing 800 to 1000 rounds per battery a day in observed fire, concentrations and harassing fire. Life for them living in the open fields was not so comfortable as it had been in dug-outs. Many dead horses were lying about, most of them with portions cut off for food by the enemy or the inhabitants.

5

On the night of the 15th/16th, the 121st Brigade, R.F.A., was subjected to an intense bombardment with double-yellow-cross gas shell for some hours.   The bottom of the valley in which they were was repeatedly swept from end to end, the mean point of impact being between Brigade Headquarters and the batteries, the wind blowing towards the latter.   It was not realized in the batteries until too late that the shell were gas, and not H.E., this being the first experience of this type of gas-shell in the 38th Division, in addition they were engaged in firing harassing fire at the time. The result was disastrous.   In "A" and "B" Batteries, by 08.00 hours, every single officer, N.C.O. and man at the guns, with the exception in each case of a single corporal, was out of action, and all had to be evacuated.   "D" Battery was a little better off, but lost its B.C. and half its personnel.   "C" Battery lost one officer and about a dozen men, and Brigade Headquarters lost the medical officer killed.   The total losses were 12 officers and over 100 men. It is a curious fact that the solitary survivor in both "A" and "B" Batteries each did the same thing, and that contrary to everything that had been taught about gas; each rolled himself up in a blanket, lay down in the deepest slit trench that he could find, and went to sleep.   Battery positions were moved forward out of the gassed area, and on the 19th October, the Brigade Headquarters was established alongside the 113th Infantry Brigade Headquarters on the Le Cateau—Cambrai Road.

"D" Battery, 122nd Brigade, R.F.A. (Howitzers) also suffered heavy gas casualties on this occasion.

Owing to the bad weather the officer commanding the 122nd Brigade on the 16th October transferred his headquarters from those of "B" Battery into the Maire's house in Troisvilles, from 1900 to 3200 yards from his batteries.   This was inconveniently far for this class of warfare, but he installed a Telephone Test Point between himself and his batteries.

On 17th October there was an instance of the extreme vulnerability of horses when aeroplane bombs are being dropped, a thing noticed many times during the war.   On this night 30 horses were killed and 20 wounded in the wagon lines of "B" Battery, 122nd Brigade, R.F.A., in Troisvilles, and in consequence all the wagon lines were shifted.

[1]In addition to the field artillery, the corps heavy artillery, and the mobile 6″ trench mortars of the two divisions were also brought into action during the days of waiting. These mobile sections had been improvised by providing one of the mortars of a division with a pair of low wheels which could be hitched on to an infantry limbered wagon. The only possible positions for them were of necessity in the open ravines facing the enemy, and they could only fire at night, but it was afterwards found, when the Selle had been crossed, that this blind fire had been very successful. The difficulty of moving the mortars and providing carrying parties for the ammunition from the tired infantry, prevented more than a very small number being used in this way. But they added much noise and explosive force to the bombardments, and their use to a limited extent was justified; while the remaining personnel of the trench mortar batteries was available for drafting to the field batteries to replace casualties, as happened after the heavy hostile gas shelling mentioned above.

By the 14th October it had been possible to bring up some more of the "frightfulness" of position warfare, and gas projectors were installed by "N" Special Company, R.E. These should have been discharged that night, but the wind was unfavourable and they could not be fired till the night of the 17th. The enemy retaliated by gas shelling our forward companies in the line.

At 05.20 on the 17th October an attack by the Fourth Army began, the 66th Division being on the left, and the 38th Divisional Artillery assisting. The line of the railway was captured up to Baillon Farm. As a consequence of these operations hostile artillery was abnormally active, and Rambourlieux Farm was specially heavily shelled, and an advanced section of "D" Battery, 122nd Brigade, suffered about 30 casualties mostly from gas, the detachments having to be withdrawn from the guns in the afternoon. Troisvilles also received some very unpleasant shelling.

18th October.

The day passed more quietly on the front of the 38th Division, though the attack on the front of the Fourth Army was resumed

---

[1] The Corps Heavy Artillery was very powerful, consisting of the 13th, 17th, 22nd and 24th Brigades, R.G.A., and the 58th Army Brigade, R.G.A. More detailed mention will be made of these later.

at 05.30. The 66th Division cleared Le Cateau and made progress on to the high ground between Le Cateau and Bazuel capturing the latter place.

At night the front of the 38th Division was extended southwards to include the Montay—Forest road. This was done by the 115th Infantry Brigade and the 9th Gloucesters of the 66th Division being relieved on the new divisional front by the 113th Infantry Brigade on the right and the 114th Infantry Brigade on the left, these brigades, which were intended to carry out the impending attack, taking over their battle fronts for the forthcoming operations. The 115th Infantry Brigade moved back to Troisvilles.

THE DELIBERATE ATTACK ON THE RIVER SELLE POSITION.

19th October.

The details of the above mentioned relief were as follows :—

On the 113th Infantry Brigade front, the 13th Royal Welsh Fusiliers took over the line held by the 9th Gloucesters, and one company 14th Royal Welsh Fusiliers took over the line held by the right company 2nd Royal Welsh Fusiliers, the whole front line coming under the orders of the officer commanding 13th Royal Welsh Fusiliers. The remaining three companies 14th Royal Welsh Fusiliers and the 16th Royal Welsh Fusiliers did not move from their billets in Bertry.

On the 114th Infantry Brigade front, the 13th Welsh took over the front held by the left company 2nd Royal Welsh Fusiliers, and the 14th Welsh took over the whole of the dispositions of the 10th South Wales Borderers, the 15th Welsh remaining in their billets in Troisvilles.

The boundaries between the 38th and 66th Divisions, and between the 113th and 114th Infantry Brigades are shown on Map 4.

All posts east of the River Selle on the 114th Infantry Brigade front were ordered to be withdrawn immediately before dawn and reoccupied immediately after dusk.

[1]It had been arranged for some days that the deliberate attack on the Selle position should be carried out by the 38th Division.

---

[1] War Diary, 38th Division and 113th Infantry Brigade.

The time from the 14th to 20th was therefore spent in carrying out the careful preparations necessary to ensure success.

Reconnaissances of the river line and the enemy's position were made, and information gained from the attack of the 33rd Division was issued to units by the headquarters of the 38th Division. A narrative of that attack was issued, giving the course of the fight, the action of the enemy, the directions from which hostile fire came, together with descriptions of the river, the railway embankments and cuttings, the wire and places where cover could be obtained. The divisional headquarters also issued a map[1] compiled from air photographs showing groups of dug-out shafts organized shell holes and rifle pits, constituting centres of resistance. Brig.-Genl. apRhys Pryce, commanding the 113th Infantry Brigade, sent in a series of notes to divisional headquarters requesting that certain specified centres of resistance, machine gun positions, and groups of hostile artillery should receive special attention from our artillery before the attack, and also that wire cutting should be carried out. [2]Acting on these requests the guns daily bombarded the railway, the hostile trenches and batteries, the ravines east of the Selle and every point which might be utilized by the enemy. Gas was fired nightly into the ravines, and every hostile effort to put out wire was nullified. The result of this fire, although not apparent at the time, was clearly shown later, when the batteries on advancing found the embankment covered with the bodies of dead Germans, many of whom from their mangled state had evidently been killed by shell fire.

[3]This period of preparation was also spent in improving the crossings which work was entrusted to the 123rd Field Company, R.E., under Major Pressy. By the time of the attack twenty four footbridges and one tank bridge had been placed across the river and the approaches to them marked with tape. This was a task of considerable difficulty, for except on our left centre we had no posts across the river, so that the work had to be done in front of the outpost line. In some places it was possible to launch these bridges beforehand and leave them concealed, but in others

---

[1] Map 4 is a reproduction of this map.
[2] "History of the 33rd Divisional Artillery."
[3] "History of the 38th Welsh Division."

the bridges had to be carried down on the night of and the night before the attack. The company had only 35 men available for this work and they were employed on it for 74 hours out of 96. They were loud in their praise of the assistance given them by the carrying party of the 17th Royal Welsh Fusiliers, the reserve battalion. So successful were these bridging operations, that when the time came the railway embankment was a much greater obstacle than the river itself.

On 17th October the Third Army issued their orders for an attack on the 20th, to be directed on Le Quesnoy (see Map 1). [1]Further orders were issued on the 19th for the army to continue the advance towards the line, Englefontaine—Ghissignies—Ruesnes—Quernaing (not shown on map, last named about 7 miles to the north east of Englefontaine). If the enemy retired he was to be followed up, and if the final objective was not reached the Third Army was to attack again on the 22nd, with the zero the same for all corps and armies.

[2]The V Corps orders issued on the 17th gave the objectives for the first phase to the 38th and 17th Divisions, and detailed the 33rd and 21st Divisions for the second phase. As the Fourth Army were not co-operating the right of the 38th Division would be refused, and would be linked up with the 66th Division on the line of the railway. On gaining the final objective divisions were to exploit and push outposts beyond it.

The attack was to be carried out as a surprise without preliminary bombardment. The barrage was to open at zero and rest on the initial line for four minutes and then advance by lifts of 100 yards every four minutes. There were to be three objectives for the first phase (see map 4) and a protector barrage was to pause on each of these before continuing at the same pace.

[3]As regards V Corps heavy artillery, bombardment and barrage tables were drawn up for certain sections of the 6″ howitzers of the 54th, 22nd and 13th Brigades, R.G.A. The remaining sections and batteries of the heavy artillery (except all the 60-prs. and 6″ howitzers of the 17th Brigade which were under the orders

---

[1] Third Army No. 76/285.
[2] V Corps operations, Order No. 238.
[3] V Corps H.A. Instructions No. 215.

of the 38th Division), were placed at the disposal of the Counter Battery staff officer V Corps.

Two machine gun companies from the supporting divisions and two tanks were allotted to each of the attacking divisions.

Additional bridges for tanks and guns were to be put in hand as soon as possible after zero hour.

[1]The 38th Division's order consequent on the above gave the details of the employment of the machine gun companies, "B" and "D" companies, 38th Battalion, Machine Gun Corps, were to be under the orders of the 113th and 114th Infantry Brigades respectively for the protection of the final objective, the remainder of the available machine guns of the two divisions were to fire on certain specified targets including organized centres of resistance shown on the intelligence map, and lift from them in conformity with the artillery barrage. The whole of the trench mortars comprising four 6″ Newton trench mortars and twenty two Stokes mortars under the divisional trench mortar officer were to open on certain specified targets at zero, and also lift in conformity with the artillery barrage. On conclusion of their bombardment the 113th and 114th Light Trench Mortar Batteries were to follow their brigades on to the final objective.

The two tanks were to cross by the tank bridge at K.16.c.0.5. and operate one with each infantry brigade, a platoon being allotted to accompany each. One troop of "A" Squadron, 5th Cyclist Regiment was allotted to each brigade for employment in exploitation and communication.

Twelve foot bridges were allotted to each brigade, and the construction of the two artillery bridges in K.16.c. and K.15.d. and two more heavy bridges was to be begun at once, the track to them being marked from the road junction at K.25.a.6.0. The whole of the divisional R.E., one field company, R.E., 33rd Division, and one company Glamorgan Pioneers, all under the C.R.E., were to be employed on this work.

The position when captured was to be consolidated in depth, and the 115th Infantry Brigade was to be ready to move at 05.00 to take up the following dispositions in support :—

---

[1] 38th Division Order No. 244.

One battalion holding the line of the river on each brigade
front distributed in depth, one battalion in reserve in
Troisvilles.

The headquarters of the 113th and 114th Infantry Brigades,
the 121st and 122nd Brigades, R.F.A., and the 38th Battalion,
Machine Gun Corps, were to be established at K.25.d.7.4. (in a
bank in the main road) and a divisional report centre at the
headquarters of the 115th Infantry Brigade in Troisvilles.

The 15th Squadron, Royal Air Force, was detailed by V Corps
to send out a contact patrol at dawn and at the odd hours, e.g.
09.00 and 11.00. A counter-attack patrol was to be up continuously, and drop a red smoke bomb if any hostile assembly for a
counter-attack were seen.

The plan of the 113th Infantry Brigade who attacked on the
right, was for the 13th and 14th Royal Welsh Fusiliers to attack
the first objective with two companies each, and for the remaining
companies to leap frog and take the second objective. The right
company of the 14th Royal Welsh Fusiliers was to be responsible
for mopping up the buildings in K.16.c. and 22.a.

Two companies of the 16th Royal Welsh Fusiliers were to
follow up the 13th Royal Welsh Fusiliers and form up facing
east on a line through K.22.central and attack eastward, forming
a defensive flank along the Roman road. The remaining two
companies of the 16th Royal Welsh Fusiliers were to remain in
brigade reserve south west of the river. The battalions were to be
drawn up on a two company front, each company on a two
platoon front, and each platoon in two waves.

The compass bearing of the direction of attack of both
battalions which was given to all platoon commanders was 74°
magnetic. The tank, arriving at dawn, was to mop up as far
as the railway inclusive and then move up to K.17.

When the time arrived the 13th Royal Welsh Fusiliers, which
was already in the line, formed up with its two leading companies
on the enemy bank of the river. Rain was falling heavily, but
a moon shone through the mist, and it was sufficiently light to see
objects by which to identify one's position.

One company of the 14th Royal Welsh Fusiliers was already in the line, and the other three marched across country from Bertry after dark (20.30 hours) to the position of assembly on the east bank of the Selle. Advanced parties had gone forward at dusk under Major Wheldon and had laid out tapes from the river to the assembly positions. As a result the assembly worked without a hitch, and all the companies reached their positions undisturbed by 01.00.

Zero hour was at 02.00, at which hour the barrage of artillery, trench mortars and machine guns opened. The rate of the barrage was 100 yards in 4 minutes to give the infantry ample time to keep up with it in the difficult and slippery ground and darkness. Its density may be judged from the fact that the front allotted to the 122nd Brigade, R.F.A., was 600 yards at the opening of the barrage and 500 yards at the end (25 and 21 yards respectively to each gun and howitzer).

The 13th Royal Welsh Fusiliers advanced with "A" and "D" companies in front formed in a double wave of section columns to take the first objective wich included the railway and the ground just beyond it. The fighting for the railway was severe, but it was carried well up to time (02.30 hours) without undue losses. The 16th Royal Welsh Fusiliers under Major Dale on the extreme right, who should have been following up with a view to forming a defensive flank, joined in the attack and materially assisted in this success, reaching the railway among the first and then turning left handed to take some hostile machine guns in rear. The enemy soon began surrendering freely. On the first objective "B" and "C" companies passed through, and meeting with only slight opposition swept on to the final objective, and consolidation was at once begun assisted by a platoon of the 19th Welsh Pioneers, who dug two strong points.

Similarly "A" and "C" companies, 14th Royal Welsh Fusiliers, moving with the barrage took the railway after some stubborn resistance, but with few casualties. "B" and "D" companies passing through on the first objective attacked with vigour, and after some fighting with enemy machine gun posts reached the final objective with remarkably few casualties (1 officer and 7 other ranks killed and 1 officer and 27 other ranks wounded).

The plan of the 114th Infantry Brigade was to attack with the 13th Welsh on the right and the 14th Welsh on the left. One company of the 15th Welsh was to be attached to the 13th and two to the 14th Welsh, the remainder of the battalion being in brigade reserve. The attacking infantry were to assemble on the enemy side of the river, between it and the road. It was doubtful if the 14th Welsh could do so, unless the house at K.15.b.7.8. and the quarry at K.15.b.5.9. could be captured beforehand.

The attack was to be on the "leap frog" system, two companies of each battalion taking the first objective, the third and fourth companies passing through them to capture the second objective and advance later to the third. The pioneers and attached companies of the 15th Welsh were to follow the rear companies of the attacking battalions, and the latter were to take over the area about the railway. Each attacking battalion was to detail an inner flank guard of about one section to advance level with the leading waves along the edges of the ravine in K.16.a., while the right battalion was to detail a mopping up party to advance up the ravine itself.

The position was to be consolidated in depth, the leading sections on or just west of the crest line about the final objective. Two sections of machine guns and two Stokes mortars were attached to each battalion for use in consolidation. After the capture of the final objective posts were to be pushed forward to get as good a view as possible to the north east.

As regards the assembly for the attack of the 114th Infantry Brigade, the 13th Welsh had one company in the front line and the other three in support and reserve. After dark the company commanders went forward for a final reconnaissance of the position of assembly and the bridges, and battalion headquarters moved to a dug out at K.20.b.9.2. It rained continuously throughout the night and there was intermittent hostile shelling, while machine guns were active at intervals from the railway, covering the ground to the south west of the river. At 23.00 the covering party of one platoon proceeded across the river and took up its position near the road from K.16.c.4.4. to K.16.a.1.1., without being detected by the enemy. The remainder of the battalion and attached troops followed by the same bridge, and were deployed across the river by 01.00. At that hour they moved forward quietly in succession until the leading companies were under the bank on the east side of the road, about 150 yards from the enemy, still without detection. It is probable that the heavy rain drowned the sound of movement though it made the ground slippery and heavy. Artillery and machine gun fire was also used to drown the sound of assembly.

The assembly of the 14th Welsh was more complicated. On the night of 18th/19th October they had captured with some difficulty the house at K.15.b.7.8., but after a heavy fight in which they sustained casualties to 1 officer and 12 other ranks they failed to drive the enemy out of the quarry at K.15.b.5.9. The battalion was therefore compelled to assemble west of the Selle, and do its best to cross the river and close up to the barrage after zero.

When the barrage came down at zero it rested on the railway for four minutes, and as soon as it lifted the 13th Welsh rushed into the cutting and got possession before the enemy could recover from their surprise. The 14th Welsh had difficulty in crossing the river and some confusion developed, they however succeeded in closing up to the barrage, and also rushed the railway when the barrage lifted. Four rows of single wire fence ran between the road and the railway, but these did not cause great inconvenience. Lieut.-Col. G. Brooke, commanding the battalion, states that fortunately the enemy's machine guns were badly sited being on the top of the embankment so that they fired over our men's heads when they were getting through the wire.[1] The railway was found to be heavily defended by machine guns, and about 30 of the enemy were killed here and about 60 taken prisoners. The enemy put up a good fight in the quarry, where three trench mortars were captured and several of the enemy killed and taken prisoners.

The barrage checked in front of the first objective for ten minutes and the leading companies began digging in. The third and fourth companies quickly followed on, while the attached companies of the 15th Welsh remained on the railway to mop up.

The two sections of the 13th Welsh detailed to clear the ravine came under hot fire from the ravine and suffered severe casualties,

---

[1] It will be remembered that the same thing happened to the Glasgow Highlanders during the attack of 12th October.

only three men remaining unwounded. The lower end was subsequently cleared by another party of moppers up, and a machine gun higher up was knocked out by a section of one of the leading companies. At 02.34 the third and fourth companies passed through, without being checked by the resistance in the ravine, and the only opposition met with was from scattered infantry and machine gun posts. By 03.15 the leading troops of the battalion had reached the second objective. From now until 04.15 the artillery maintained a protective barrage, and the troops consolidated in depth. When the barrage again lifted at 04.15 the leading companies again advanced to the final objective. In the dim light they got beyond the crest, and when dawn came they had to withdraw just behind it, leaving Lewis gun posts on the forward slope. This was practically the line of the second objective, and touch was established on both flanks of the brigade.

The 17th Division on the left continued fighting all day near Amerval, which changed hands constantly and remained at evening in the hands of the enemy. The patrols of the 38th Division during the night reported the enemy on the outskirts of Forest, Croisette and Richemont. Hostile shelling with gas and high explosive was heavy on the railway and river up to mid-day, and there was scattered shelling by field guns over the rest of the forward area. A 5·9″ howitzer battery fired most of the day at Rambourlieux Farm.

By evening 1 officer and 211 other ranks had passed through the prisoner's of war cage of the 38th Division, and 225 enemy dead were counted. 4 field guns, 3 trench mortars and about 40 machine guns were captured. The casualties of the division were about 18 officers and 400 other ranks.

This attack with its comparatively light casualties and methodical advances carried out strictly to time offers a great contrast to that of the 12th October on the same position. In the one case every effort had been made to locate enemy centres of resistance and to deal adequately with them both before and during the fight. In the other little assistance was given to the infantry, and it was hoped that they might be able to deal with a strong position by means of their own weapons alone. The results of the two methods can be clearly seen in the pages that have gone before.[1]

It also offers a contrast to the attack of 10th October, where the artillery support was of an impromptu nature, by means of observed fire and without a time programme in the morning attack.

A further comparison may be made with the attack on the Masnieres—Beaurevoir line on 8th October, where though the means for assisting the infantry were present, they were insufficiently or improperly used.

To compare the strength of the two positions; at the Beaurevoir line the German position was provided with very strong wire; as against this their position on the Selle was a naturally strong one, difficult of approach down a long slope, with a river in front of it and along a railway, the steep earthwork of which gave good cover and command. The superiority of one over the other was certainly not sufficient to account for the infliction of treble the number of casualties on the attackers in the earlier fight, where the 38th Division lost 1200 men against 400 on the Selle.

The History of the 105th Infantry Regiment for these few days throws some light on German methods. From the 12th to 15th October it held the line near Neuvilly, then :

"On the morning of October 16th the I/105 were relieved by Reserve Infantry Regiment 64 of the 1st Guard Reserve Division. The 105th Infantry Regiment withdrew to Vert Baudet, and was there held in readiness to counter-attack in the event of an enemy attack. As there was no attack on either of the following days the 105th Regiment marched to billets in Englefontaine.

The regiment rested in Englefontaine, was re-organized, and equipment and uniform replenished.

The 105th Regiment was again re-formed into two battalions (I, and III/105) each with three companies of infantry and one machine-gun company. They then became the counter-attack regiment of the 1st Guard Reserve Division of the IV Reserve Corps.

On October 20th a practice alarm by the 30th Infantry Division took place to practise the occupation of the Hermann-III-position, which ran north and south, west of the road from Englefontaine to Landrecies. During the practice news came that the British had attacked and broken through along the length of the road between Amerval and Neuvilly. The

---

[1] It is probable that the capture of Le Cateau a few days before by the Fourth Army had a considerable effect on the resisting power of the enemy on 20th October.

30th Infantry Division was placed in readiness to attack north of the road between Englefontaine and Forest, the 105th Infantry Regiment being in position south of Ovillers. The 143rd Infantry Regiment was deployed to counter-attack, I/105 took possession of the southern half of Ovillers, III/105 the hollow and the district south-west of Ovillers, the battle head-quarters of the 105th Infantry Regiment was established in Vendigies aux Bois. At 2.35 p.m. word came from the 60th Infantry Brigade that the 105th Regiment was to co-operate in the attack with the 143rd Regiment, III/105 was to advance in the first line, the 5th Field Battery being attached to them as supporting battery. Just as the firing line of the III/105 were deploying for the attack, the counter order came from the 30th Division that the 105th Regiment was not to take part in the attack, but to stay in corps reserve on the southern side of Ovillers."

After this it appears to have remained for the next two days in close support in Ovillers, part of it being used to fill a gap between two other regiments in the front line.

21st October.

The positions captured were consolidated with the help of two companies of pioneers, and were held without any serious counter-attack. On the left the 17th Division carried out a local attack at dawn, and succeeded in capturing Amerval with prisoners.

During the afternoon and evening the 115th Infantry Brigade relieved the 113th and 114th Infantry Brigades, and the two relieved brigades moved back to Bertry.

22nd October.

The situation remained unchanged. During the night the enemy artillery probably fearing a further attack carried out a counter-preparation on the valley of the Selle, firing much mustard gas.

A section of "C" Battery, 122nd Brigade, R.F.A., was pushed across the Selle on the evening of the 20th, and the remainder of the 121st and 122nd Brigades were moved across the river during the night of the 21st/22nd. The going was very bad owing to the rain and the slope of the ground on the east of the Selle. But the batteries were helped by a moonlight night. The position was a cramped one as the front line was only 1500 yards from the river, and the most advanced batteries were within 700 yards of our front line. 122nd Brigade headquarters were in an old farm on the

Bridge over LE CATEAU—CATILLAN Road as left by the Germans.

INTELLIGENCE MAP ISSUED TO UNITS.

Red markings show groups of dug-out shafts, organized shell holes and rifle pits, probable centres of machine gun resistance likely to be met with on 38th Division front only.

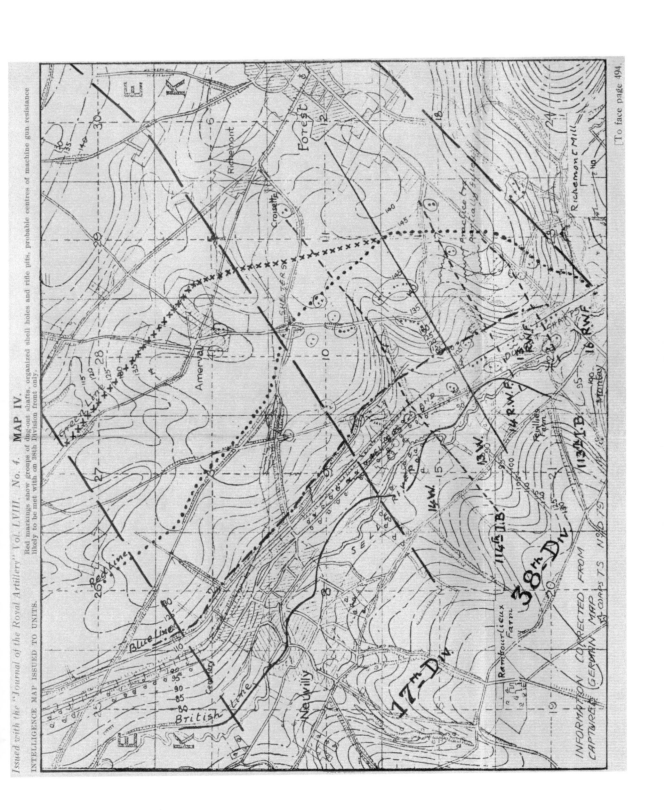

Montay—Neuvilly road and their wagon lines at Troisvilles, three miles away. During these days the artillery in this confined position and the engineers working on the bridges were naturally a target for the hostile artillery and suffered a number of casualties.

Next evening (22nd) the 98th Infantry Brigade on the right and the 19th Infantry Brigade on the left relieved the 115th Infantry Brigade in the line, and on relief the 115th Brigade moved back to Troisvilles.

THE 38th (WELSH) DIVISION

IN THE LAST FIVE WEEKS OF THE GREAT WAR.

By Major-General H. D. DePree, c.b., c.m.g., d.s.o., *p.s.c.*

CHAPTER IV.

The 33rd Division continue
the advance to the Mormal Forest.

ON 20th October, shortly after the battle of that day which resulted in the capture of the high ground east of the Selle River, V Corps Headquarters issued "Preliminary Instructions No. 1"[1] for the advance of V Corps to the line Western edge of Mormal Forest—Ghissignies. This advance was to form part of a great attack by the Fourth, Third and First Armies. Zero hour was ultimately fixed for 02.00 on 23rd October, and in order to carry out the attack the 33rd and 21st Divisions relieved the 38th and 17th Divisions in the front line. In the 38th Division sector the 98th and the 19th Infantry Brigades relieved the 115th Brigade on the evening of 22nd October, as already stated.

The details of the operations were discussed by Major-General Sir R. Pinney with his brigadiers and other officers concerned at a conference on 20th October, and the operation order confirming the arrangements was issued on the 21st October.[2]

The plan was an ambitious one embracing five objectives, the fifth including the village of Englefontaine on the edge of the Mormal Forest, which entailed an advance of 10,000 yards. (See Map No.V). This objective was due to be reached in 11 hours and 40 minutes after zero hour. The first, second, third and fourth objectives were to be captured by the 98th and 19th Infantry Brigades advancing abreast. The 100th Infantry Brigade was then to capture the fifth. It will be noticed that the zone of the 98th Infantry Brigade was the more difficult, as it included the houses along the Roman road, and was likely to be the area of

---

[1] G.S. 515/4.
[2] 33rd Division Order No. 367.

the heaviest shelling, as such a long straight road was sure to have a great attraction for the enemy's guns.

The attack on the first and second objectives was to be covered by an artillery and machine gun barrage moving at the rate of 100 yards in 4 minutes. The four brigades of the 33rd and 38th Divisional Artilleries, and the 223rd Brigade, R.F.A. (Naval Division), were available on a front of 2000 yards, which gave each gun and howitzer a front of about 17 yards. The 156th and 121st Brigades were to cover the 98th Infantry Brigade, and the 162nd and 122nd Brigades the 19th Infantry Brigade, whilst the 223rd Brigade was superimposed on the whole divisional front. After the first two objectives the brigades were to be pushed forward and brigade commanders were given their own discretion as to firing. One battery of field artillery and two 6 inch trench mortars were allotted to each infantry brigade to give close support. But in addition the 156th, 162nd and 223rd Brigades were to be pushed forward in close support immediately the barrage had been fired, covered by the 121st, 122nd Brigades and 13th Brigade, R.G.A. The 6 inch howitzers of the V Corps heavy artillery were detailed to bombard selected points in advance of the barrage, and the whole of the heavy artillery to engage in counter-battery work and distant harassing fire.

Two machine gun companies of the 38th Division had remained in the line to fire a barrage along with those of the 33rd Division. As soon as this was finished one company of the 33rd Machine Gun Battalion was to be placed at the disposal of each of the 98th and 19th Infantry Brigades, and the remainder were ordered to come into divisional reserve and move forward under the orders of the O.C. 33rd Machine Gun Battalion. Four points along the middle of the divisional zone of advance were fixed as communication centres, and the O.C. 33rd Divisional Signal Company was ordered to connect these with cable and also by means of wireless and visual signalling. In the later stages of the advance these points were to be used as divisional report centres. Three tanks of the 11th Tank Battalion were to assemble in K.16.a. on the night of the 21st/22nd, and to move forward along the central line of the 33rd Divisional advance at zero hour. Two were to be specially detailed to co-operate with the 98th Infantry Brigade, and one with the 19th ; but all three were to be available to operate as the situation required up to the fourth objective. After this they were to be attached to the 100th Infantry Brigade for the capture of the fifth. Brigadiers were to ensure that at least one platoon was always available to secure prisoners and localities that surrendered to a tank.

The 18th Division was to attack on the right of the 33rd Division, and as its front line was about 1000 yards to the right rear of the forming up line of the latter, its attack was to commence at 01.20 hours, so that the infantry of the 18th and 33rd Divisions should reach the various objectives at the same time. The 21st Division was to attack on the left at the same time as the 33rd.

At midday on October 22nd the 19th and 98th Infantry Brigades were in Troisvilles, and the 100th in Bertry. The march of the two former to their assembly positions began at 16.00 hours and of the last named at 20.00 hours. Divisional Headquarters moved to Troisvilles at 16.00 hours. The relief of the 115th Infantry Brigade in the front line by the two brigades was reported complete at 21.30 hours, and the assembly of 100th Infantry Brigade in its assembly position just east of the Selle at midnight.

23rd October.

The night was fine with bright moonlight, but the valleys were full of mist. The ground was wet and sticky making movement difficult. There was considerable enemy shelling during the night on the assembly positions and along the valley, and as soon as our barrage came down for the attack of the 18th Division, it increased to great intensity, causing many casualties. The 98th Infantry Brigade on the right had the 2nd Argyll and Sutherland Highlanders holding the front line before the attack. The brigade commander's plan was for the 1st Middlesex Regiment to pass through them at zero to the attack of the first objective, closely supported by the 4th King's Liverpool Regiment. The 2nd Argyll and Sutherland Highlanders were then to reorganize. The 4th King's were to pass through the 1st Middlesex on the first objective and capture the second and third objectives, supported by the 2nd Argyll and Sutherland Highlanders, who in their turn were to pass through the 4th King's to the capture of the fourth objective, supported by the 1st Middlesex.

[1]The 1st Middlesex moved off at zero (02.00 hours) close behind the barrage with "C" company on the right and "A" company on the left to envelop the village of Forest, while "B" company in the centre mopped it up. The enemy in considerable strength was holding an organized line of well sited rifle pits, supported in depth by numerous machine guns. These were overrun under cover of the barrage without great loss. The first message, received from the O.C. "B" company, read "On outskirts of Forest. Everything going splendidly, enemy retiring, very few casualties". The first objective was reached and the village mopped up, as intended, three field guns and many prisoners belonging to the 8th German Division being taken. The 4th Kings in accordance with the programme passed through the 1st Middlesex on the first objective and gained the second objective taking 200 prisoners, 5 field guns and many more machine guns. Their casualties amounted to 50 including one officer killed and one wounded. The two tanks allotted to the brigade were of little use in the advance, one becoming ditched and the other being struck by shell fire immediately after zero.

[2]On the left the 19th Infantry Brigade had been holding the line with the 1st Scottish Rifles (Cameronians). In their case the first and second objectives were allotted to the 5th Scottish Rifles, the third objective to the 1st Queen's Regiment, and the fourth to the Cameronians. This brigade also suffered from the heavy counter preparation by hostile artillery at zero, a company of the 1st Queen's suffering especially severely. After a hot meal at the point of assembly the 5th Scottish Rifles lined up on their jumping off tapes, and although the enemy barrage greatly disorganized them, they were able to move off at zero, with "C" company on the right, "D" in the centre and "B" on the left. The attack on the left progressed very well but the right was soon held up by machine gun fire. This temporarily checked the right wing, but the opposition was eventually overcome by the outflanking of the German machine gun posts. The left now continued very much in advance of the right until the first objective was reached, where the pause of 40 minutes enabled the right to come up into line.

---

[1] War Diaries 98th Infantry Brigade and 1st Middlesex Regiment.
[2] War Diaries and narrative, 19th Infantry Brigade and battalions.

4

During this advance valuable assistance was received from the attached tank.

The first objective was reached at 03.40 hours and at 04.20 the barrage moved forward again with the 5th Scottish Rifles close behind it. The left of the battalion succeeded in getting through to the second objective arriving there at 05.30 hours. The right of the battalion was held up by strong opposition in the vicinity of the Slaughter house, but this was finally outflanked and overcome and most of the battalion was on the objective and consolidating the position by 07.00 hours. The losses were 1 officer and 20 other ranks killed and 6 officers and 128 other ranks wounded.

[1]The machine gun units of the 33rd Division moving in close support of the infantry saw a good deal of fighting on this occasion. The first to be engaged were two sections of "D" company assisting the 19th Infantry Brigade on the left. Moving forward from their assembly positions along the road to Richemont they came under machine gun fire from the village. Limbers were withdrawn under cover and a party from each section went forward to reconnoitre. One reached a cottage on the southern outskirts, met with resistance and forced the enemy into a cellar, drove them out again with bombs and secured a score of prisoners. Two guns were then mounted on the outskirts of the village to cope with enemy machine gun fire. The infantry advanced assisted by the fire of these two guns and the enemy fled abandoning their guns, kit and casualties. Three sections of "B" company supporting the 98th Infantry Brigade became involved in close fighting on the right about this period. When they reached a spot a little north east of Forest the second objective had not been taken, and considerable fire was coming from the front while the enemy was trying to outflank the 4th King's, Lieut. Coleman brought the guns of all three sections into action and frustrated this movement killing many of the enemy. Afterwards these sections supported the advance up to the second objective firing from the house tops. "C" company came into action in the centre. Owing to the difficulties of the country and losses in mules, the limbers were moved by the Forest road, while the detachments moved across country. Lieut. Bedson having observed that the troops on his left had been checked went

---

[1] Narrative of machine gun operations, 33rd Division, October 22nd—26th, 1918.

forward to reconnoitre.   He came under fire from a sunken road
and adjoining houses.   He returned to his men, formed for attack,
fixed bayonets and charged, killing many of the enemy and forcing
the remainder to surrender.   34 prisoners including 2 officers and
5 N.C.O's, two machine guns and two light trench mortars were
captured.

As regards the artillery B/156 and one section D/156 crossed
the Selle at 05.30 hours and followed up the leading battalion of the
98th Infantry Brigade working in close touch with them throughout the day.   By 06.45 the 162nd Brigade was also across the Selle,
both brigades of the 33rd Divisional Artillery being now across the
river.   Shortly afterwards the 156th came into action 1000 yards
west of Croix and the 162nd west of Forest.   The two brigades of
the 38th Division, which were already east of the river before the
attack started, remained in their position covering the advance.
The heavy hostile shelling of the Selle valley slackened about 06.00
hours and practically ceased an hour later, which meant that the
enemy's guns had retired.   ·

The 4th King's were due to advance from the second objective
at 07.20, but the war diary of the 98th Infantry Brigade states that
the advance was delayed owing to the troops not having come up
on either side, thus leaving the enemy in rear of both flanks.   The
diary also states that owing to the delay the barrage was lost, and the
attack was consequently held up from the spur running north west
to Vert Baudet.   As a matter of fact no barrage had been arranged
after the second objective.

Brigade headquarters came forward to Richemont at 09.00,
and as soon as the above situation was definitely established two
companies of the 1st Middlesex were ordered to turn the enemy's
flank from the south.   For some reason this movement did not
materialize, but the 4th King's reached the third objective by noon[1]
assisted by the 19th Infantry Brigade on the left who had made
good progress.   News was later received from the 55th Infantry
Brigade, 18th Division, on the right, that they had made good
progress and that they had taken Bousies by 11.00 hours.

---

[1] The scheduled time for reaching this objective was 08.00 hours.

On the 19th Infantry Brigade front the second objective is stated to have been taken by the 5th Scottish Rifles at 07.30 together with some field guns and machine guns. The Cameronians were now ordered to push forward and assist the 1st Queen's to take the third objective as the 1st Queen's who had been detailed to take it were very weak, having already been seriously engaged on the second objective.[1] These two battalions advanced together to the third, which they took at 10.11 hours.

---

[1] The doings of the 1st Queen's are given in considerable detail in the report of the battalion's operations and are worth following. "The battalion moved out of their billets at Troisvilles at 19.30 the companies following one another by platoons at 50 yards distance, with battalion headquarters in rear. They were led across country to the bridge over the Selle at K.15.b.5.5. and thence to the ravine in K.16.a., which point was reached at 22.30.

At 23.00 hours a heavy barrage was put down by the enemy along the ridge north-east of the railway, and was particularly heavy on the ravine. At midnight another heavy barrage caused considerable difficulty in keeping the men together, and in moving the arms and Lewis guns, many of which were put out of order. This barrage lasted an hour. The battalion moved to a position of deployment on a tape running N.W. & S.E. in K.10.b., and K.11.a., on a frontage of 850 yards. "B" and "C" Companies were in front and "D" and "A" in support, with battalion headquarters in rear in the centre. On reaching the tape it was found that "C" Company had suffered so many casualties that "A" was ordered into the front line on the left. The advance was then begun in accordance with the time-table as far as the second objective, from which point the attack of the battalion on the third objective was to be carried out at 07.20. The night was misty at times with a late moon, and direction was kept by compass on a magnetic bearing of 57°.

On approaching the enclosures of Croisette and Richemont heavier shelling was encountered, and the battalion was halted at 06.00 in the sunken road in E.30.c. and K.6.a. It was then discovered that the enemy were still occupying Richemont and Forest, and the battalion was subjected to heavy enfilade machine gun fire at 900 yards down the road from a point at K.6.d.8.2. "B" Company was ordered to form a defensive flank and opened fire on the enemy. At this juncture (07.00 hours) Lt.-Col the Hon. H. Ritchie commanding the battalion went down the road towards Forest to reconnoitre and was badly wounded by a machine-gun bullet. (He had only returned a few days before, having been twice wounded previously). Two attempts were made to reach him but without success. (He subsequently died of his wounds). Troops were seen coming back over the ridge and the situation appeared critical. An enemy aero-

---

[1] Operations N.E. of Selle River 22nd/26th October, 1918, 1st Bn., Queen's Regt.

plane flew over the position and soon after the road was shelled with shrapnel. At this moment the brigade on the right advanced and the enemy were seen streaming out of Forest in a north-easterly direction, but at too great a range for effective Lewis Gun fire. The command of the battalion now devolved on Captain N. B. Avery, who withdrew it south-west of the road and organized it into three companies, there being no survivors of "D" Company at the time.

At 08.15 hours the advance towards the second objective was continued with "B" and "C" Companies in front line in section columns, and "A" Company in support. Some shelling was encountered during the advance and the Slaughter-house was reached at 09.12 hours. The 5th Scottish Rifles were found to be in position along the road running north of the Slaughter-house, and the Queen's took up their position on the right flank, being subjected to heavy machine-gun fire and the fire of 77$^{m/m}$ guns at close range from the direction of Harpies Mill. A request was made to brigade headquarters for assistance from the Cameronians who were following up the advance. The Tank allotted to the battalion reached the Slaughter-house at 09.30, but was found to be broken down and unable to proceed. At 09.45 the advance was continued towards the third objective assisted by the Cameronians, and this was gained at 09.50. The Cameronians then proceeded to go through towards the fourth objective, and the Queen's dug in at the south-west edge of the Bois de Vendegies".

Of the machine guns closely supporting the advance, No. 4 section of "B" company on the right were placed on the roof of a house standing high on a rise in Croix and engaged the enemy in Caluyaux and on the road beyond it. Almost as soon as the infantry advanced three hostile field guns opened direct fire on them. Two sections of "B" company were manoeuvred to a flank, came into action and succeeded in forcing the field guns to withdraw. They were shortly afterwards discovered in column of route retiring along the road, and the same sections fired upon them again, and inflicted such casualties that two of the guns had to be abandoned. Meanwhile No. 3 section, slightly in rear, observed an observation balloon about Harpies Mill opened fire on it, and forced it down. "D" company on the left co-operated with the infantry by placing a barrage on the ridge just north of Vendegies Wood, and "C" company in the centre as soon as the infantry had begun to move forward from the Slaughter-house joined in the engagement by firing barrages and silencing machine guns.

[1]To turn now to the 98th Infantry Brigade, who were on the third objective. The 2nd Argyll and Sutherland Highlanders who had been following up the 4th King's from the first objective on the south of the Roman road, with "B" and "D" companies leading, followed at a considerable distance by "A" and "C" companies, found that "B" company had lost their direction and had strayed too far to the right, where they carried out an attack in conjunction with a front line battalion of the 18th Division. The attack was successful but they incurred many casualties, and no touch was regained with them till 14.00 hours. The remainder of the battalion advanced with many halts and delays in rear of the 4th King's to the second objective and finally to the third objective east of Vert Baudet. At 12.30 the 4th King's reported to the Argyll's that the whole of the third objective had been captured. "A" company, 2nd Argyll and Sutherland Highlanders thereupon sent forward patrols and followed them closely to the line held by the 4th King's north west of the main road, taking up the same line in preparation for a further advance at 14.30. "C" company, having ascertained that the 4th King's were not on their objective south east of the main road as they claimed, were ordered to move up into line with "A" company. At 15.30 the O.C. "C" company was able to report that this had been done, and that all three companies were pushing forward in close touch with one another.

During this time the Cameronians on the other flank who had left the 1st Queens consolidating on the third objective pressed forward round the northern side of Vendegies Wood. At 13.50 they reached a line east of the above wood and came under heavy machine gun fire from Poix-du-Nord, Wagnonville and the sunken roads west of those villages. It was decided to wait for more effective covering fire next day, and to consolidate the line gained, a few hundred yards short of the objective, as it gave good cover.

This advance of the Cameronians was of assistance to the 2nd Argyll and Sutherland Highlanders on their right. By 17.00 hours the latter were on the road running south east and north west in F.16.d., in touch with the Cameronians on their left and with the 18th Division coming up on their right. The whole were held

---

[1] Argyll and Sutherland Highlanders account of operations from 23rd to 26th October, 1918.

·up by heavy machine gun fire from a line running through Paul
Jacques Farm.   Touch was now at last established with "B"
company who were with the 18th Division, and at 21.00, as they
had been reduced to 3 officers and 25 men, they were withdrawn
into battalion reserve.

At 18.30 the 100th Infantry Brigade advanced and assembled
prior to pushing through, but owing to the lateness of their arrival
on the fourth objective their further advance was cancelled.   As
the night grew darker "A" and "C" companies, 2nd Argyll and
Sutherland Highlanders gradually dribbled their men across the
road in F.16.d. and at 19.30 captured Paul Jacques Farm together
with a few prisoners by an enveloping movement.   An outpost
line was then established with "A", "C" and "D" companies all
in line 100 yards short of their final objective, which was found
to consist of a continuous belt of wire protecting numerous machine
gun posts.   These three companies then numbered from 35 to 40
rifles apiece.   During this phase the machine guns again co-operated closely with the infantry.

As regards the artillery the 121st and 122nd Brigades, R.F.A.,
were moved forward from the positions in which they had fired
the original barrage at 11.00.   The 122nd came into action 1000
yards north west of Croix with the headquarters in the Slaughter-
house.   Lieut.-Colonel Williams states that few shell were fired,
and the History of the 33rd Divisional Artillery states that the
batteries found themselves being left too far behind.   So it is
probable that the bulk of artillery did little to co-operate with
the infantry in the latter stages of the fight.   At 12.30 the 162nd
Brigade advanced from west of Forest and came into action 1000
yards north of Croix and remained there the rest of the day
neutralizing machine gun fire and doing what they could to assist
the infantry who were making their way slowly through and past
Vendegies Wood.   Unfortunately on this day Lieut.-Colonel B. A.
B. Butler, commanding the 156th Brigade, was mortally wounded
while riding up from his headquarters at Richemont to visit his
batteries near Croix.

The 38th Division had been ordered to support the 33rd
Division, and its leading infantry brigade the 115th, followed the

latter up closely. About 10.30 V Corps received reports that the enemy were blowing up roads in front of the 33rd Division, and an air reconnaisance reported that the enemy appeared to be concentrating on Englefontaine in considerable numbers, but that eastward movement appeared to be stopped east of this. As this might mean a counter-attack from this direction the 115th Infantry Brigade was ordered at 11.30 to the general line Caluyaux— Slaughter house where it took up a defensive position and the supporting brigade the 113th was ordered to the Forest area.

The 100th Infantry Brigade remained close in rear of the 98th and 19th Infantry Brigades in Vendegies Wood. The left of the 18th Division was somewhat in rear about F.21.d.5.1. and the right of the 21st Division was on the road running east and west through F.8.b. Up to 17.00 hours 12 officers and 315 other ranks had passed through the divisional prisoners' cage; and two batteries of field guns, two single field guns, 60 machine guns and two anti-tank rifles were reported captured.

The History of the 105th Infantry Regiment gives a long description of the fighting of 23rd October. At the time of the British attack the regiment was holding a position slightly to the north of the sector on which the attack of the 33rd Division fell, and it was only in the evening that the regiment actually came onto the front with which we are dealing. But the narrative gives a very good idea of how severely the relentless advance of the British divisions hustled the enemy, and the great straits to which they were put. Even in the short period dealt with two or three reorganizations of units are mentioned, caused by the devastating casualties suffered; and the story finishes with the final withdrawal of the regiment from the front. Indeed withdrawal or disbandment was the fate of a considerable proportion of the German units which faced the British armies at this time.

"On the morning of October 23rd very heavy drum fire started on the section of the right neighbouring division, and on the right flank of the 30th Infantry division. The enemy fired a great many red lights, whereupon the German artillery put up a heavy barrage in front of the section where the 30th Infantry Division lay. As the enemy fire ceased and no attack followed, the German barrage died down at about 2.0 At 3.15

a.m. the enemy drum fire broke out again. [1] At 4.0 a.m. followed a terrific enemy attack, which was directed mostly against the left wing of the 105th Infantry regiment and the right wing of the 99th Infantry regiment in the direction where Ovillers lay. 11 and 12/105 held back the enemy for a considerable period with rifle and machine gun fire, but in spite of it they broke through. III/105 tried to hold on and bent their left wing back towards the east to avoid being surrounded. Towards 5.0 a.m. information came from the 117th Infantry regiment that the British had also broken through in their sector, and were already in possession of Ovillers. I/105 tried in vain to join up again with the 117th regiment. Patrols were sent out and reported that the enemy were already in possession of Ovillers, and that there were already enemy tanks on the outskirts. The British were advancing from north to south, and in this way were threatening to cut off the whole position of the regiment. The headquarters of I/105 in attempting to escape through the gardens of the village of Ovillers, which had already been a long while in the hands of the British, were exposed to heavy rifle and machine-gun fire, in which Haupt. Leimbach and the greater part of the staff lost their lives, while Adj. Lt. Dietze, Ord. Offz. Lt. v. Reitzenstein, and the trench mortar officer Schall with the others, practically without exception, fell wounded into the hands of the enemy. In spite of this the I/105 held on to their position in the hopes of a German counter-attack. Meanwhile the companies of III/105, i.e., 11 and 12/105, under pressure from the south and south-west, fell back on to the reserve company (9/105) in the hollow road at the battle headquarters. Major Schultze here ordered his companies, as they were unable to hold their position, to retire towards the north-east to Vendegies aux Bois, and to attempt to occupy as a rallying position the high ground where regimental headquarters were. While doing this the staff of the III/105 with Major Schultze together with the troops under their command ran into hostile detachments, not being aware that the British had turned the position from the north at Vert Baudet, and were disarmed and taken prisoners. One half of the disarmed prisoners were sent back by the British unescorted towards the West, where they were to report themselves to a headquarters. On their way west from Ovillers, they met the company of the I/105 who on account of the darkness had not realised that they were almost surrounded by the enemy; The prisoners took this wonderful opportunity to escape. They placed themselves under the command of the I/105, reporting that the British occupied the whole position backwards from the front line, and that such troops as had not fallen back had been taken prisoners. Under these circumstances, Lt. L. Lewitzky, being the senior, assumed command over the troops left in position and determined to try to fight his way through towards the east. At 6.30 a.m. he gave the order to retire by platoons. The battalion was then to rendezvous on the eastern edge of the village of Ovillers. In the uncertain light of the approaching dawn they saw the outline of enemy tanks, and that the western edge of Ovillers was under heavy artillery fire. Lt. Lewitzky

---

[1] The 105th Infantry Regiment were in support some 1,500 yards behind the German front line. This probably accounts for their thinking there was no attack at 2.0 a.m. (zero hour).

decided to join up with a company of the pioneer battalion 5, which he met holding the artillery position, south of Vendegies aux Bois, and got into communication with the regimental staff of the 105th regiment.

At 8.30 a.m. the British opened heavy artillery fire[1] on the position occupied by Lt. Lewitzky and his men, and caused heavy casualties among them.   Also on the right flank of the position, where the enemy under cover of artificial mist had penetrated further, machine guns appeared which further increased the casualties.   As they could get no touch on the north, and there was the danger of being again surrounded, Lt. Lewitzky decided, in consultation with the headquarters of the 105th regiment, to take his men, and the 5th Pioneers back into the Hermann-II-Stellung; the headquarters of the 105th infantry regiment went back to near Paul Jacques Farm.   An order then came from the 60th infantry brigade that the 105th regiment were to occupy and hold the line from Erpies Mill to Vendegies aux Bois, but this was not possible, as the officers had only 2 or 3 platoons left, and the enemy was already in possession of the point which they were to hold. The remainder of the 105th Regiment was therefore withdrawn with the consent of the brigade and division, back into the Hermann-II-Stellung, to the sector held by the 30th Infantry Division, which was occupied by remnants of the 143rd and 99th Infantry Regiments and two companies of the 5th Pioneer Battalion.   They were in touch on the right with the 117th and 115th Regiments.   The troops were so mixed that it was first necessary to re-organize.   From the remainder of the three infantry regiments of the division a regiment was formed under the command of Lt.-Col. Haupt, commander of the 99th Infantry Regiment.   The command of the remnants of the 105th Infantry Regiment was undertaken by Lt. Uber.   Lt.-Col. Haupt occupied the Hermann-II-Stellung, about the cross-road 600 metres south of Wagnonville, the rest of the 105th Regiment were on the right flank in touch with the 117th, the centre of the position was held by the 143rd regiment and the left flank by the 99th regiment.   The remnants of the 105th regiment was made up into a full-strength company out of men drawn from the first and second line transport.

On the morning of October 25th the 30th division was to have been relieved by the 116th Infantry Brigade.   The 105th, strength 3 officers, 27 N.C.O's and 30 men went back to Hecq in reserve.   The next morning about 2 a.m., after a short but heavy artillery bombardment, there was a strong attack, in which the enemy succeeded in penetrating the German position.   The portions of the 105th in reserve in Hecq were subjected to heavy flank fire.   At 7 p.m., 99th Infantry Regiment and 103rd which was on its right had to retire, and the 105th dug itself in east of Hecq.   Hostile artillery fire died down and no more attacks were made.   On October 28th the 105th was at last relieved by the 103rd, and withdrawn towards Locquignol, where it occupied rest billets.   For the last time in the World War the regiment had stood armed against the enemy.   The heavy casualties of this rearguard fighting, had reduced it to a mere remnant of the proud regiment which once stood before its commander and which now again stood before him on parade for the first time since the retreat''.

---

[1] Evidently the barrage had now reached them.

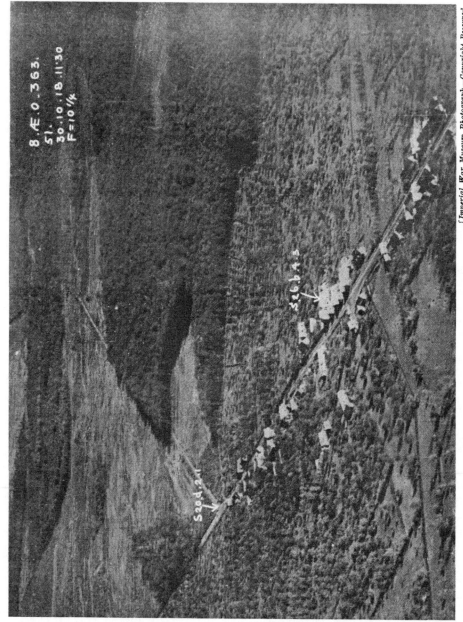

FOREST OF MORMAL (S. of Louvignies-lez-Quesnoy).

The Germans had cleared the villages close behind the Hermann-Stellung of civilians, and the only ones met with here were three men and a woman who had lived for 24 days in a cellar, hiding after the order for them to be evacuated had come out. They had had nothing to eat but raw potatoes, and were in a very bad state.

Orders were issued at 19.00 by the 33rd Division for the advance to be continued at 04.00 next morning in conjunction with the XIII and IV Corps on the right and left respectively. The 98th Infantry Brigade on the right and the 19th Infantry Brigade on the left were to capture and entrench the line Englefontaine (inclusive)—Le Coupe Gorge, refusing the right flank south of Englefontaine to connect with the left of XIII Corps, and to gain touch with the right of the 21st Division on the road Le Coupe Gorge—Grand Gay Farm. The 100th Infantry Brigade were then to pass through the 98th and 19th Infantry Brigades, form the advance guard of the division and move onto the line S.28.a.—S.21.central—Futoy. [1]In order to carry out these orders, arrangements were made by the 98th Infantry Brigade for the 100th Infantry Brigade to relieve the 2nd Argyll and Sutherland Highlanders in the front line to allow that battalion to reform and continue the attack. The attack was to be covered by heavy bursts of fire 500 yards in advance of the infantry by all the available artillery and machine guns. The 2nd Argyll and Sutherland Highlanders were to attack on the right and the 1st Middlesex on the left, with the 4th King's in close support. On the 19th Infantry Brigade front the 5th Scottish Rifles were to pass through the Cameronians' outposts at zero (04.00) attack Wagnonville and establish themselves 600 yards north east of the village. The Cameronians were then to pass through them in their turn and seize the line of the Englefontaine—Ghissignies road. The 1st Queen's were to remain in brigade reserve.

The enemy had erected a good deal of wire, in places five rows deep, on the line F.16.central and F.9.c and d., and a line of posts had been constructed behind it. A German map captured afterwards shewed that this position was called Hermann-Stellung

---

[1] 98th Infantry Brigade order No. 282.

II. Towards the south, on the Fourth Army front, it was continued south of Landrecies and east of the Sambre canal. It had
been intended by the enemy to organize it as a defensive system,
with a second system in rear on the general line F.12.a.o.o—
F.4.central. No work had been observed on this line from the
air up to 14th October, so that such preparation as had been
carried out was of a hurried nature.

24th October.

The 2nd Argyll and Sutherland Highlanders attacked with "D"
company on the right, "A" on the left and "C" in support.
Strong opposition was encountered by them and the 1st Middlesex
on their left; but the German position was overrun, and a large
number of the enemy killed or captured, though further advance
either by the Highlanders or the 1st Middlesex became very
difficult owing to the shortage of men. Captain Broad of the 1st
Middlesex, who was killed later in the day, reported at 06.05 that
the machine-gun fire from the front was extremely heavy, but that
he believed that some of the battalion were in front of him,
though he could not get into touch. At 07.25 he reported that
he had got "C" and "D" companies totalling 50 men with him.
By 07.30 "A", "D" and "C" companies of the 2nd Argyll and
Sutherland Highlanders were on the road running south east in
F.17.a., with the 1st Middlesex on their left, but no troops had
come up on their right, and much artillery and machine gun fire
was being encountered. The difficulty of the situation was reported to the 98th Infantry Brigade, and passed to the 33rd
Division. Several parties of the enemy had not been mopped
up, and were offering strong resistance to the supporting battalion
the 4th King's. This caused touch to be lost with the leading
battalions, but these parties were eventually dealt with. By 08.00
the leading battalions had reached the road in F.11.a. and b. The
enemy were then 200 yards in front and the bridge at F.11.c.5.8.,
had been blown up. The 1st Middlesex were now reorganized
into a single company numbering about 90 men. At 08.15 orders
were received for the 100 Infantry Brigade to pass through the
98th and 19th Infantry Brigades and take the final objective.

To turn now to the attack of the 19th Infantry Brigade;[1] this was supported in the same way by bursts of artillery and machine gun fire. The 5th Scottish Rifles advancing to attack Wagnonville also encountered the two lines of wire entanglements defended by machine gun posts of the Hermann-Stellung II. These after some fighting were captured successfully. In outflanking Wagnonville the 5th Scottish Rifles cleared a large part of the village of Poix-du-Nord and captured a heavy howitzer. Two thousand civilians were liberated in Wagnonville and Poix-du-Nord. By 08.00 the 5th Scottish Rifles had taken their objective, and the Cameronians were passing through.

The 1st Queen's[2] who were in reserve were ordered at 08.00 to move forward to a position in the sunken road south east of Poix-du-Nord (F.4.d.) to guard the left flank of the brigade. The companies moved off via the north west edge of the Bois-de-Vendegies. They came under heavy shell fire directed at the batteries in this vicinity and a few casualties were caused. Battalion headquarters moved at the same time by the south east edge of the wood and came under shell fire on reaching Paul Jacques Farm, F.16.central. The leading companies took up the position ordered with "A" company in support on the bank of the Fontaine—Le Comte Brook. Battalion headquarters was established in the cellar of a house in Wagnonville.

The Cameronians, after passing through the 5th Scottish Rifles, succeeded in gaining the line of the Englefontaine—Ghissignies road with two companies, while two companies remained in support about the Tuilleries. Englefontaine was found to be strongly held by the enemy and all attempts to push through were met by heavy machine-gun fire. As regards the action of the 33rd Machine Gun Battalion, "B" company on the right moved with the attack taking their limbers with them. Their chief role throughout the day was to guard the right flank of the attack. "C" company worked by sections on the 19th Infantry Brigade front.

[3]After firing bursts of fire the artillery, although all ranks were

---

[1] Narrative of operations 23rd to 26th October, 19th Infantry Brigade.

[2] Operations N.E. of the Selle River 22nd/26th October, 1918 (1st Queen's).

[3] History of the 38th Divisional Artillery.

now very exhausted, began to advance at dawn. At 06.00 the 162nd Brigade had reached the southern outskirts of Vendegies, and was directing fire upon the eastern outskirts of Poix-du-Nord, where the enemy was reported to be retreating. By 08.00 the same brigade had again advanced to a position in observation 1,000 yards further on, the 156th Brigade reaching the edge of the Bois-de-Vendegies one hour later. From here harassing fire was kept up on the approaches to Englefontaine, while A/156 kept in close touch with the leading battalion of infantry. News was then received that, in spite of strong opposition Wagnonville had been captured and Englefontaine itself was being threatened. Upon receipt of this information the guns were moved up, the 156th Brigade coming into action between Poix-du-Nord and Wagnonville, and the 162nd Brigade in Poix-du Nord itself. [1]Lt.-Colonel Williams, commanding the 122nd Brigade, started his batteries forward about 06.30 when the situation seemed to be clearing and brought 3 batteries into action 1,500 yards south west of Poix-du-Nord, with the fourth on the northern outskirts of the village within a few hundred yards of our front line to work with the leading infantry unit. Firing was carried out on information received from our infantry, the country being too enclosed and the visibility too bad for successful observation. About 16.00 the rear batteries were moved up. During the last few days there had been a good many casualties in the brigade, among them Major A. D. C. Clarke, whose battery was first across the Selle, and whose resource and gallantry have been mentioned on several occasions. He was severely wounded after crossing the Selle. Major Carr and two other officers of D Battery were also sent away gassed. The horses of the brigade too had suffered severely, and were 135 short of establishment. The 121st Brigade advanced to positions south of Vendegies with headquarters in the village.

At 07.45 hours the 33rd Division on being informed of the difficulties of the 98th Infantry Brigade, had issued orders for the 100th Infantry Brigade to pass through the 98th and 19th Infantry Brigades when these could go no further, capture the line Englefontaine—Le Coupe Gorge and, then advance to the line S.28.a.o.o.

---

[1] Personal narrative of Lt.-Col. Williams.

—S.21.central—Futoy. On the 98th Infantry Brigade front as already stated the 2nd Argyll and Sutherland Highlanders with the 1st Middlesex, greatly reduced in numbers, on their left, had reached the road in F.11.a. and b., at 08.00, had there re-organized and taken up a defensive position. On the left of the divisional front the Cameronians of the 19th Infantry Brigade had passed on to the attack at the same time, and had later reached the Engle-fontain—Le Coupe Gorge road with two companies at some un-stated time. The [1]Brigade Major of the 19th Infantry Brigade who had made a personal reconnaissance reported at 11.00 hours that the leading troops of his brigade were on the main Coupe—Gorge road in X.30.a., and those of the 98th Infantry Brigade on the road in X.30.c. The leading troops of the other two brigades had thus already reached the left of the first objective of the 100th Infantry Brigade soon after it started. The brigade diary puts this hour at about 10.00. The 100th Brigade moved with the 9th High-land Light Infantry (Glasgow Highlanders) on the right and the 16th King's Royal Rifles on the left. There seems to have been considerable delay, on the right at any rate, as the 2nd Argyll and Sutherland Highlanders in their report on the operations state that the 100th Infantry Brigade started to move at 12.00 and were not through them till 13.00.

The war diary of the Glasgow Highlanders states that the Brigade Major, 100th Infantry Brigade, brought them verbal orders at 10.00 to push on to their objective and to take the high ground in F.12.a., on the way, by an enveloping attack, as the enemy were holding up the advance from there. The plan seems to have been for the Worcesters who were in support to advance direct on the high ground and for the Glasgow Highlanders and 16th King's Royal Rifles to make flanking movements to take it. On reaching F.11.b., the Glasgow Highlanders received a message that the Worcesters had found the high ground clear, the battalion there-fore changed direction and made for the next objective the Engle-fontaine—Ghissignies road. On reaching the road in X.29, they received information that the Cameronians were occupying a posi-tion along the road in X30. They were then in touch with the Worcesters on their right and the 21st Division on their left, and

---

[1] Report on the operations of the 33rd Division, October 22nd—30th.

were making preparations to proceed to their objective when they discovered that the Cameronians did not appear to be on the Coupe Gorge road in X.30. as reported (?). At the same time the road in X.29. was under direct fire from a battery of field guns in X.18.c., and was also under heavy machine gun fire. In these circumstances it was decided that it would be inadvisable to attempt to proceed further without artillery support. Shortly afterwards the 64th Infantry Brigade of the 21st Division, attacked the Coupe Gorge road further to the north under a barrage and took it.

The 16th King's Royal Rifles diary states that that battalion started about 12.00 (which agrees with the 2nd Argyll and Sutherland Highlanders report), and by 16.00 they were within 600 yards of their objective. The situation now was that the 16th King's Royal Rifles held a position near the Tuilleries, and the Glasgow Highlanders held from there to F.6.a.4.1. The number of rifles available in the latter battalion at the end of the day was 130. At 15.00 the 100th Infantry Bde. reported to the 33rd Division that their troops had taken the high ground in F.12.a., and were mopping up Englefontaine, but this report proved inaccurate as regards Englefontaine. The truth was as stated by the 19th Infantry Brigade in their narrative of operations, that Englefontaine was strongly held by the enemy, and all attempts by the 100th Infantry Brigade to push through it were frustrated by heavy machine gun fire.

During all this time the enemy were not passive, and at 12.30 it was discovered that they were advancing through a gap between the 33rd and 21st Divisions. Two machine guns were quickly got into action on the high ground north of Tuilleries and the enemy dispersed with loss. No further advance was made during the rest of the afternoon. At 23.15 hours orders were accordingly issued by the 33rd Division for the 100th Infantry Brigade to establish themselves during the night on a line running round the east side of Englefontaine to Le Coupe Gorge. The first definite and reliable information of the situation was obtained next morning, when as a result of personal reconnaissance by the Brigadier of the 100th Infantry Brigade (Brig.-Genl. A. W. F. Baird), it was ascertained that the enemy were still holding Englefontaine, and that the 100th Infantry Brigade held the road F.6.c. and a., and X.30.c.

EXAMPLE OF A RAILWAY DEMOLITION.

and a., the troops of all these brigades being considerably mixed up.

At nightfall the 18th Division which had been held up all day in F.17.c., reached the road in A.7.a., and were now in touch with the 100th Infantry Brigade. While on the other flank the right of the 21st Division which had not been able to advance beyond l'Arbre de la Croix, X.28.b., until 16.00 hours, advanced at this hour under an artillery barrage as already stated and took the road between Le Coupe Gorge and Grand Gay Farm. The prisoners that passed through the divisional cage during the 24 hours ending 17.00 on October 24th amounted to 5 officers and 187 other ranks.

25th October.

Soon after daylight the hostile shelling which had been kept up all night became very heavy on Poix-du-Nord and the area west and south-west of Englefontaine. At 07.30 the enemy attacked the left of the 16th King's Royal Rifle Corps and the right of the Glasgow Highlanders and drove in four posts. An immediate counter-attack was organized with two or three sections of the 16th King's Royal Rifle Corps, and about 75 of the enemy were driven back with the loss of 3 machine guns. "B" company of this battalion was also sent up to reinforce the Glasgow Highlanders who were very weak. The enemy again attacked in the afternoon at 13.00 but were driven off, after which "B" company 16th King's Royal Rifle Corps commenced operations to clear the Englefontaine—Le Coupe Gorge road of the enemy, and touch was established all along it by 18.00 hours. The machine gun covering this part of the front did good work in repelling these attacks; spare numbers of one gun section were posted in houses, and with their rifles knocked out a German light machine gun which was trying to come into action.

Early in the day it must have become quite evident that Englefontaine could not be taken or further progress made without a well organized attack. At 10.30 therefore, the divisional commander (Maj.-General Sir R. J. Pinney), held a conference at the 100th Infantry Brigade headquarters in Wagnonville to arrange this. The three infantry brigadiers, the C.R.A., G.S.O.I., and the O.C.

33rd Machine Gun Battalion attended.   The plan was for the 98th
Infantry Brigade to attack round the village from the south, and
the 19th Infantry Brigade to encircle it from the north west, and
join hands east of the village, while the 100th Brigade starting later
were to attack the village direct and clear it, finally relieving the
98th and 19th Infantry Brigades along the whole divisional front.
Zero was fixed for 01.00.   [1]To go into detail :—

(a).   One battalion 98th Infantry Brigade was to form up facing
east in F.6.c. and F.12.a., on the left of the 18th Division, attack
eastward and establish a strong post about the road junction
A.2.a.1.1.   A strong patrol was to be sent forward to meet troops
of the 19th Infantry Brigade at the track junction A.2.a.8.9. where
another post was to be formed.

(b).   One battalion 19th Infantry Brigade was to assemble in
S.24. and attack south east along the road through S.19, and establish two posts about the road junctions in S.26.a.   A strong patrol
was to be sent forward to join hands with the 98th Infantry Brigade
at A.2.a.8.9.

(c).   The 100th Infantry Brigade at zero + 21 was to send forward its left battalion to guard the rear of the 19th Infantry
Brigade attack along the road in S.19., and establish posts along
that road.   Its two other battalions were to clear Englefontaine,
also moving at zero + 21.

The whole attack was to be covered by artillery creeping
barrages, moving at 100 yards in 7 minutes, to give the infantry
plenty of time to keep pace with them when moving and mopping
up in the village and its outskirts in the darkness.   The attack of
the 19th Infantry Brigade was to be covered by a standing barrage
on its left in addition to the creeping barrage in front of it, and
a protective barrage was to be put down in front of the whole
objective.   The heavy artillery were to bombard selected points
east of the objective.[2]

Three machine gun companies were to strengthen the barrage,

---

[1] 33rd Division Order 369.   Issued at 16.30 hours in confirmation of the divisional
conference.

[2] The programme for the barrage was worked out almost entirely by Brig.-Genl.
G. H. W. Nicholson, as his staff had been depleted by "Spanish influenza".   He tackled
the work single handed and with such skill that the barrage was a complete success.   The
epidemic was part of the wave which swept Europe and Asia at this time and caused
enormous losses, both to the civil populations and the armies.

paying special attention to roads. After this, one company was to be placed at the disposal of the brigade commander of the 100th Infantry Brigade to move forward and cover the final objective, and two were to remain in position to defend the general line—high ground in F.12.a.—Tuilleries—Spur in X.24.c., and also cover the line of the new objective with barrage fire in case of an S.O.S. signal being sent up. The medium (6″) trench mortars were to take part in the preliminary bombardment, and two of the Stoke's mortar batteries were to support the 100th Infantry Brigade attack through the village. During the day defended localities were constructed in F.12.a., and about Les Tuilleries and garrisoned by one battalion of the 98th and 19th Infantry Brigades respectively.

26th October.

The Brigadier of the 98th Infantry Brigade selected and gave verbal instructions to the 4th King's to carry out the attack round the south of the village. The attack was entirely successful, and about 70 prisoners of the 18th German Division were taken. At dawn, after the objective had been reached, it was found that the 18th British Division had not come up into line on the right. The 1st Middlesex were therefore ordered up to form a defensive flank between F.12.a. and the houses in A.2.c. [1]In the case of the attack on the north of the village the Brigadier of the 19th Infantry Brigade sent for Captain N. B. Avery, on whom the command of the 1st Queen's had fallen, at noon on October 25th and gave him verbal orders for the carrying out of the attack by the battalion. The battalion was to assemble for attack on the flank of the 21st Division near Le Coupe Gorge. The battalion paraded at 22.45 and marched to the headquarters of the 2nd East Yorks Regiment (21st Division), at the quarry in X.29.a.

The battalion formed up with "A" company on the right of the road in S.19.b., and "B" company on the left, to attack down each side of it, with an officers' patrol out on each flank. The remains of "C" company were divided up between the other two companies to make each up to about 65 rifles. (It will be remembered that the battalion had been reorganized into three companies). The attack was completely successful, and the casualties

---

[1] Narrative of Operations, 1st Queen's, N.E. of Selle 22nd—26th October.

only numbered 17. The enemy seemed surprised and demoralised by the suddenness of the attack, which was vigorously pressed home, and a report was received at 04.45 that all objectives had been taken at 02.30. The enemy gave themselves up in large numbers, all of whom it was impossible to collect, and though the battalion took well over 150 prisoners including four officers, they were only credited with 115 and 3 officers. The 16th King's Royal Rifle Corps of the 100th Brigade quickly relieved the battalion on the final objective, and it was back in billets by 07.00.

The frontal attack of the 100th Infantry Brigade for the purpose of clearing the village, which started 21 minutes after zero was also completely successful. The Worcesters reached their objective with a loss of 1 officer and 4 O.R's killed, and 1 officer and 33 O.R's wounded.

The attack of the Glasgow Highlanders was led by a party from the headquarter company under Lieut. Bennett. The attack of this party proceeded along the main Forest—Englefontaine road, and "A" "C" and "D" companies followed and mopped up the village. The success of the attack and the casualties inflicted on the enemy were increased by the fact that the garrison of Englefontaine, the 58th German Division was caught in process of relief by the 14th German Division. Many of the enemy were killed, and our machine and Lewis guns got excellent targets by the light of burning houses. The fighting took place under the most extraordinary conditions owing to the presence of the civil population. There were said to have been 2,000 civilians in Poix-du-Nord; luckily the Germans did not make much of a stand there; but at Englefontaine, where there were several hundred civilians and the Germans put up a stubborn resistance, the civilians were all among the fighting. The Highlanders were routing Germans out of the cellars and fighting through the houses while the people looked on, and the women were actually giving our men baked apples while the fighting was going on.

The captures of the 33rd Division on this day were 5 officers and 425 other ranks.

The two battalions of the 100th Infantry Brigade which had cleared Englefontaine immediately relieved the two battalions of the 98th and 19th Infantry Brigades which had carried out the enveloping attack, and they themselves were relieved by the 115th Infantry Brigade of the 38th Division during the early part of the following evening and marched back to rest at Forest. V Corps had originally issued a warning order directing the 38th Division to relieve the 33rd on the night of the 25th/26th October, but as the 33rd Division had been unable to take Englefontaine on the 25th as expected, the relief was postponed till the night of the 26th/27th. It was carried out in the evening and the 33rd Division marched back to a well earned rest in the neighbourhood of Forest, Montay and Troisvilles. After dusk the 121st and 122nd Brigades, R.F.A., drew out of the line and marched back to Bertry, about eleven miles distant for 72 hours rest; the only relief which they got during the whole advance. Unfortunately Major Thompson of B/121 was killed when getting his wagons under cover. He had been with the 38th Divisional Artillery since its formation.

Napier in his "Peninsular War" speaks of the majesty with which the British soldier fights, but never in history has more sustained endurance, determination and courage been shown than by the innumerable men who went into battle day after day on the Western Front between August and November 1918. Among the many great deeds of this time, the advance of the 33rd Division from the Selle to the Mormal Forest will always hold an honourable place. The infantry battalions of the division had moved out of billets for the attack on the afternoon and evening of 22nd October, and from that time they had been continuously fighting and manœuvring in close touch with the enemy till relieved on the evening of 26th October. Their casualties had been :—

Killed	...	13 Officers	210 O.R.
Wounded	...	51 ,,	1109 ,,
Missing	...	3 ,,	94 ,,

Some of the battalions had been reorganized into three, two and even one companies. In spite of small numbers and fatigue, they rounded off their task by taking the big village of Englefontaine crowded with Germans in triumphant style on the fourth night of the operations.

6″ GUNS IN ACTION IN FLANDERS.

THE 38th (WELSH) DIVISION

IN THE LAST FIVE WEEKS OF THE GREAT WAR.

By Major-General H. D. DePree, c.b., c.m.g., d.s.o., p.s.c.

CHAPTER V.

The Last Set-Battle of the War.

27th October.

The 38th Division had been in close support during the four day's fighting which comprised the advance from the Selle River to the Mormal Forest, and the 115th Infantry Brigade which took over the front line and the 113th Infantry Brigade which was in support had to come up from the neighbourhood of Forest. The 2nd Royal Welsh Fusiliers of the 115th Infantry Brigade took over the right of the line and the 17th Royal Welsh Fusiliers the left, while the 10th South Wales Borderers moved into brigade reserve in the outskirts of Poix-du-Nord.

The 113th Infantry Brigade took up a position with one battalion in Poix-du-Nord, and two battalions about Paul Jacques Farm. While the 114th Infantry Brigade in divisional reserve was billeted in Croix.

Prisoners taken the previous day reported that the enemy intended to hold the Englefontaine position at all costs, and it was not long before he counter-attacked. At 05.45 hours on the very first morning a heavy barrage was put down on the front held by the 17th Royal Welsh Fusiliers and an enemy attack on a front of about 1000 yards quickly developed. On the left company front the enemy emerging from a hedge in S.19.b. (see Map VI), some 150 yards away was held up by rifle and Lewis gun fire, and was also caught in the British counter-barrage and made no progress.

On the right company front the country was much more enclosed, and a few of the enemy succeeded in passing between two of our posts in S.26.a., and in surprising and capturing ten men of the 115th Light Trench Mortar Battery, two of whom subsequently escaped. Two battalion stretcher bearers who were attending to

wounded men were also captured.   At every other place the attack
was driven back with loss.   The country, especially in the outskirts
of the village, consisted mainly of orchards and farm buildings,
and it was hard to tell which belonged to the enemy and which
to the British.   Consequently the line on which there had been
little time for work was no easy one to hold.

28th October.

During this day the Brigade continued to hold the line without
any change in the dispositions.   The intention[1] of Sir Julian Byng,
commanding the Third Army, was that on reaching a line running
north through Englefontaine the main bodies of Corps should make
no further advance until the state of the rear communications was
more secure.   Meanwhile troops were to be rested, but Corps
were to be prepared to resume the advance at short notice.   Advanced guards of all arms were to be pushed forward with the
following general instructions :—

   (1)   Touch to be maintained, if the enemy retired, by Corps
         cavalry or cyclists supported by the artillery and infantry
         of the advanced guards.

   (2)   If the enemy did not retire advanced guards were to push
         past the enemy rearguards up to a distance of 2 or 3 miles.
         If the opposition was so strong as to hold up the advanced
         guards, the advance was not to be pressed without further
         orders from Army Headquarters.   Meanwhile the main
         position was to be organized for defence.

In order to carry out these instructions the[2] 115th Infantry
Brigade ordered the two leading battalions to entrench the main
line of resistance, leaving one company free to act as advanced
guard and to make ground wherever and whenever possible.
When the advanced guard companies gained any ground an outpost
line was to be formed covering it.

The 10th South Wales Borderers in support were to entrench
a line through the orchards in F.6. and F.5., west of Englefontaine.

The 2nd Royal Welsh Fusiliers in the right sector spent the
27th and 28th endeavouring to carry out a policy of "infiltration",

---

[1] Third Army G.S. 76/320 of 23rd October.
[2] 115th Infantry Brigade Order No. 283.

but were checked by heavy machine gun fire, and only succeeded in advancing their line by 150 yards. On the extreme right our men made no advance. The enemy and our own men held nearly adjacent houses in the Route d'Hecq, and kept up a continued fire on one another while a number of unfortunate civilians were imprisoned in their cellars between them.

The 17th Royal Welsh Fusiliers spent the 28th preparing for a raid to be carried out next day with the object of preventing the enemy from feeling moral superiority after his partial success in his counter-attack of the previous day.

The plan for the raid was as follows :—

[1]The attacking infantry (2 companies) were to start from our front line between S.26.a.3.8. and S.19.d.9.5., and clear the area up to the line S.20.d.1.5. to S.20.a.3.8., and return to our lines by zero plus 60 minutes. A special party was to follow up the right flank and when this had reached its objective to advance south-east and clear the houses on the Roman road. If these were successfully cleared they were to be held.

The operation was to be covered by a powerful artillery, consisting of three brigades of field artillery, two 6″ howitzer batteries and a battery of 60 pdrs., besides trench mortars and machine guns. These were to form a creeping barrage of shrapnel with 10% smoke shell, and box barrages with 50% smoke and 50% shrapnel.

29th October.

Zero was at 08.00. The left company reached their objective and inflicted severe casualties on the enemy besides capturing about 30 prisoners and six machine guns. Some men of the 115th Light Trench Mortar Battery acted as infantry and acquitted themselves very creditably. The attack of the right company was thrown into confusion by two very unusual circumstances and never matured.

A short distance behind the line on which the infantry formed up there was a row of poplar trees 50 or 60 feet high. The shrapnel shells of the barrages failed to clear these trees, exploded on the infantry and threw them into confusion. This was intensified by a

---

[1] 115th Infantry Brigade Order No. 284. 38th Divisional Artillery operation Order No. 117.

column of French civilians, who were being evacuated, emerging from the village with their household effects on carts just as the enemy counter-barrage came down. The men, women and children scattered into the fields to escape it. The Germans now turned machine guns on them, and they fled leaving their carts where they stood and some dead and wounded. The presence of civilians in villages which were constantly being shelled was a most painful feature of these operations.

The raid resulted in the capture of 33 prisoners and 70 killed mostly from our barrages. Our casualties were 15 killed and 55 wounded.

During the evening of the 29th October the 114th Infantry Brigade relieved the 115th, the 15th Welsh taking over from the 2nd Royal Welsh Fusiliers and 14th Welsh from the 17th Royal Welsh Fusiliers. The 115th Infantry Brigade then withdrew into rest billets in the Forest area.

30th and 31st October. 1st November.

Throughout these three days the 114th Infantry Brigade remained in the front line without any change, the line of resistance running through the orchards east and north-east of Englefontaine as shown on Map VI, with posts 150 yards in front. During this time the 156th and 162nd Brigades, R.F.A., of the 33rd Division, marched back for 72 hours rest at Bertry; but the 156th Brigade actually only got 24 hours rest, as both were back in the line by 2nd November. The 121st and 122nd Brigades, R.F.A., had been brought back to the line from their short rest on the 28th and 29th October respectively. The 121st came into action west of Wagnonville and Poix-du-Nord, and the 122nd Brigade one battery north-east and the three others south-east of Poix-du-Nord, with brigade headquarters in that village.

The support and reserve infantry brigades during the wait in front of Englefontaine took every opportunity of practising attacks through the orchards and woods. Time in reserve after the first day of rest was devoted to accustoming the men to find their way in the very enclosed country which lay in front. For this purpose Vendegies Wood was a perfect godsend, and many

were the attacks which were practised through it. The 115th
Infantry Brigade had only three days in rest, two of which were
given up to tactical training in wood fighting, and to practising
platoons in marching on compass bearings.

All this time British activity in the air grew continually greater.
On the Third Army front 3 tons of bombs were dropped on
Bavai Railway Junction on 30th October, 6¼ tons on 31st, and
2 tons on troops and transport on the road on 1st November.

2nd November.

The situation was unchanged. The shelling of Englefontaine,
Poix-du-Nord and Wagnonville was heavy as usual. Most of the
German high explosive shells at this period had a proportion of
lachrymatory gas which made the shelling particularly unpleasant.

In the afternoon and evening the 115th Infantry Brigade relieved the 114th in the line, taking over on a three battalion
front with the units in the positions they were to occupy in the
forthcoming operations. The 2nd Royal Welsh Fusiliers were on
the right as before, the 10th South Wales Borderers in the centre,
and the 17th Royal Welsh Fusiliers on the left in their old position.
The 114th Infantry Brigade on relief moved back into the Forest
Area.

Lieut.-General Shute, commanding V Corps, had held a conference at Ovillers on 30th October attended by Maj.-General
Cubitt, and after it V Corps on 31st October issued their orders
for the advance. The First French Army, and Fourth, Third and
First British Armies were to attack together. It was destined to be
the last attack on the grand scale.

    (a)   The first phase of these operations was to be the capture
           of the Green Line—the road which runs north-east and
           south-east through the Foret-de-Mormal from Les
           Grandes Pâtures. (See Map VI.)

    (b)   The second phase was to be the capture of the Avesnes—
           Bavai road which crosses the Sambre at Pont-sur-Sambre.

The first phase of the attack on V Corps front was to be
carried out by the 38th and 17th Divisions.

[1]The intermediate objectives for brigades were given in the

---

[1] V Corps G.S. 518/6.

orders, and the 38th and 17th Divisions were to exploit forward on gaining the final objective, and to establish outposts in front of it. On Z + 1 day the advance was to be continued by the 33rd and 21st Divisions.

The artillery instructions were to be communicated later, when the initial barrage line, rate of the barrage, etc., had been arranged with the neighbouring corps.

[1]The Divisional Orders were issued on 2nd November. The plan was perfectly straightforward. The 115th Brigade was to take the first objective (Blue Line), the 113th Brigade the second (Red Line), and the 114th Brigade the third and fourth (Brown and Green Lines). Owing to the very enclosed nature of the country the execution of the plan was not so simple.

The division was attacking on a front of 2000 yards, and the frontage and objectives are given in the attached Map VI.

The 115th Brigade were to form up on a three battalion front and commence the attack at Zero + 45 (06.15 hours). The 18th Division on the right was to begin its attack at the same time, but the 17th Division on the left was to start three quarters of an hour earlier, at Zero (05.30).

[2]The 113th Brigade was to assemble south-west of Englefontaine

---

[1] 38th Div. Order No. 250.

[2] The following time-table was issued by H.Q., 38th Division as a rough guide to assist all officers and men to follow the progress of the barrages and to arrive at and depart from the various objectives as intended.

TIME TABLE FOR ATTACK.
4th November, 1918.

115th Infantry Brigade advance				06.15
,,	,,	,,	arrive Blue Line on Right	08.00
,,	,,	,,	,, ,, ,, Left	07.15
113th	,,	,,	assemble West of Blue Line	08.30
,,	,,	,,	pass through Blue Line on Right	09.05
,,	,,	,,	,, ,, ,, ,, Left	08.50
,,	,,	,,	arrive on Red Line on Right	10.20
,,	,,	,,	,, ,, ,, ,, Left	10.30
114th	,,	,,	assemble West of Red Line	12.00
			(Left may be refused at discretion of Brigadier).	
,,	,,	,,	pass through Red Line on Right	12.20
,,	,,	,,	,, ,, ,, ,, Left	13.00
,,	,,	,,	on Brown Line on Right	14.20
			,, Centre	14.10
			,, Left	14.00
114th	,,	,,	pass East of Brown Line	14.40
,,	,,	,,	arrive Green Line on Right	15.40
,,	,,	,,	,, ,, ,, Left	17.10

in F.11. and 12., and afterwards form up for attack on the Blue
Line moving thither by the south of Englefontaine, but keeping
north of the Ruisseau des Eclusettes. The brigade was to be in its
assembly positions west of the Blue Line at Zero + 180, and was
to assault on a three battalion front at Zero + 215 on the right,
and Zero + 197 on the left. If the attack of the 115th Brigade
should be held up the 113th Brigade were to push through and
capture the Blue Line prior to advancing on the Red Line.

The 114th Brigade was to assemble in F.11. and 12. as soon
as the 113th Brigade had moved forward. The brigade was to form
up for attack west of the Red Line on a two battalion front at
Zero + 390 and begin the assault at Zero + 410 on the right, and
Zero + 450 on the left. On arrival on the Brown Line there
was to be a pause of 20 minutes, and the third battalion was to
pass through to occupy the left of the Green Line while the right
battalion continued its advance and occupied the right of the Green
Line. After occupying the Green Line the 114th Brigade was to
establish outposts in advance, and exploit the success by means
of strong patrols.

[1]The advance was to be covered by a creeping barrage moving
100 yards in 6 minutes to give the infantry plenty of time to work
their way through the enclosed country and forest. It was to be
constituted as follows : —

(a) 300 yards in front of the infantry, two fifths of the 18 pdrs.
firing shrapnel with one round in three smoke.

(b) 100 yards in front of barrage (a). All 4·5″ Hows. with
101 fuze.

(c) 300 yards in front of barrage (a), the remaining 18 pdrs.
firing H.E. with 50% thermite, fuzes set to give 20%
on graze.

(d) 60 pdrs. firing shrapnel and 6″ Hows. with 106 fuze on
tactical points not closer than 700 yards in front of
barrage (a).

The barrage was to fired by the usual four brigades of field
artillery together with the 169th Army Brigade, R.F.A., and the
13th Brigade, R.G.A. Owing to the lesson learnt in the raid of
29th October the barrage was placed 300 yards in front of the

---

[1] 38th Divisional Artillery Operation Order No. 123.

infantry through the wooded country. In order to regulate the advance of the artillery the following orders were given:—

(1) Brigades firing barrage (a) to cease fire on arrival of the barrage at the Blue Line protector, and advance to positions east of Englefontaine, there to pick up the barrage again in conformity with the barrage map as batteries came into action.

(2) Two of the three brigades firing barrage (c) to halt on the Blue Line protector changing from H.E. and thermite to shrapnel and replacing the brigades firing barrage (a) which will have commenced to advance. The remaining 18 pdrs. to continue firing barrage (c).

(3) The barrage from the Blue to the Red Line to be fired by three brigades of field artillery only, two brigades firing barrage (a) with 1 round in 6 smoke, and the third firing barrage (c) using thermite as far as available.

(4) On the capture of the Red Line the three rear brigades to commence to move forward by batteries to squares S.27. and A.3.

(5) The long halt of the infantry on the Red Line should give time for the bulk of the artillery to advance into action, and the barrage from the Red to the Green Line should be fired by such batteries as were in action, each one taking up the line according to the barrage map, on that line which gives safety clearing limits dependent on the range.

In this ingenious and skilful manner Brig.-General Topping, C.R.A. 38th Division arranged a powerful barrage to break the crust at the opening of the attack, and the infantry were provided with a reasonable barrage continually in front of them afterwards. An attack like this through a forest earlier in the war would have entailed desperate and long continued fighting, even if it were not considered practically impossible. The arrangement made provision for the infantry to have the help of a barrage for nearly 6000 yards, as against 3000 yards which was the depth to which the barrage advanced on 23rd October on the occasion of the advance from the Selle. It also enabled the infantry to advance without a very long halt on any of the objectives, which proved to be of great importance during the actual attack. The commander and C.R.A. of the 17th Division on the left were of opinion that their infantry should be covered by the full amount of their artillery throughout. This necessitated in their case a pause of two hours on the second objective while the artillery were being moved, and during this pause the enemy got up machine guns, which prevented the further advance of that division till the advance of the 38th Division enabled it to get on.

The covering fire was to be strengthened by the whole of the Stokes mortars of the division, 4 mortars each from the 113th and 114th Infantry Brigades to be placed at the disposal of the 115th Brigade for the opening crash. They were subsequently to rejoin their own brigades and move forward with them. The mobile sections of 6″ trench mortars were also to assist. They had been in action since the 2nd November, and had been utilized on each day to blow gaps in the big overgrown hedges interlaced with wire. They had expended two hundred shells each day from each section, and fired the same number on the morning of the battle causing great commotion and provoking strong retaliation.

The powerful heavy artillery of V Corps[1], unseen by the divisions, was also to assist. Special tasks in advance of the barrage were given to twenty-eight 6″ Hows., the 60 pdrs. of the 13th Brigade, R.G.A., and the 6″ guns. The tasks for the 60 pdrs. of the 17th Brigade, R.G.A., were given by the divisions, and the rest of the heavy artillery, comprising ten 6″ Hows., ten 8″ Hows., ten 9·2″ Hows., and two 12″ Hows., was placed at the disposal of Counter-battery Staff Officer, V Corps. The 13th and 17th Brigades, R.G.A., were to be in liaison with the right and left divisions of the corps respectively. A special point was made of the importance of balloon observation, and a 60 pdr. battery was attached to each balloon. Special attention was also ordered to be given to the far edges of any clearings in the forest.

The machine gun battalion of the 38th Division was as usual to join in the barrage firing over Englefontaine from squares F.12., and X.29. and 30. Their targets were to be first the edge of the forest and second the Blue Line. One company was to move forward under the orders of each of the 113th and 114th Brigades

---

[1] V Corps H.A. Instructions No. 217.   V Corps Artillery Instructions No. 219.

to protect the positions occupied. The other two companies under Lieut.-Colonel Lyttelton, commanding the battalion, were to follow up the 114th Brigade to the Green Line and there be joined by the company attached to the 113th Brigade, the whole battalion then acting under the orders of the Brigadier of the 114th Brigade.

One section of four tanks was allotted to the division and was placed under the orders of the Brigadier of the 115th Brigade. They were to rendezvous on X/Y night in Vendegies Wood, and on Y/Z night immediately west of Englefontaine. They were to advance with the infantry and assist them by breaking down hedges and by engaging any hostile posts holding up the advance among the orchards, on the edge of the forest or in the houses in A.2.c. and S.26.a. As soon as the infantry had entered the forest they were to withdraw to their rendezvous of the night before.

All the Field Companies R.E., and the 19th Welsh Regiment (Glamorgan Pioneers) were to work under the orders of the C.R.E. and to be employed on clearing the roads and tracks and improving the Englefontaine—Hecq—Route d'Hecq road. This road was one of those wanted for motor transport. They were also to clear the main cable route, mentioned below.

As regards communications a cable was to be laid by the Divisional Cable Company. Artillery and Infantry Brigades were to establish their headquarters as near as possible to test points on it. Infantry Brigades were to maintain one wireless loop set continuously manned, and the 114th Brigade was allotted one wireless trench set to work with the Divisional Report Centre. The Divisional Aeroplane dropping station was established at A.1.b.6.0., the Divisional Report Centre being at A.1.b.5.2. (to become Advanced Divisional, M.G., and R.E. H.Q. as soon as the Red Line was occupied).

One troop of the 5th Cyclist Regiment was attached to each of the 113th and 114th Brigades, and the half section of the 183rd Tunnelling Company attached to the brigade in the line for the purpose of dealing with delay action mines, etc., was placed under the orders of the 114th Brigade from Zero hour. Careful arrangements were made for the exact location of brigade head-quarters during the advance, and also for liaison posts with neigh-bouring divisions.

3rd November.

During the night of 2nd/3rd November the battalions of the 115th Infantry Brigade sent out patrols which returned with useful information as to the position of some of the hostile posts. The day was spent in preparation for the attack, and the Divisional Commander visited a number of the battalions of the Division.

[1]Tactical instructions were issued by the 38th Division, the most important feature of which was, that through woods the only method of making sure that direction would be maintained, was to keep units well concentrated under the personal command of platoon, company, and if necessary battalion commanders, wide extensions being quite out of place. The importance of getting forward as fast as the barrage would permit was also emphasized, and it was pointed out that it was to be expected that pockets of the enemy would be left, but this was of little account as other troops would be continually passing through from front to rear, which would ensure the surrender of these small parties.

During the day the attack orders[2] of the 115th Infantry Brigade were issued The attack was to be on a three battalion front, the 2nd Royal Welsh Fusiliers on the right, the 10th South Wales Borderers in the centre, and the 17th Royal Welsh Fusiliers on the left. The forming up line, objective and divisional boundaries are given on Map VI. Each battalion was to attack with two companies in the front line, the western edge of the forest being their objective. The two rear companies were to leap-frog on this line and move direct to the final objective, the Blue Line. The original leading companies were to mop up the defences on the edge of the forest, reform quickly and move in support of the companies which had passed through.

It was pointed out that though the frontage allotted to battalions was about 700 yards, they were not to move on a greater front than 200 yards per company, the gaps thus caused between companies and battalions being filled by troops working to their right and left on the edge of the forest and on the final objective.

---

[1] Tactical Instructions to accompany 38th Division Order No. 250.

[2] 115th Infantry Brigade Order No. 287.

All battalions companies and platoons were to do their utmost to help forward any troops on their flanks, who might be temporarily held up. As the division on the left of the 38th Division would be attacking three-quarters of an hour earlier, orders were given for the forming up line, decided on at a meeting the previous night, to be marked out and deep slits cut on it during the day. It lay some two to three hundred yards behind the front line, along the eastern edge of Englefontaine, and all troops were to be in position on it, and all posts in advance of it were to be withdrawn half an hour before Zero, i.e. the time of attack of the division on the left. The barrage was to pause for four minutes on the opening line, but troops were warned not to get too near to it when entering the forest, till they saw where the shell were bursting.

Eight guns of the 115th Light Trench Mortar Battery and eight guns from the two other brigades, working under the orders of the officer commanding the 115th, were to fire at Zero on points near the opening line of the artillery barrage, which had already been notified to him. One mortar was to be prepared to go forward with each battalion.

One Tank was allotted to each battalion and one Tank if available was to be held in brigade reserve ready to help any battalion that might need its services.

The success signal was to be a Very light bursting into three white lights.

The absolute necessity of every officer making full use of his compass in keeping direction was pointed out. The direction of the attack was due East, 102° Magnetic.

Brigade headquarters were moved forward into the cellar of a house in Englefontaine at 17.30 hours. During the night the enemy, who was firing away his dumps of ammunition, put down one of the heaviest bombardments on Englefontaine that was experienced throughout the advance, and brigade headquarters were lucky to escape without casualties, their billet being hit by shell many times.

4th November.

The first seven hundred yards was across the very small strongly fenced orchards lying between the village and the forest, and the final brigade objective was a ride running roughly north and south seven hundred yards inside the edge of the forest.

[1]The 2nd Royal Welsh Fusiliers on the right were formed up as ordered by 05.00 hours, "C" and "D" companies in front with "B" and "A" companies in support. The task allotted to the battalion involved two changes of direction and the length of front varied by some 300 to 800 yards, owing to the right resting on a winding stream the Ruisseau des Eclusettes. The front on the forming up line was about 500 yards and on the final objective about 1200 yards, the greater part of which was in a clearing. This meant that on reaching the leap-frog line a third company had to push into the front line. The dispositions ordered, therefore, were that "B" company on reaching it should become the right front company, "C" company the centre front company, and "A" company should leap-frog through "D", the last named remaining in the leap-frog line in reserve. As the number of troops required to go forward without delay to the final objective left too few to mop up the houses encountered at the beginning of the attack, battalion headquarters was made responsible for mopping up these houses.

The battalion moved to the attack at 06.15 behind a heavy and accurate barrage. The morning was very misty and though it made keeping direction more difficult, it hampered the enemy's movement and fire still more. This will always be the case and fog will always be an advantage to the attacker, so long as his troops are well trained in the use of compasses. The Tank allotted to the battalion failed to appear, but a Tank allotted to the 18th Division which had lost its way was intercepted and rendered valuable service. During the whole of the advance there was a gap of 400 yards between the right of the battalion and the left of the 18th Division, and from this gap the enemy enfiladed the battalion with machine gun and trench mortar fire. It was owing to the skilful leading of Captain Butler, commanding "B" company on the right, and the dash exhibited by his subordinates that the company won through to its objective. The Tank also helped in keeping down this fire, and once again proved, as was many times de-

---

[1] War Diary, 2nd Battalion, Royal Welsh Fusiliers.

RIFLE PITS IN THE ORCHARDS AT ENGLEFONTAINE.

monstrated in the later battles of the war, the great value of Tanks for covering the flank of an advance. On the final objective being captured, the reserve company, "D", crossed the Ruisseau-des-Eclusettes and cleared the enemy from just beyond the right of the final objective and the ground in rear as far back as the village of Hecq. This company during the manœuvre, dropped posts which formed a defensive right flank. Battalion headquarters meanwhile moved into the position formerly occupied by "D" company as reserve. The battalion killed about 40 of the enemy and captured four officers and 120 O.R., together with 1 field gun, 6 trench mortars and 28 machine guns (light and heavy). The casualties were 1 officer and 10 O.R's killed, 65 O.R's wounded and missing. The operations reflected very great credit on the commanding officer, Major de Miremont.

The 10th South Wales Borderers in the centre of the brigade attacked with "A" and "B" companies in front and "C" and "D" in support. They must have collected the stray Tank from the 2nd Royal Welsh Fusiliers, as they were assisted by two, which helped them up to the edge of the forest and turned and swept the edge right and left. The opposition offered by elements of the 16th and 58th German Divisions was weak and easily overcome. The final objective was reached at 07.15, one hour after the start. The casualties amounted to 42, including two officers killed and one wounded.

The attack of the 17th Royal Welsh Fusiliers was also completely successful, both objectives being captured well up to time. The battalion lost 1 officer, and 7 O.R's killed and 3 officers and 41 O.R's wounded. All along the brigade front the little columns got through gaps in the enemy's line, and in many cases took the hostile posts from the rear. The enemy were completely overpowered, and retired in disorder leaving many machine guns and prisoners in our hands. Touch was established on the left with the 17th Division, and the battalions dug themselves in during the day on the line which they had captured, but in the evening they were withdrawn to billets in Englefontaine.

The machine guns suffered considerably whilst firing their barrage. A counter barrage was put down by the enemy when the 17th Division on the left attacked at 05.30, and another when the 38th Division attack began at 06.15. This was especially heavy on the right, and the casualties were very severe in "C" company.

The 6″ trench mortars fired 200 rounds during this part of the bombardment. They also suffered from the enemy retaliation, losing 7 men wounded.

The task of the 113th Infantry Brigade required careful preliminary arrangements and accurate staff work. 38th Division Order No. 250 ordered them to assemble south-west of Englefontaine in F.11 and 12, and afterwards follow up the 115th Infantry Brigade and form up for the attack west of the Blue Line by zero + 180. [1]As the result of careful reconnaissance by the brigade headquarters and by battalions, other assembly positions further north and closer to the starting off line were thought to be better. [2]The battalions were to attack—13th Royal Welsh Fusiliers on the right, 14th in the centre and 16th on the left. They were therefore ordered to assemble :—13th Royal Welsh Fusiliers about A.7.b.4.8., and F.12.a.7.7. 14th Royal Welsh Fusiliers in the southern part of F.5.c. and d, and 16th Royal Welsh Fusiliers in the northern part of these squares. They were to be in position by 05.00 hours and to start forward, 16th Royal Welsh Fusiliers. not later than 06.45, 14th Royal Welsh Fusiliers not later than 07.00, and 13th Royal Welsh Fusiliers not later than 07.15. On arrival in the assembly position, units were to dig in for protection against the counter barrage, though the time available for this was only half an hour.

[3]Reveille for the 13th Royal West Fusiliers was at 02.00 hours and the battalion moved at 03.00 hours, companies moving independently. The attack of the 17th Division at 05.30 drew retaliation and a certain number of casualties were incurred. Companies were reported in position at 05.45. When the 115th Infantry Brigade went forward to the attack at 06.15 it was evident that they were meeting with considerable opposition on the fringe of the forest. As soon as it was seen that this had been overcome,

---

[1] 113th Infantry Brigade No. BM/S/2077 and 2080.

[2] 113th Infantry Brigade Orders No. 270.

[3] War Diary, 13th Royal Welsh Fusiliers.

the battalion left its assembly position, "D" company on the right, "C" company in the centre and "A" company on the left, with "B" company in support on the right. Crossing the orchards in A.2., all the companies were much harassed by machine gun fire and by batteries firing at very close range. The 14th Royal Welsh Fusiliers moved across country by companies from Poix-du-Nord, starting at 01.45. They assembled on a north and south line in square A.1., 200 yards in rear of the 10th South Wales Borderers, "C" and "D" companies in front and "A" and "B" companies in rear. On arrival they dug in for protection. They moved forward to the Blue Line in artillery formation and were in position there by 08.30. While leaving his headquarters at Poix-du-Nord, Major Wheldon, who had just taken over command of the battalion was wounded and two other officers were killed. Major Wheldon carried on for some hours till Lt.-Col. Collier who had started on leave could be recalled to take command again. The 16th Royal Welsh Fusiliers suffered heavy casualties in the assembly position but few afterwards.

The method of attack of the 13th Royal Welsh Fusiliers as ordered by the 113th Infantry Brigade was necessarily somewhat different from that of the other two battalions. One company moving along the Ruisseau-des-Eclusettes to about A.9.b. were to attack and occupy the high ground in A.10.a., and form an "international post" with the 8th Berkshires, 18th Division, about A.10.b.3.0. The remainder of the battalion moving by the stream in A.3.d. and A.4.c. and d., were to occupy the wood in the battalion area, establish an international post with the Berkshires at A.10.b.9.1. and thus pinch out the open ground in A.3.d., A.4.c. and d. and A.10.a. and b.

The 14th and 16th Royal Welsh Fusiliers were to make a straightforward attack with two companies each in front and two behind. The leading companies were to capture the line of high ground between A.4.a.0.0. and S.28.b.0.2., and thence along the road to S.27.b.6.7. The two rear companies were then to leap-frog through to the final brigade objective.

Three sections of "C" company of the 38th Machine Gun Battalion were to follow up the 115th Infantry Brigade and bring their guns into action in the clearing in A.3. and A.9.b., from whence they were to support the advance of the 113th Infantry Brigade by firing direct on any enemy who shewed themselves, or on the far edge of the clearing. The remaining section was to follow the 16th Royal Welsh Fusiliers and come into action about S.27.b.8.4. On the Red Line being captured the whole company was to entrench itself in depth. Four Stokes mortars were to move with the infantry; a section of two each with the 13th and 16th Royal Welsh Fusiliers.

Direction generally was to be kept by compass; but in addition the 13th Royal Welsh Fusiliers had streams to help them, and certain landmarks were pointed out to guide the other two battalions. On the Brown Line being captured by the 114th Infantry Brigade the 113th Brigade was to be ready to support it or to move forward.

On advancing to the attack from the Blue Line, the 13th Royal Welsh Fusiliers on the right encountered very little determined resistance in spite of the numerous batches of the enemy still hiding in the undergrowth, and the companies swept on to their objectives well up to time. They then dug in along the road forming the final objective. A battery of $10^{c/m}$ guns and a total of 65 prisoners were captured. The casualties were one officer and 14 O.R. killed and one officer and 64 O.R. wounded, the great majority having occurred during the early stages of the attack.

The 14th Royal Welsh Fusiliers advanced at 08.45 hours with "C" and "D" companies in front, they attacked the high ground in A.4.a. and S.28.a., and thence along the road in S.27.b. They captured it and the two rear companies passed through and went forward to the final objective without serious opposition. The 16th Royal Welsh Fusiliers on the left advanced at 08.30 hours in the same formation, leap-frogged on the high ground, and went on to the final brigade objective without difficulty.

The attack of the 114th Infantry Brigade was possibly even more difficult to arrange than that of the 113th Brigade. It had to advance to a greater depth through enclosed and forest country before it was called upon to take up the running, with the consequent greater chance of units losing direction and going astray.

Detailed orders (114th Infantry Brigade Order No. 223) were issued on 3rd November and will be found in Appendix II.

Battalions marched from their billets at Croix and Cailuyaux at 07.00, battalions at 500 yards and companies at 100 yards interval. The order of march was 14th Welsh leading, 15th Welsh, 13th Welsh.[1] They marched by a track to the first assembly position. The morning was fine but there was a thick mist which lasted till 08.30 hours. The units reached the assembly position between that time and 09.00 hours. Brigade Headquarters had already been established at 05.00 in one of the outlying houses to the south of Englefontaine at F.6.c.8.3. It had been intended to move forward to positions of deployment in the forest at 09.30. The situation in front, however, being obscure, orders were issued by the brigade to await further instructions. During this time the assembly position was subjected to a certain amount of shelling with 4·2 and 77$^{c/m}$ shell, and most of the casualties occurred at this time. During the wait all units kept touch with the situation by means of reconnaissance parties.

The plan of the 114th Infantry Brigade differed from that of the other two brigades in that much more reliance was to be placed on roads and rides in the forest for keeping direction than on the compass. It was not easy to do so, as these mostly ran diagonally to the direction of the attack, but still it was accomplished. The plan was for the brigade to march with the battalions following one another in the order mentioned above along the road running east through squares F.11.b. and F.12, then through the houses lying between the villages of Hecq and Englefontaine on to the road running east in square A.2.d. up to the north and south road at A.3.central. From this point the battalions were to separate and take up the positions from which they would attack. The attack was to be carried out by companies advancing on allotted localities, each company being given its special route and moving along either flank of a main ride through the forest, leading companies to be covered by their own advanced guards. The routes of the companies and all the company objectives were shewn on a sketch map issued with the orders. (Map VII). From A.3. central the 14th Welsh, which was to attack on the left, was to move by the

---

[1] War Diary 13th Welsh.

Route du Chene-Couplet to its position of deployment in A.10.b. The 15th Welsh followed by the 13th Welsh were to move astride the Route-d'Hecq to their positions of deployment in rear of the Red Line by moving across the clearing in the forest. The 15th Welsh followed at 500 yards interval by the 13th Welsh were to commence the assault at zero + 410. The 14th Welsh were to commence the assault at zero + 450. Companies of the two battalions were to make for the points allotted to them on the map. A pause of 20 minutes was to be made on the Brown Line, when the 15th Welsh was to continue its advance to the Green Line, and the 13th Welsh was to pass between the 15th and 14th Welsh on to its objectives on the left half of the Green Line. The final objectives were then to be consolidated, the companies' positions were to be prepared for all round defence, and patrols were to be pushed out. The 14th Welsh were then to become brigade reserve. [1]In conformity with these orders the brigade left its assembly position in F.11.b. at 10.00, when news of the success of the two leading brigades had come through. It was led by the Brigade Commander, Lt.-Colonel C. C. Norman, who had commanded the 2nd Royal Welsh Fusiliers at Villers Outreaux.

The 14th Welsh were in their position of deployment by noon, and the other two battalions in theirs astride the Route d'Hecq fifteen minutes later. (See Map VII). At 12.20 the brigade began its attack behind a creeping barrage. The 15th Welsh attacked on a two company front astride the Route d'Hecq accompanied by two sections of machine guns and two Stokes mortars. The 14th Welsh on the left started their attack at 13.00, two companies in front and two in support each leading company being covered by its advanced guard. The opposition was slight and consisted mainly of small isolated posts of infantry, with occasionally a machine gun post. The left battalion met with some opposition from machine guns firing across the open space in A.5.d. By 14.15 both leading battalions had reached the Brown Line. The right battalion arrived in front of time, but the barrage allowed of it. Prisoners from the 103rd, 107th and 115th Infantry Regiments, and the 68th Artillery Regiment were captured by both battalions.

---

[1] Narrative of operations carried out by 114th Infantry Brigade in Foret de Mormal, 4th and 5th November, 1918.

The right battalion captured ten guns in A.11.b., which were handed over to the artillery who turned them on the enemy. Touch had been gained with brigades on the right and left. At 14.30 the mobile 6" trench mortars reached the Brown Line, a fine performance for a weapon designed for trench warfare.[1] These were directed to shoot at the houses in Les Grandes Patures, and opened fire an hour later with good effect. After a twenty minutes pause on the Brown Line the support companies of the 15th Welsh passed through the leading companies at 14.40, and on the left the 13th Welsh advanced on the north side of the Route d'Hecq on a one company front, for the advance to the Green Line.

The hostile resistance was of a similar character to that encountered up to the Brown Line. The right battalion captured six more guns. The left battalion encountered machine gun fire down the road running south from Locquignol through T.25 central. By 15.40 the 15th Welsh were established on the Green Line on the right, and a few minutes later the 14th Welsh, the reserve battalion, pushed advanced troops into the orchards on the south-western outskirts of Locquignol—in the face of desultory shooting from the houses in the village. By 17.15 the 13th Welsh on the left were also established on the Green Line. Consolidation was immediately started and patrols pushed out. Touch was not established on the flanks for some hours. The right battalion established outposts along the Laie de Locquignol in B.2., and the left battalion about 250 yards east of the Green Line. Patrols reported the enemy in B.8.a., B.2.a., T.26.d., in very small numbers, mostly isolated machine guns. A patrol from the left battalion proceeded as far as Locquignol church, and found the village unoccupied. They fired a few shots to attract attention, but with no result. At 22.30 the 13th Welsh reported that they could find no enemy within 2,000 yards of the cross roads on their left flank at T.26.b.1.8.

By this time 114th Infantry Brigade Headquarters had been established further back in the forest at A.3.b.9.2., and thanks to a particularly efficient signal officer, Lt. Bowen, telegraphic communication had been quickly established with the 38th Division

---

[1] The 6' mortar of the 38th Division had moved out of Englefontaine in close support of the 16th Royal Welsh Fusiliers under Captain Shurman. It came into action twice and fired 18 rounds.

and also with the front line battalions. The reports from the patrols to Divisional Headquarters showed Major-General Cubitt that the enemy was slipping away from in front. About 00.30 or 01.00 he rang up Capt. Bucknall, the Brigade Major, to find out whether it was not possible to push on to the Sambre River, and eventually the 13th Welsh on the Divisional Commander's instructions, though almost worn out with their long and tiring day were ordered to take on the task.

In accordance with these orders and largely owing to the personality and drive of Lt.-Col. H. Hobbs, commanding the 13th Welsh, "A" and "B" companies of that battalion advanced at 02.30, under Captains H. Wilcoxon and W. B. Morgan respectively, one via La Tête Noire to La Croix Daniel, and the other via the road junction T.22.c.0.0., and the cross-roads at B.5.d. to Sarbaras, each company covered by its own advanced guard. The advance was particularly difficult as it was very dark and raining hard. The troops surrounded the above villages and took the enemy completely by surprise, capturing 40 prisoners. In addition a Field Ambulance with 32 wounded Germans and 1 wounded soldier of the 14th Royal Welsh Fusiliers and a staff of 10 was taken in Sarbaras. The two companies entrenched themselves before dawn on the general line of the road T.30.c.8.0., T.30.b.4.0., La Croix Daniel, with flanks refused. Both companies pushed out patrols, and one from "B" company on the left consisting of two sections, which was sent to find out if the Germans were still in Berlaimont, succeeded in entering the village about 07.00. Helped by information from the inhabitants this patrol captured 60 prisoners. These companies were on the move from 07.00 on the 4th November, till the same hour on the 5th, during which time they had covered a distance of $11\frac{1}{2}$ miles, the first half of which was traversed under shell fire, and the second in continuous contact with the enemy. As a result of their efforts troops of the 38th Division had penetrated to a depth of about four miles further than the divisions on the right and left, and had over-run the first objective of the next day's attack.

The final advance of "A" and "B" Companies, 13th Welsh was a very good example of a commander promptly seizing an opportunity as soon as it presented itself. The advance through the forest in the middle of the night, in darkness and heavy rain, was a really fine performance. The casualties of the 114th Infantry Brigade were very light—1 officer and 4 O.R. killed, 2 officers and 122 O.R. wounded and missing. The strengths of the battalions and the numbers going into battle are recorded, and are of interest : —

	13th Welsh.	14th Welsh.	15th Welsh.
Battalion strength ...	29 Offs. 837 O.R.	27 Offs. 775 O.R.	30 Offs. 855 O.R.
Numbers going into the line	14 ,, 543 ,,	17 ,, 558 ,,	16 ,, 537 ,,

The prisoners amounted to 215 and the captured materiel to 16 guns and 20 machine guns. 66 of the enemy were killed.

To turn now to the other arms. [1]The whole of the machine gun companies fired the first part of the barrage. Then as soon as the 115th Infantry Brigade had taken the first objective (Blue Line) "C" company went forward with the 113th Infantry Brigade. It will be remembered that this company was heavily shelled during the firing of the barrage. Consequently only seven guns were able to move owing to casualties. "A" company (12 guns) went forward with the 114th Infantry Brigade. At 11.00 "B" and "D" companies were ordered to limber up and advance. Some delay was caused by casualties to officers, and "B" which had only one officer left did not start for some hours. "D" were established in battery positions covering the Green Line by 16.30. Getting the limbers through the forest was a difficulty, as bye roads and paths were blocked by trees blown down by shell fire, and the main roads had been ruined by the enemy.

As regards the Divisional Artillery the whole of the brigades fired the original barrage at 06.15. [2]At 08.15 the 156th and 162nd Brigades began to advance one battery at a time as soon as the 115th Infantry Brigade had taken the Blue Line. They were directed on positions already chosen east of Englefontaine. At this time the enemy's artillery fire was still heavy, but the 162nd Brigade, although shelled on the way, was successful in reaching

---

[1] War Diary, 38th Machine Gun Battalion.
[2] History of the 33rd Divisional Artillery.

the new positions. On the other hand the 156th Brigade following up the infantry closely was prevented from doing so by intense machine gun fire. Only A/156 was able to get through, the other batteries having temporarily to drop into action west of the village till the machine gun fire slackened. The move was then completed, the whole of the 156th Brigade lying 1,000 yards south-east of Englefontaine on the outskirts of the forest, close alongside the 162nd Brigade. From here the barrage was continued till the final objective was taken. Positions were then reconnoitred 3,000 yards further forward, and at dusk all the batteries advanced again. Great difficulty was experienced by the artillery in getting forward on account of the fallen trees and the craters blown in the roads, but all the batteries were again in action in the positions which had been reconnoitred round a cross road in the forest by 20.00 hours.

The 121st and 122nd Brigades continued firing the barrage from their original positions, the war diary of the 121st Brigade gives noon as the hour at which it moved into action in the Forest east of Hecq. It was followed by the 122nd Brigade. Lt.-Col. MacClellan commanding the 121st Brigade, gives the following description of his doings on this day :—

I rejoined on the 3rd November, the brigade then being in action W. of Wagnonville and Poix du Nord. On the 4th November the brigade supported the attack of the 113th Infantry Brigade (as usual), with the usual creeping barrage. As soon as this was well under way I rode to Brig.-Genl. apR. Pryce's H.Q., and remained there until he had information, at, I think, about 10.30 that his brigade had progressed. I galloped back to my H.Q., and obtained the C.R.A's (Brig.-Genl. Topping) permission by phone to advance the 121st Brigade by batteries to positions E. of Hecq to support the infantry advance through the forest. This appeared to be the first information that he had that our infantry had gone on, which points to the fact of the 113th Infantry Brigade communications with division having been cut. Of course, I cannot say for certain.

(As a matter of interest I may mention that on my way up to the infantry brigade H.Q., I found a battery R.F.A., which had been detailed for close support, completely held up because the roads were being barraged by the enemy, and the guns could not get across country; an example of the necessity of something like Pack Artillery for that work in close country).

Not having had anything to eat that morning I sent forward the leading battery while I got something, and followed close on its heels, to find Major P. M. Balfour, the B.C., red from head to foot with the blood of his horse, which had been shot under him at a range of a few yards, he having ridden into a pocket of Germans while he was reconnoitring. He was unhurt, and the Bosches having been rounded up, the remaining batteries came into action unmolested.

The infantry meanwhile had gone right on. It was absolutely impossible to get field guns along to support them, the only type of battery which could have competed with the situation being pack, or mountain, of which there were, of course, none. The enemy had blown huge craters on every road and track, most carefully sited where the ground on each side was a bog, and making passage by wheels impossible until they had been dealt with by the Pioneers, which was done during the night.

[1]The twenty-four hours fighting resulted in the capture by the 38th Division of 8 officers, 522 O.R., and 23 guns, of which the 115th Infantry Brigade took over 200 prisoners and 2 guns. The casualties amounted to about 600. The 411 wounded were evacuated by the 131st Field Ambulance on the 4th and 5th November by means of relays of bearers established through the forest. All the field companies and pioneers got to work at daybreak on the 5th making the only two roads available for the whole corps, which had been most methodically destroyed by the enemy, passable for artillery. They soon succeeded in this, but to make the roads fit for motors was a colossal work, and it was some days before motor traffic could move through the forest.

On the German side there was by this time great confusion of formations. On the 22 miles front attacked by the British Armies on 4th November the Germans had 15 divisions in the line, and reinforced them with 8 more, making a total of 23 divisions engaged. On the 38th Division front, the *14th Division* was opposite its left and the *58th Saxon Division* on its right, but prisoners were taken from 22 battalions of 10 regiments from five different divisions.

The regimental history of the 3rd Westfalian Regiment No. 16, describing the battle and the two or three days preceding it, which is given below, shows that the enemy intended to hold their position to the last, a fact which was elicited at the time from prisoners, but the loss of the road from Jolimetz to the cross

---

[1] History of the 38th Welsh Division.

roads in A.10.b. decided them to retreat, and during the night a
mounted orderly was captured by the 114th Infantry Brigade, who
was bringing orders to the troops in the line to withdraw. This
withdrawal became a part of the large scale retirement of the
German armies opposite the British front. No signs of any defence lines further to the rear could be discovered from air reconnaissance, and the intelligence branch at G.H.Q. deduced from
the location of aerodromes, the movements of wireless sets and
preparations for demolitions of railways, etc., that the enemy had
no intention of standing for long except on some great natural
obstacle, such as the Meuse. The correctness of this deduction
is confirmed by the following narrative which states that the
Infantry Regiment No. 16 on 6th November commenced the
retreat to the Antwerp—Meuse position.

Extract from the History of the 3rd Westfalian Regiment No. 16.

"The front near Raucourt (S.15.d.) was held by battalions of the 16th
and 57th Regiments interspersed, with the heavy machine guns of the
regiment behind the front line. The whole position consisted of rifle-
pits connected up irregularly. There were no dug outs. There was no
field of view owing to hedges, houses, wall and gardens. The battle headquarters were in small cellars hardly splinter proof. In these inadequate
positions the weakened and used up troops awaited the attack of an overwhelming enemy. The hostile artillery and air activity were so great that
attacks were expected hourly and the division was in a constant state of
readiness.

On the 29th October[1] from 9.15 a.m. onwards there was a heavy
bombardment of the front line and back areas on the Roman Road and
the enemy attacked north of that road with strong forces, but was everywhere repulsed . . . .

*   *   *   *   *   *

Under cover of artillery he attacked in dense masses thinking our
infantry had been annihilated and got into this area where there was
no field of view under murderous fire at very short ranges.

During these last weeks the Regiment fought with a strong front line
and the supports close up in tactical localities. The defence and organization was elastic. Elastic retreats and counter-attacks on the flanks were
constantly made use of. The machine guns and the artillery which constantly increased were the essence of the defence. . . .

The increasing activities of the enemy pointed to a big attack in the
near future. Enormous numbers of hostile airmen continually encircled

---

[1] The German version of the 38th Division raid.

A FIRST AID POST IN THE FOREST.

the battlefield, engaging batteries and attacking the rearward communications . . . .

On 4th November at 6.30 a.m., the enemy's great attack began with an enormous expenditure of ammunition and supported by numerous aeroplanes and tanks. It fell on opponents thoroughly exhausted by the hardships of the past few months. The regiment maintained itself with the courage of despair and only succumbed to superior force when both its flanks had been turned. No reserves were available to counter-attack. The portions of the regiment which had not already succumbed to the effects of the bombardment were over-run and killed. A few were taken prisoners and still fewer were able to escape to bring back news of the glorious end of the regiment. From 9 a.m., the regiment had no longer any communications to the rear. About 1 p.m., Capt. Peipe reported from the artillery protective position that he had repulsed the enemy; but on his right flank long columns of artillery, infantry, and tanks were on the march. Notwithstanding this orders were issued by the regiment to offer further resistance. Five minutes later a despatch rider from the brigade reported that British cavalry and tanks had occupied Jolimetz. Col. von Abercron thereupon decided to give the order to retreat; but the battalion was not any longer in a position to do so . . . . An hour later the regiment had the account of the last stand of the 1st Battalion from scouts who had fought their way back . . . . The remnants of the 3rd Battalion succeeded in fighting their way out. About 2.30 p.m., it was reported from all sides that the enemy was advancing. As there were now only about 30 or 40 men left, Col. von Abercron retired with about 20 men. A few officers with two machine guns and about 20 men covered this retirement. This detachment was attacked about 3 p.m. in rear and flank and was forced to retire pell-mell. At the same moment the enemy emerged everywhere from the wood under cover of his barrage. On the Herbignies—Grande Carriere road the remnants of the regiment fell in with fresh troops. The casualties sustained by it were 16 officers and over 500 men. The remnants of the regiment (57 men) were placed under Cavalry Captain von Hesse in readiness to protect the right flank of the 18th Reserve Division.

On 6th November the regiment was organized into three companies, fighting strength 150 rifles, and commenced the retreat to the Antwerp—Meuse position.

* * * * * *

Col. von Abercron who had been ordered to O.H.L. (G.H.Q.) returned from there on the 9th with the news of the revolution . . . .

On the 11th the regiment marched to Lu'ttre. Here the news was received at 1 p.m. "Armistice between Germany and the Entente was concluded at 11 a.m. to-day".

The troops of the 33rd and 21st Divisions passed through the outposts of the 114th Infantry Brigade about 07.00 hours on the 5th, and all available information was handed over to them by the brigade.

APPENDIX II.

114TH INFANTRY BRIGADE ORDER NO. 223.   3RD NOVEMBER, 1918.

Ref. Map 1/20,000, sheets 51A S.E., 51.S.W., 57B N.E., 57A N.W.

1. *Information.*

(a) Map 3 (not attached) shews the nature of the forest and roads and rides through it. Aeroplane photographs have been issued to infantry battalions. Copies can be seen at brigade headquarters at any time by other units. No definite line of resistance between the Red and Green Lines (see Map 1. not attached) is known to exist, but there are indications of rifle and machine gun pits in the clearing in A.5.d. and A.6.c. It is probable therefore that machine gun nests will be encountered.

(b) At zero on Z day the attack of the Third Army, together with the armies on its flanks will be continued.

(c) The 18th Division will attack on our right and the 17th Division on our left.

2. *Intention.*

Ref. Map. 1. (Not attached, information will be found in Map VII). The 115th Infantry Brigade will capture the Blue Line, the 113th Brigade will pass through the 115th Brigade and capture the Red Line; 114th Brigade will pass through the 113th Brigade and capture the Brown Line, and then the Green Line. Times of arrival and departure are shewn on Map 1.

The 33rd Division will pass through the 38th Division on Z +1 day.

3. *Orders to Troops.*

(a) *Infantry.*

(i) Infantry Battalions and 114th L.T.M.B. (less 4 guns and personnel) will march from billets in Croix to the first assembly position at F.11.b. in accordance with the attached March Table. (Not given. Battalions marched in following order :—14th Welsh, 15th Welsh, 13th Welsh, starting at 07.00, battalions at 500 yards and companies at 100 yards interval).

(ii) At zero + 195 battalions followed by machine guns and Stokes guns attached to them will move to positions of deployment in the following order :—14th Welsh leading followed by 15th Welsh and 13th Welsh. Route will be as follows :—Via road from F.11.b.2.4., A.7.a.9.3., A.2.c. 2.2., A.2.c.7.5., A.2.c.8.4., thence along road to A.3.b.1.0. From this point 14th Welsh will move to its position of deployment in A.10.b., via Route du Chene Couplet; 15th Welsh followed by 13th Welsh to their positions of deployment astride the Route d'Hecq in rear of the Red Line, by moving across the clearing in the forest.

(iii) Battalions will be formed up by zero + 390.

(iv) 15th Welsh followed at 500 yards by 13th Welsh will commence the assault at zero + 410. 14th Welsh will commence the assault at zero + 450.

Companies of the 15th and 14th Welsh will make for objectives on the Brown Line as indicated on the attached Map 2. (Not attached, information embodied in Map VII.)

A pause of 20 minutes will be made on the Brown Line, when 15th Welsh will continue its advance to the Green Line, and the 13th Welsh will pass between the 15th and 14th Welsh and on to its objectives on the Green Line.

14th Welsh will become the Brigade Reserve when the Green Line is captured. All final objectives will be consolidated, and positions of companies prepared for all round defence. Patrols will be pushed forward and to the flanks.

(v) Liaison posts will be established as follows :—

(a) On the right with the 7th Queen's on the Brown Line at B.7.a.1.4., and with the 8th Surrey's on Green Line at cross roads at B.8.c.6.9.

On the left with 17th Division on Green Line at T.26.b.0.9.

5

(b) *"A" Company 38th M.G. Battalion* will join the brigade at the assembly position in F.11.b. at zero + 165. Two forward sections will march with the 15th Welsh to its position of deployment, and will follow this battalion during the advance. One section will be specially detailed to cover the advance of the 14th Welsh across the clearing in A.5.d. if required. This section will subsequently move to the Green Line and assist in its consolidation with the 13th Welsh. The other section will accompany the 15th Welsh throughout.

Two reserve sections will follow in rear of the 13th Welsh and will move to localities as follows :—

One section to S.30.d.3.2.

,,   ,,   ,, A.6.c.9.2.

(c) 114th L.T.M.B. (less 4 guns and their personnel) will be attached to battalions as under :—

2 guns to 15th Welsh.

2   ,,   ,, 14th Welsh until Brown Line is captured, when they will move forward to the Green Line and assist in the consolidation of the 13th Welsh.

4. *Artillery.*

The advance will be covered by an artillery barrage :—

18 prs. (shrapnel and smoke) 300 yards ahead of infantry.
4·5 Howitzers   400   ,,   ,,   ,,
18 prs. (H.E. and Thermite) 500   ,,   ,,   ,,
6″ Howitzers   700   ,,   ,,   ,,

Barrages will lift at 100 yards every 6 minutes. When moving under trees infantry must keep at least 300 yards behind the barrage.

5. *Headquarters and Report Centre.*

Battalion Headquarters of all 3 battalions will move with their units from the assembly position and will establish themselves at A.4.c.1.9. when units are on positions of deployment and until Green Line is captured. They will then move forward to A.6.c.9.2. Brigade Headquarters will be at F.6.c.8.3. until Green Line is captured with advance report centre moving first to A.4.c.1.9. when

Brown Line is captured, and to A.5.a.3.5. when Green Line is captured.

6. *Communications.*
   (a) By runners and cyclists to Brigade Advanced Report Centre.
   (b) Contact aeroplanes will call for flares on Brown and Green Lines. White canvas strips will be exposed, officers and N.C.O's will spread their maps, electric torches should be flashed.
   (c) Success signals will be fired on reaching objectives.
   (d) SOS rockets, green over red over green.

7. *Advanced Dressing Station* at Brewery, F.6.c.0.3.

8. *Prisoners.* To advanced Brigade Report Centre.

Issued through Signals
at 06.30.
Distribution.

(signed) G. C. Bucknall, Captain,
Brigade Major,
114th Infantry Brigade.

THE 38th (WELSH) DIVISION

IN THE LAST FIVE WEEKS OF THE GREAT WAR.

By Major-General H. D. DePree, c.b., c.m.g., d.s.o., p.s.c.

CHAPTERS VI and VII.

Chapter VI.

The Pursuit to the Frontier.

5th November.

The Third Army issued orders during the battle on 4th November (at 13.00 hours) that its corps were to continue operations on 5th November to gain the St. Remy Chaussee—Pont sur Sambre —Bavai Road. [1]V Corps accordingly issued orders at 18.00 for the 33rd and 21st Divisions to pass through whatever line might be held by the leading divisions at 06.00 or at latest at 06.30. These instructions stated that it was of the utmost importance that the Yellow Line,[2] which on V Corps front included the passages over the river from Aulnoye southwards, should be gained immediately. It was therefore considered that no pause should be made, or leap-frogging carried out on the Black Line which ran through La Tete Noir and Sarbaras. (As a matter of fact this line was in possession of the 38th Division some hours before the time arranged for the rear divisions to pass through.) The first leap-frog of a brigade was to take place on the Yellow Line, which was timed to be reached at 13.30 and the advance resumed at 14.30 to the final objective, the Avesnes—Pont-sur-Sambre road, which was due to be reached at 17.00. In actual fact the advance was a good deal less rapid than V Corps expected, and this road was not reached till the afternoon of 6th November. The 33rd Division which was to carry out the advance on the right had one brigade group in Forest, one in Montay and one in Troisvilles; with the Divisional Artillery

---

[1] V Corps G. 664.
[2] See Map VI.

ARMISTICE DAY. BRITISH SENTRIES AT THE PORTE DE MONS, MAUBEUGE.

in action under 38th Division. [1]The plan of the division was that after passing through the 38th Division the 100th Infantry Brigade should capture the Black Line, the 98th Infantry Brigade passing through the 100th Infantry Brigade on or beyond the Black Line should capture the Yellow Line and 19th Infantry Brigade should then go on and capture the Dotted Brown Line. The leading brigade was to be supported by two companies of the 33rd machine Gun Battalion and such artillery as could be got forward. One Field Company and one company of Pioneers was to be attached to the leading brigade.

The assembly of the division was carried out on 4th November without trouble. By night-fall the 212th and 22nd Field Companies R.E., and the Pioneer Battalion were at work on the Route d'Hecq. The 100th Infantry Brigade was in the area A.10.a. and b., and the 98th and 19th Infantry Brigades and 11th Field Company R.E. in Englefontaine, with the 33rd Battalion Machine Gun Corps in Hecq. Divisional headquarters were at Forest with a report centre at Englefontaine. About 01.00 hours on 5th November General Cubitt telephoned to the 33rd Division report centre to the effect that he believed the enemy to be in retreat along his whole front, and that he had ordered two companies to be sent forward to Tete Noire and Sarbaras. On receipt of this information instructions were issued for the 100th Brigade to support the advance of the companies of the 38th Division and to move forward as early as possible. At the same time the 19th and 98th Infantry Brigades were warned to be prepared to move an hour earlier than originally intended.

The Brigadier-General commanding the 100th Infantry Brigade moved forward to the headquarters of the leading brigade of the 38th Division in A.4.c., and reported about 03.45 hours that his brigade was beginning to advance. On this orders were issued by the division for the 98th and 19th Infantry Brigades to move forward as early as possible, each brigade keeping touch with the brigade in front of it.

At 06.30, 33rd Divisional Headquarters moved to Englefontaine and a report centre was opened at Les Grandes Patures at 09.20.

---

[1] Account of operations carried out by 33rd Division from 4th November to 8th November, 1918.

The companies of the 38th Division having made such good progress the 100th Infantry Brigade met with little opposition until the leading troops reached the western bank of the Sambre. They marched by the main road through Les Grandes Patures and Sarbaras and after clearing part of Berlaimont dug in approximately on the line C.2.d.central—U.26.d.central with the 2nd Worcesters on the right, the Glasgow Highlanders on the left, and the 16th King's Royal Rifle Corps in support. All the bridges over the Sambre were found to be broken, and the enemy held the eastern bank in considerable strength with machine guns. The river was a serious obstacle being 70 feet wide and 6 feet deep.

The 98th Infantry Brigade,[1] owing to the time taken for orders to reach battalions in the dark and the distances to the starting point, was not closed up and ready to start till 05.40. It then found the roads badly blocked by artillery and transport. It reached the point where it had been decided to deploy (south east of Les Grandes Patures) at 11.30, and from there the 4th King's were directed on Sassegnies, the 1st Middlesex on Berlaimont and the 2nd Argyll and Sutherland Highlanders on Sarbaras. By 12.30 all three infantry brigade headquarters were established in close touch with one another at Sarbaras.

By 13.30 the 4th King's had passed Sassegnies and were pushing north east along the railway in C.8. and 9., in touch with the enemy on their front and the 18th Division on their right. The 1st Middlesex were closed up on the Ribaumet—Berlaimont road in touch with the 21st Division on their left, and were reconnoitring the river with a view to crossing.

At 14.00 hours Sir R. Pinney held a conference at Sarbaras which was attended by the C.R.A., all the infantry brigade commanders, and the O.C. Machine Gun Battalion. During the conference a report arrived from the 1st Middlesex stating that it was considered that the bridge at U.27.a.2.4., which had been blown up, could with R.E. assistance and the material available on the spot be made passable for infantry.

Sir R. Pinney gave instructions :—

(a) That the divisional front was to be divided into two

---

[1] War Diary 98th Infantry Brigade.

Brigade Sectors, the dividing line being the east and west grid through C.2.central.

(b) The 100th Infantry Brigade on the right and the 98th Infantry Brigade on the left, supported by harassing fire from the artillery and machine guns, were to endeavour during the night to establish crossings over the river and seize the general line Petit Maubeuge, inclusive, to the road in U.28.c and a.

(c) The 19th Infantry Brigade were to be prepared to move across the river and advance through the other brigades and through the Dotted Brown Line.

(d) The 222nd and 212th Field Companies R.E. were to be attached to the 100th and 98th Infantry Brigades respectively for the purpose of constructing bridges.

As a result of continued rain, the roads were in very bad condition and were badly blocked by transport and guns, but sufficient bridging material was got up to enable a footbridge to be constructed on the 100th Infantry Brigade front, and a pontoon bridge on the 98th Infantry Brigade front.

[1]Immediately after the conference the 98th Infantry Brigade issued hurried written orders for the 1st Middlesex to effect the crossing in the left sector

(a) if possible by local enterprise with the material on the spot, if not

(b) by an organized attack when the R.E. material arrived.

Officers of the 212th Field Company R.E. were reported to be on the way to supervize the bridging.

The first objective was the Railway in U.27.c. and C.3.b., to cover the bridging, and the second the sunken road in U.28.c.

"B" Company, 1st Middlesex effected the crossing, which was reported to brigade headquarters at 19.45, and a bridgehead was established across the river. "A" and "D" Companies crossed at midnight, while "C" remained on the near bank to cover the crossing. By 02.30 the report came through that the 1st Middlesex had made good their objective, taking about 30 prisoners and several machine guns. The enemy shelling inflicted some casualties.

---

[1] 98th Infantry Brigade Order No. 286.

[1]During the night the 212th Field Company put across one cork float bridge, one foot bridge across the demolished French bridge, and one pontoon bridge with bad approaches.

6th November.

The 2nd Argyll and Sutherland Highlanders who had been warned to be ready to push through the 1st Middlesex and seize the high ground in U.28.c., were ordered to advance as soon as news was received that the 1st Middlesex had reached their objective. They crossed the footbridge at 03.30, passed through the 1st Middlesex outposts at 05.30, and attacked the enemy with the object of enlarging the bridgehead and joining up with the 21st Division on the left who were making a similar attack. The attack was carried out by three companies in front and one in reserve and was completely successful. Touch was established on the left with the 21st Division, who had not advanced, although two battalions were assembled on the east bank of the river.

On the front of the 100th Infantry Brigade, the 222nd Field Company R.E. put a cork float bridge across at C3.c.8.3 No pontoon was possible, as the ground was too marshy to get pontoons to the site. The 2nd Worcesters followed by the Glasgow Highlanders commenced crossing at 05.30 hours under cover of a short weak barrage. In this order the two battalions advanced quickly over rising ground and took the villages of Petit Maubeuge and Leval with small loss by 08.30 At 09.45 the fact that the 100th and 98th Infantry Brigades had taken their objectives was established, and the 33rd Division ordered the 19th Infantry Brigade to move forward and pass two battalions over the river at Berlaimont and one by the footbridge in C.3. for the capture of their objective, the Dotted Brown Line.

[2]A conference of commanding officers was immediately assembled at 19th Infantry Brigade Headquarters, the scheme was explained and orders issued as follows :—

The Cameronians on the right to cross the Sambre by the foot bridges in the vicinity of the Sassegnies—Bachant railway, and passing through the 100th Infantry Brigade at Petit Maubeuge take

---

[1] War Diary, 33rd Divisional R.E.

[2] 19th Infantry Brigade narrative of operations from 4th to 8th November, 1918.

the southern portion of the brigade objective. The 5th Scottish Rifles to cross by bridges immediately south of Berlaimont, and passing through the 98th Infantry Brigade capture Aulnoye station buildings from the north west. The 1st Queen's to follow the 5th Scottish Rifles and direct two companies on Aulnoye station from the south, the remaining two companies to push on and take the northern part of the brigade objectives.

The brigade moved off at 11.00 hours, brigade headquarters moving to Ribaumet.

The Cameronians assembled in artillery formation south of the railway and advanced through the 2nd Worcesters at Petit Maubeuge and on to the Bavai—Avesnes road with slight opposition.

On the left the 5th Scottish Rifles advanced with slight resistance and took Aulnoye station by 13.40, with a loss of 1 officer killed and 1 officer and 12 other ranks wounded.

At 13.00 a message was received at 19th Infantry Brigade headquarters from the 33rd Division that the enemy were reported to be withdrawing, and the brigade was ordered to continue the advance on Pot de Vin.

The brigade commander and the brigade major went forward to the battalion headquarters of the 5th Scottish Rifles and the officer commanding was ordered to advance on the line Pot de Vin—Ecuelin as advanced guard to the brigade, as soon as the capture of Aulnoye station buildings had been completed. Meanwhile brigade headquarters moved to the vicinity of Aulnoye station, but before the battalion could move the plans were altered.

The weather throughout the 5th and 6th November had been of the worst, with continuous heavy rain, and darkness fell early. In view of this and of the stiffening resistance of the enemy it was finally decided to wait for dawn before continuing the advance.

About this time the 98th and 100th Infantry Brigades began to concentrate at Aulnoye station and Petit Maubeuge respectively.

The prisoners taken during the day amounted to 1 officer and 58 other ranks.

As regards the Divisional Artillery on these last two days: during the night of the 4th/5th the batteries again advanced and were deployed in the squares A.5., A.10., A.11., A.8., and S.26.

Early on the morning of 5th November the batteries of the 156th and 162nd Artillery Brigades pushed forward sections to keep in close touch with the infantry. These moving through Les Grandes Patures took up positions east of Sarbaras, which gave easy command of the crossings and of the ground beyond the Sambre. From these successful observed fire was carried out on enemy movement. Meanwhile the remainder of the batteries endeavoured to get forward, but much delay was caused by congestion on the roads, by craters, felled trees, and finally the execrable weather. During the course of the day the 121st and 122nd Brigades got into positions of readiness near Le Croisil Inn (B.10.). During the night of 5th/6th these two brigades again moved forward and took up positions in and near the village of Sarbaras. The whole divisional artillery was now deployed from Sassegnies northwards covering the river.

During 6th November the artillery was unable to get across owing to lack of bridges and heavy hostile shelling of the crossings, which prevented the construction of more bridges, and the infantry soon got out of supporting distance.

The 162nd Brigade had been ordered to move across the river on the night of 5th/6th, while the other brigades remained to the west of it. But it was not till dawn on the 7th that the batteries could begin crossing. The proper approach had been hopelessly blocked and the batteries had to move down a steep narrow winding track, while on the eastern bank the only route was along a tortuous towing path, and necessitated the cutting of gaps in hedges, and the man-handling of guns across rivulets and swamps.

The 60-pdr. batteries of the 13th Brigade, R.G.A., which was attached to the Divisional Artillery, were got forward during the 5th to B.6. (south of Sarbaras), but the 6″ Howitzers were unable to move on account of the state of the roads. As a matter of fact the 60-pdr. batteries of the 13th and 17th Brigades, R.G.A., were the only part of V Corps Heavy Artillery which it was possible to move forward even to the river Sambre before the Armistice. The remainder stayed in the positions they had occupied for the battle of 4th November. An attempt was made on 8th November to get the 60-pdrs. across the river but it was found to be impossible.

[1]As a result of an effort to get the 60-pdrs. across on 9th

---

[1] War Diary V Corps.

November, the bridge at Sassegnies was completely blocked, and a footbridge had to be repaired to get even infantry and pack animals across.

7th November.

At 21.07 hours on 6th November orders were received from V Corps for the 33rd Division to advance next morning to secure the line Floursies—high ground in W.27. Orders were therefore issued to the following effect :—

(a) The advanced guard consisting of the 19th Infantry Brigade, 11th Field Company R.E., 2 companies 33rd Machine Gun Corps, and "A" Squadron 5th Cyclist Regiment, to move forward at 06.00, capture Pot de Vin and Ecuelin and advance on Floursies and the high ground in W.27.

(b) The 98th and 100 th Infantry Brigades to follow one after the other.

(c) As many batteries as could be got across the river to support the leading troops.

In order to carry out these instructions the 19th Infantry Brigade ordered the Cameronians to advance on Pot de Vin and thereafter on the Avesnes—Maubeuge road. The 5th Scottish Rifles to advance on Ecuelin and clear it of the enemy, after which the 1st Queen's to pass through, take Eclaibes, and then advance to the Maubeuge—Avesnes road.

The weather was fine but there was a thick mist which made it difficult to find the way in a strange country and keep touch with neighbouring troops. The advance progressed rapidly to the line Pot de Vin—Ecuelin. The Cameronians met with some opposition at Pot de Vin, but cleared it and continued through the wood to the east till they were met on emerging from it by strong machine gun fire from Dourlers. After some delay the 4th King's Royal Rifles of the neighbouring division of the Fourth Army came up and cleared Dourlers. The battalion then pushed on along the edge of the wood still meeting with some opposition from machine guns.

On the left things did not quite work out as intended. The 5th Scottish Rifles should have passed through the 1st Queen's who were holding the outpost line. But the latter found that only one company of the Scottish Rifles passed through them and thought that the remainder had lost their direction in the fog. The 1st Queen's therefore themselves advanced to attack Ecuelin. On reaching Ecuelin heavy shell fire was encountered, and small parties of the enemy were met with in the village. These were overcome, but progress was impeded by machine gun fire from the left flank, from Limont Fontaine, and from the edge of the wood. Both battalions were engaged in fighting for the village and for the edge of the wood east of it throughout the morning.

At 10.30 hours the reports received by 33rd Division indicated that the right battalion of the 19th Infantry Brigade (Cameronians) was making good progress, while the other two battalions were held up fighting in Ecuelin. It was therefore decided that the 98th Infantry Brigade should pass through the Cameronians and capture the Maubeuge—Avesnes Road. Here the 100th Brigade was to come up on its left and the two were to capture the line Floursies—high ground in W.27. At 11.30 hours the G.S.O.1. of the division arrived at Pot de Vin where the headquarters of all three infantry brigades had been established and gave them verbal orders confirmed in writing for the operations.

By about the same time the whole of the 162nd Brigade, R.F.A., was got across the river and two of the batteries came into action just west of Pot de Vin at the moment when the infantry were assembling along a sunken road for an attack. The gratitude of the infantry for this close support was very marked, and several infantry officers came up to thank the batteries for their support. All the batteries suffered a number of casualties owing to the enemy shelling of the roads.

Fighting for the wood east of Ecuelin continued throughout the afternoon, and a concerted attack about 15.45 failed owing to the strength of the enemy, but when the operation was repeated at 22.00 hours it was found that the enemy had retired. The fighting while the enemy held his ground was quite severe, and the 5th Scottish Rifles lost 1 officer wounded and 20 other ranks killed, wounded and missing; while the 1st Queen's lost 1 officer and 6 other ranks killed and 4 officers and 52 other ranks wounded and missing.

The Cameronians on the right continued to advance till their objective, the Maubeuge—Avesnes road was reached about dusk, when one company was established on it with the three others in close support. Considerable opposition was encountered at the Maubeuge—Avesnes road, and it was subsequently ascertained from a prisoner, that a fresh regiment had been moved up to hold the line of it. The battalion lost 4 killed and 18 wounded and missing.

The leading battalion of the 98th Infantry Brigade (the 4th King's) passed Pont de Vin at 12.30 with the other two following closely, but it never actually passed through the Cameronians. The position at dusk was that the 33rd Division was on the Maubeuge—Avesnes road, but the enemy still held Belle Hotesse Farm. After dark, troops of the 38th Division arrived and relieved or passed through the 33rd Division with a view to continuing the advance.

On relief the 33rd Division marched back to Petit Maubeuge, Sarbaras and Sassegnies.

We will turn now to the movements of the 38th Division as it came up in relief.

Owing to the great difficulty of supplying the troops caused by the thorough way in which the enemy had destroyed the roads and railways the Third Army had given orders after the battle of the 4th November that supporting divisions should be echeloned as far back as the situation permitted. On 6th November, however, V Corps ordered the 38th Division to close up to a position from which it would be able to pass through the 33rd Division that night. The infantry brigades of the 38th Division had remained in the positions which they had captured in the battle, the 113th and 114th being in the forest with very little cover against the weather and the 115th in Englefontaine. On the 6th, therefore, the 113th was ordered up to Ribaumet and Sarbaras, and the 115th was ordered up to take its place, while the 114th remained partly in bivouacks and partly in billets in Les Grandes Patures.

Owing to the check on the river the 33rd Division was ordered to continue operations on the 7th, and the 38th was therefore ordered not to pass through it till the night of 7th/8th.

The relief of the 33rd Division offered some difficulties, as all that was known about it was that it was somewhere beyond Dourlers and continually pressing on; while there was only one bridge at Berlaimont by which the 38th Division could cross, and that was under shell fire. However, all three infantry brigades were across the river by 16.00 on 7th November.

[1]The 113th Infantry Brigade was ordered to act as advanced guard with two sections of machine guns, and to pass through the leading brigade of 33rd Division at 21.00 under arrangements to be made mutually between the two brigadiers. The 114th Brigade was to follow up the 113th to the Maubeuge—Avesnes road, and was to be followed by the 115th to Pot de Vin.

The advanced guard group was allocated such artillery as was available which consisted of the 162nd Brigade and the 169th Army Field Artillery Brigade. The objective was the line Floursies—wood in W.27.

The 113th Brigade moved forward from Berlaimont at 08.00 crossed the river and halted for the day at Aulnoye. At 15.30 it moved forward again to Pot de Vin. The enemy shelling on the roads was severe and the 13th Royal Welsh Fusiliers suffered 14 casualties besides considerable damage to their transport. Another halt was made at Pot de Vin, after which the 19th Infantry Brigade of the 33rd Division was relieved some little distance short of the main Maubeuge—Avesnes road by 22.00. The 114th Infantry Brigade moved in the morning to Petit Maubeuge, and, leaving its first line transport there, moved on again at 19.00 to Pot de Vin in support. The enemy were said to be still in V.28., 29., and 30. The 14th Welsh were therefore ordered to relieve the Queen's and the 5th Scottish Rifles of the 19th Infantry Brigade in the front line north of Ecuelin to cover the left flank of the division. The 13th and 15th Welsh were instructed to follow up the 113th Infantry Brigade through Dourlers to E.8., west of Floursies, from there they were to attack due north past La Belle Hotesse Farm, and establish a line through W.19. and 20.central. As a matter of fact the 113th Infantry Brigade did not gain sufficient ground to enable this attack to be carried out during the 8th.

The 115th Infantry Brigade marched during the afternoon of the 7th November to billets in Aulnoye, and moved forward again at 05.30 next morning to Pot de Vin.

---

[1] 38th Division Order No. 253.

GERMANS TRYING TO RETAKE A STRONG POINT IN THE WOOD.

Some idea of the movements of the German formations opposed to the 33rd Division between the 5th and 7th November can be pieced together from the histories of such regiments as have published them. From these it is evident that 2nd German Army received orders on the night of 4th/5th November, immediately after the battle, to retire to the Antwerp—Meuse position. As a first step it was ordered to fall back to the Hermann—Stellung III which lay immediately behind the Sambre river. While the direction of advance of the British corps was due east, the line of retirement of the German corps was north east. This brought the LI Corps (Gen. von Bulow) on to the line of advance of the 33rd Division. The greater part of the divisions of this corps crossed the Sambre in the neighbourhood of Landrecies (5 miles south west of Noyelles) and moved north east through the latter place to take up a position from Aulnoye through Leval to Noyelles. The 243rd the 121st and the 204th Divisions were ordered to occupy it from right to left with 1st Guard Reserve Division in support. The movement was covered by the 54th Division as rear guard. The march along the valley across the British front was carried out during 5th November. It could never have taken place if it had not been for the very wet thick weather.

The part of the position which interests us here is the right from Aulnoye to Leval. It was held by the 243rd Division with the 478th Wurtemburg Infantry Regiment on the right from Aymeries southwards along the river. The line was continued from Aulnoye bridge by the 479th Infantry Regiment as far as Merremont Farm C.3.central., from there it was continued by Fusilier Regiment No. 122 on both sides of the Aulnoye—Landrecies railway.

The 479th Regiment state that when they were sure there were no more German troops between them and the enemy they blew up the bridges and sluices at Aulnoye and Berlaimont at 11.40 on 5th November. The 479th Regiment headquarters seem to have been badly let down by their battalions, because the first news they received of the British being on the eastern bank of the river was at 03.00 on 6th November, when they heard that they had crossed on the front of the 122nd Regiment on their left. As a matter of fact the 1st Middlesex of 98th Infantry Brigade had established a bridgehead at the Aulnoye bridge at 19.45 on the 5th and the whole battalion was across by midnight.   The 479th Regiment hearing nothing from their own battalions refused to believe the report of the British being across at 03.00 hours.   At daybreak they received a report that the British were across and had already captured Merremont Farm.   This was the attack of the 100th Infantry Brigade who had crossed just south of the farm near the railway on a cork float bridge at 05.30.   The 2nd Worcesters followed by the Glasgow Highlanders had crossed here, and quickly took Leval and Petit Maubeuge.   The 479th Regiment withdrew its left and took up a position facing south ; but by 08.00 the British appeared in the group of houses north of Aulnoye, and hurried orders were given for the whole regiment to retire by the shortest way in the direction of Bachant.   A position was however taken up along the Bavai—Avesnes road in U.30.   The 479th Regimental Headquarters seem never to have discovered how the British got across the river ; but the truth is told in the history of the 478th Regiment which says that the British suddenly attacked the bridge south of Berlaimont in masses without artillery support and overpowered the weak detachment of the 479th Regiment.

After this the 243rd Division seems to have taken up a position near St.Remy—Mal—Bati with the 54th Division on its left on the Limont Fontaine—Bachant road.   This latter division was attacked here on the 7th and driven back.

The 7th Brandenburg Infantry Regiment No. 60 of the 121st Division speaks of the sudden attack without artillery preparation of the 2nd Worcesters on the 122nd Fusilier Regiment, which taking Leval, turned the flank of the 121st Division who retired to take up a position at Pot de Vin.   They did not wait here long, and finally retired towards the Meuse on the night of 6th/7th.   A little incident reported to the 115th Infantry Brigade next day by the innkeeper at Pot de Vin possibly shows the reason for this. He stated that a German infantry officer of a battalion which was passing the inn shouted some order and his men then began jeering at him.   He drew his revolver, but the men at once covered him with their rifles, and he quickly cleared off.   From this it is evident that many German units were by this time unfit to make a serious resistance.

[1]The final retirement to the Meuse of the divisions in the St. Remy-Mal-Bati position began on the night of the 7th/8th. They had a terrible long night march, several columns marching side-by-side on a bad country road, with troops even on the plough, while railway stations and trains were burning on all sides. On the 9th November the troops heard of the abdication of the Kaiser.[2]

8th November.

The 113th Infantry Brigade after relieving the 19th Infantry Brigade moved forward during the night to the Maubeuge—Avesnes road. The attack on the line of the road was carried out by the 14th Royal Welsh Fusiliers and was launched at 03.15 under a slight bombardment. This was the first objective and was taken easily; but the second objective the road in E.3.c. and a. was not gained till the afternoon owing to the severity of the machine gun fire. The 16th Royal Welsh Fusiliers who were working on the left of the 14th moved to the attack of the road in W.26 at 12.00, and later advanced to the second objective. The battalion lost 3 men killed and 25 men wounded or missing during this small operation. The casualties in the various battalions during these last three days of the fighting show how expensive it is to advance without adequate artillery support in the face of modern weapons, even when the enemy is thoroughly demoralized.

The enemy were found to be holding La Belle Hotesse Farm in strength, and a minor operation by one company of the 13th Royal Welsh Fusiliers was therefore ordered to capture it. The attack was carried out at noon, but on the advance of our troops the enemy fled, and the farm was taken with a loss of 5 wounded. At 21.00 the 13th Royal Welsh Fusiliers passed through the other two battalions, which bivouacked where they lay, and advanced through the woods in W.27. No trace of the enemy could be found and it was evident that he had retired. At 22.30 therefore the 113th Infantry Brigade issued orders for an advanced guard consisting of the 13th Royal Welsh Fusiliers, "C" Squadron Oxford Hussars, which had now been attached, and "A" Company 33rd

---

[1] History of the 90th Reserve Infantry Regiment (54th Division).

[2] For the extracts from German regimental histories the writer is greatly indebted to Lt.-Col. T. Carew Hunt, who has been good enough to translate them.

Machine Gun Battalion, to assemble next morning on the eastern edge of the wood in E.4.b. with a view to pursuing.

As the opposition was no longer formidable, the 114th Infantry Brigade moved into billets in Ecuelin and the 115th Infantry Brigade marched back to Aulnoye. This latter place was a most important junction on the main lateral line of communications of the Germans. The permanent way had been most effectively destroyed by the Germans; and in addition the place shewed remarkable signs of the British aerial bombing. In all directions round the station were craters large enough to take a motor omnibus, and the remains of two ammunition trains which had been blown up were to be seen. The great station yards were full of enormous dumps of briquettes and other forms of compressed coal many acres in extent, which had been set on fire by the enemy, and the battalions of the 115th Infantry Brigade were quickly set to work saving the coal and preventing the fires from spreading.

9th November.

By 07.00 cavalry patrols had reported that Wattignies was clear of the enemy, and the 13th Royal Welsh Fusiliers advanced through it and put out an outpost line along the stream in X.25.central. Cavalry patrols still advancing reported that there was no trace of the enemy in Dimont, Dimechaux and Solrinnes. At 12.30 the 16th Royal Welsh Fusiliers therefore passed through the 13th Royal Welsh Fusiliers and put out outposts in front of Dimechaux, the latter going into billets in Wattignies together with the 14th Royal Welsh Fusiliers.

10th and 11th November.

During the afternoon the 14th Royal Welsh Fusiliers moved into billets at Dimont, but with this exception the units of the 38th Division remained in the same position, while the cavalry and cyclists kept touch with the enemy. At Hestrud on the Belgian frontier they lost touch with him, and the duty of following him up was taken over along the whole Third Army Front by an advanced guard under the G.O.C. VI. Corps.

From the moment that the pursuit began after the battle of 4th

November, the chief obstacle to a rapid advance was the difficulty of supply caused by the thorough manner in which the enemy had destroyed the roads and railways, rather than the action of his fighting troops.

Early on the morning of 11th November, orders were received by the troops that hostilities would cease at 11 a.m. on that day. Defensive precautions were to be maintained and no intercourse was to be held with the enemy. And so the great struggle ended on this part of the front, not amidst the clash of arms, but with the enemy vanished across the frontier. The troops could scarcely be expected to realize at once the meaning of the great event, and the news was received in quiet and weary thankfulness.

CHAPTER VII.

SOME TACTICAL AND OTHER LESSONS.

An attempt has been made in the preceding pages to write a description of the daily doings of a division in the line during the last offensive of the Great War in as great detail as the records which have been preserved permit. This detail allows a study to be made of minor tactics, of methods of command and of the handling of units. It may be of interest if some of the lessons are summarized. It would appear to be self-evident that the tactics and methods of this campaign, the last in which great armies of the first rank have been engaged, are worthy of the closest study. Especially is this the case when it is remembered, that these methods were the result of the experience of four years of the most relentless warfare, which had long since winnowed the wheat from the chaff, and that they led to unqualified success against the greatest and most efficient army which the world has ever seen.

In applying these lessons to the present day or to any possible war which may take place in the near future it is necessary to take note of certain factors. Though no new weapons have been introduced, there has been considerable improvement since the Great War in armoured fighting vehicles, in weapons to counteract them, in aeroplanes and in wireless telegraphy. The chief problem at that time for infantry, artillery or cavalry attempting to move in close proximity to the enemy was how to deal with the hidden machine gun. That problem still remains, and has only been partially dealt with by such advances as have been made in mechanization.

Again as has been shown several times, the German army in the last few months was not what it had been. The resistance offered was of a mixed nature, some units such as Jägers, marksmen machine gun detachments, &c., fought as stubbornly as ever, while others by no means did so. Even so the general efficiency of the German army at that time was probably not inferior to that of any other army in the world, except the British and French.[1] On the other hand the units of the British army had not been trained for open warfare. Infantry battalions were not adepts at making ground under cover of their own weapons. Batteries of artillery frequently took two hours to move their position, and after a move were very slow to get into touch with the forward observing officer. But whether those war worn units were inferior to the units of a large national army at the beginning of a war is more than questionable. Still due weight must be given to these facts.

FIELD ARTILLERY.

In the case of every deliberate attack, and in fact whenever it was possible, a creeping barrage with every available gun was used. In no other way could casualties be kept down or a reasonable rate of advance maintained.

In the battle of October 8th at the Masnieres—Beaurevoir line, the barrage up to the first objective advanced to a depth of 1,800 yards on the 38th Division front. There was then a long pause of something like five hours, during which the field artillery moved, and at the end of it fired the final barrage which had a depth of about 3,500 yards, making 5,300 yards barraged on that day.

On 23rd October when the 33rd Division advanced from the heights above the Selle river towards the Forest of Mormal, the whole of the artillery covered the attack with a creeping barrage up to the second objective a distance of 3,400 yards.

---

[1] A proof of this would appear to be the small headway which the American army could make against the German army during the same period.

On 4th November when the 38th Division attacked through the Forest of Mormal, the whole of the artillery fired a creeping barrage up to the time some of the batteries had to move, and from that time onwards approximately half of the field artillery at a time fired the remainder of the barrage, thus obviating any long pause. The whole of the planned advance, 6,000 yards, was covered by a barrage.

On the other hand the attack of the 33rd Division across the Selle river on 12th October which was to be supported by observed fire alone was a failure. The same attack was repeated by the 38th Division on 20th October under a barrage, after a careful preparation, and was a complete success.

No barrages or time programmes were arranged for the advance on 9th October when the enemy had been driven from his position in the Masnieres—Beaurevoir line or on 23rd October and subsequent days after he had been driven from his position on the heights above the Selle. This was on account of the rapidity of the advance and the difficulty of getting up ammunition

On the 9th October the 33rd Division advanced with the 19th Infantry Brigade leading, on a two battalion front. Four brigades of field artillery were affiliated to the 19th Infantry Brigade, of which the 156th was actually placed under the infantry brigadier's orders. As a matter of fact all five artillery brigades belonging to the 33rd Division followed the 19th Brigade up closely, and came into action when the check occurred at Clary. It is on record that the 121st Bde., R.F.A., was ordered to operate under the orders of the infantry brigadier as well as the 156th, and it seems probable that all the brigades received similar orders. The 156th and 162nd Brigades sent forward advanced sections from some of their batteries; while the 121st and 122nd Brigades moved as brigades though the batteries of the 122nd Brigade were placed under battery control owing to difficulties of communication.

The best system of command in order to obtain the maximum of effect from five brigades of field artillery operating in support of a single infantry brigade offers a nice problem in artillery tactics. It is suggested that one artillery brigade might have been affiliated to each of the leading infantry battalions, and that the remaining three brigades might have worked under the orders of the C.R.A., in close liaison with the infantry brigadier.

On the 23rd October the advance of the 33rd Division commenced under a barrage of all the artillery up to the second objective. On the capture of this the 121st and 122nd Brigades, R.F.A., which were already across the Selle remained covering the further advance, while the 156th and 162nd and 223rd crossed the Selle and moved forward in close support of the infantry. The division was on a two brigade front and the officers commanding the 156th and 162nd Brigades were each placed in close liaison with one of the infantry brigadiers. One 18-pdr. battery and one section of howitzers of the 156th Brigade reported to the 98th Infantry Brigade and were ordered to follow up the leading battalion, which they did all day. The remainder came into action to cover the infantry advance. The 121st and 122nd Brigades moved up during the advance on the 4th objective, and by nightfall all the artillery brigades were again covering the front. The advance was so rapid that the infantry were soon out of range, and little was done by the artillery in the way of co-operation, though they took up successive positions. On 24th October the further advance was covered by heavy bursts of fire from all the available artillery 500 yards in front of the infantry. The artillery followed up the infantry and took up successive positions, but the country was too enclosed for successful observation, and firing could only be carried out on information from the infantry. The advance was finally brought to a stand at the village of Englefontaine, where the opposition was so serious that a properly mounted attack became a necessity. This was prepared, and the much weakened and tired infantry took the village without a hitch under creeping barrages.

On 23rd October the two attacking infantry brigades advanced each on a one battalion front, and it is possible that better co-operation with the artillery might have been effected if an artillery brigade had been affiliated to each leading battalion.

On 24th October the division was on a three battalion front and possibly a brigade or even two batteries might have been affiliated to each front line battalion. When a large force of artillery is available, these operations seem to point to the fact that it would be advantageous to affiliate up to a brigade of artillery to each leading battalion if opportunities are not to be missed. It may only be possible for single batteries to act in close support in very enclosed country like that round Englefontaine; but still it would ensure artillery being close at hand, and in touch with events happening in the front line.

One of the artillery brigade commanders of the 38th Division (Colonel R. C. Williams) has made the following notes of his experiences in this campaign :—

(1). It is an advantage to get one's batteries as far forward as possible, more so in moving warfare than in stationary. It enables closer touch and easier communication to be maintained with one's advanced troops. It enables targets to be engaged outside the range of guns further back or to engage with more deadly effect targets closer in. It has a good moral effect on the infantry. On the other hand, it increases the difficulties of communication to the rear and of ammunition supply. It also tends to increase casualties. But the advantages out-weigh the disadvantages.

(2). To save time it is a good thing to make extensive use of rendezvous to send batteries to during an advance, when the exact destination is vague.

(3). Extensive use should be made of officers' patrols for keeping touch with the advanced troops and with the general situation. The O.C. Brigade should be continually reconnoitring for positions further forward. He should be very chary of moving into action without adequate reconnaissance however insistent the demands of the infantry.

(4). The advantages of direct observation are very great; but it is no use relying on it at a time of day when it will probably be impossible to see. Vide the operations of 10th and 12th October.

As regards O.P's; after the crossing of the Ancre on 25th August an attempt was made to keep four O.P's going, one per battery, one of the four only being manned at night as a Brigade O.P. After a few days a system was instituted of having a joint O.P. for "A" and "D" batteries, and another for "B" and "C", one of these being manned at night as a brigade O.P. On special occasions such as 10th October each battery had an O.P. by day. In the enclosed country east of the Selle a single brigade O.P. alone was used. In such country it is doubtful whether it is worth risking lives at all in an O.P.

(5). The artillery brigade commander should have his H.Q. with or near that of the infantry brigade commander with whom he is working. This is easier said than done as easy communication with one's own batteries and with one's own battalions is the first consideration. Batteries should be kept close together and artillery brigade headquarters close to them if possible. Wagon lines should not be too far from the gun line, but this should not be overdone, and it should be remembered that horses are very vulnerable to aerial bombs. They should therefore be kept clear of well defined places such as roads and railway cuttings.

6

(6). A good method of communication between divisional artillery and artillery brigades is for the former to issue beforehand the location of divisional artillery telephone exchanges along the line of advance. Artillery brigades are then responsible for laying lines to those places.

(7). Water supply for horses was at times a great trouble, and several horses died from want of water.

(8). Ammunition dumping is one of the chief difficulties, owing to harassing fire on the roads and the great number of teams in the forward area at the same time.

(9). Slit trenches between and behind guns, generally dug at night before guns moved into action, were much used and saved many casualties.

HEAVY ARTILLERY.

Not much mention has been made in the narrative of the Vth Corps Heavy Artillery as they were not a divisional organization, and their handiwork was beyond the view of the troops in the line. This does not mean that they did not exercise a most potent effect on the operations with their five brigades of heavy howitzers and guns, and their powerful bombardments and counter-battery work.[1] All the German histories testify to the value of the continual British bombardments in destroying the moral of the German army, and their contribution towards thickening and deepening the creeping barrages was no small one.

The heavy artillery were under the Brigadier-General R.A., V Corps, Brigadier-General R. P. Benson, who exercised command

---

[1] The following order of battle of V Corps Heavy Artillery, taken from the location list of a day late in October, shows what a powerful adjunct the heavy artillery was to the offensive value of the Corps.

22nd Brigade, R.G.A.
2 Batteries 6″ howitzers (10)
1 ,, 9·2″ ,, (3)

54th Brigade, R.G.A.
2 Batteries 6″ howitzers (6)
2 ,, 8″ ,, (8)

13th Brigade, R.G.A.
1 Battery 60-pounders (5)
2 Batteries 6″ howitzers (8)

17th Brigade, R.G.A.
1 Battery 60-pounders (3)
2 Batteries 6″ howitzers (5)
1 ,, 9·2″ ,, (4)

58th Army Brigade, R.G.A.
1 Battery 6″ guns (2)
1 ,, 12″ howitzers (2)

Affiliated to Right Division of Corps.

Affiliated to Left Division of Corps.

Resting.

1 Battery 6″ howitzers   22nd Brigade, R.G.A.
1 ,, ,, ,,   54th ,, ,,
1 ,, 60-pounders   13th ,, ,,
1 ,, ,,   17th ,, ,,

through the commander of the heavy artillery, Brigadier-General A. M. Tyler and the Counter-battery Staff Officer Colonel J. Waring. One brigade containing 60-pdrs. and 6″ howitzers was affiliated to each of the two divisions in the line, and the remainder were distributed between bombardment and counter-battery work as the situation demanded. For instance on 23rd October for the advance from the Selle river twelve 6″ howitzers from each of the 54th and 22nd Brigades, R.G.A., were given a bombardment and barrage programme by V Corps, Heavy Artillery, the 21st and 33rd Divisions gave orders to the 6″ howitzers and 60-pdrs. of the 17th and 13th Brigades, R.G.A., and the remainder (the heavier howitzers and guns) were placed at the disposal of the Counter-Battery Staff Officer, V Corps.

The barrages were usually put down by 6″ and 8″ howitzers and started some 500 yards in rear of the German front line; as far as possible there were four 6″or 8″ howitzers to each 500 yards of front. For the bombardment programme road cuttings, fences, and other points likely to conceal guns were selected from air photographs by the Brigadier-General R.A., and a section of 6″ howitzers placed on each of these, shifting their objectives to further points as the infantry advanced.

The 9·2″ howitzers took a long time to dismantle and get back into action and were therefore less in the picture during this class of warfare than the others.

Colonel J. Waring, has given the following notes on the counter-battery work during this period :—

"The system employed as regards counter-battery and bombardment work by the V Corps H.A. was as follows. No definite brigades or batteries were told off permanently for either branch, each phase was dealt with on its merits and the best use made of the available guns, in close cooperation between the counter-battery and H.A. Staffs. The method had both advantages and disadvantages. At times it meant a very great increase of guns for any particular work in hand at the moment. Again there were times when it caused a certain amount of friction and necessitated a good deal of personal insistance to obtain the use of guns to deal with the number of known or suspected hostile batteries, and usually entailed a modification of the bombardment programmes originally laid down in Corps R.A. Instructions. But for this strong insistance and the good relations which existed between the various staffs, the counter-battery work might well have suffered. It is this reason which led many corps to the definite allotment of certain guns solely to counter-battery work. But on the whole the V Corps system justified itself.

In each operation the allotment of guns, as shown in the operation orders, was only applicable to the initial bombardment phase, and the C.B.S.O. always had the call on all guns not otherwise engaged. Consequently the number of guns available was far in excess of anything suggested by reading R.A. Instructions.

From the time we crossed the Ancre (21st August) the rigidity of control of counter-battery work of necessity broke down, and I had to decentralize, taking complete control again only for short periods when things became static, and complete communications had been established. Our main source of information, the sound rangers, never really came into working order again after the Ancre, although they were just established on the Selle. They were not provided with the transport necessary to compete with a quick move.

The Observation Group of the Field Survey was self contained in this respect, and with a little assistance from one of the H.A. Brigades, owing to the great energy of the officer in charge, Lt. Lysons, was able to keep up with the rate of advance and always had a couple of stations in action in any pause. This group was attached to the 17th Brigade, R.G.A., on the left of the corps front and gave its information to the brigade who passed it on.

During periods of movement the method adopted was to allot the front roughly to whatever H.A. Brigades were in action in zones with a slight overlap for counter-battery purposes. I and my staff went round by car and horse, collecting and disseminating such information as came to hand from various sources, leaving the actual action in the hands of brigade commanders.

In each brigade one or more batteries were told off to work with the Royal Flying Corps on what we then called the M.Q.N.F. system, i.e., the Airman had a definite battery to call on in various zones; but the selection of the target was left in his hands. Much good work was done in this way.

Set piece programmes in support of definite operations became more difficult as the advance continued, and locations became less definite. I had to do a good deal of guess work, and treat suspicious areas in which there were indications from the various sources, i.e., planes, air-photos, flash spotters, R.A. O.P's, which with an intelligent comparison with the map gave pretty fair evidence of hostile battery localities. The same sort of method was applied to machine gun areas for treatment by H.A. bombardment. In the final stage at the Forest de Mormal this was almost all we had to go on.

At each halt when things stabilized, I endeavoured so far as communications would allow to re-assume central control of counter-battery work, for deliberate destructive shoots and concentrations on identified locations; but found it advisable to leave full freedom for neutralization in the hands of brigade commanders.

My last attempt at a deliberate destructive shoot is of interest. It was at Englefontaine after our front had been swung round directly facing the forest, and we were very short of information, when we got an air photo shewing, in a clearing near Locquignol, close to where we had been given a flash by an airman, what looked like the trench warfare type of eight-inch howitzer position with heavily built pits. I called up our Squadron Commander and told him I wanted to deal with this with a 9·2″ howitzer battery. He was delighted and said he would do the job himself, and so he did with excellent result. We expended some 100 odd rounds of 9·2″ and obtained direct hits on all four pits. Immediately our advance was resumed I made straight for this location to see how facts compared with reports. Found the place and found the reports of the shooting fully justified, and not a bit exaggerated. However, instead of having smashed up a German 8″ howitzer battery, we had only very thoroughly untidied four fine stacks of timber, which apparently had never had a gun near them. Hence our war debts!

At every phase of temporary static conditions throughout the advance, I got help in concentrations and area shoots from the divisional artilleries, and almost nightly the 4·5″ howitzers poured out gas for me on the enemy battery areas. How they managed to do it, and fight their battles during the day is a marvel.

To sum up. During trench warfare the chief and best source of counter-battery information was the sound-ranging section, whose locations almost invariably were confirmed on photos, giving us absolutely certain targets. Second in merit and accuracy the observation group (Flash spotters). Third most prolific but not very accurate, air observers. Their results till confirmed or corrected from photos could not be relied on. However, when they caught a battery active and could deal with it straight away, by say the M.Q.N.F. method, without having to reduce it to accurate map coordinates they were very good. Also their observations were invaluable for indicating areas of activity.

As the advance went on deliberate methods decreased, and area shoots and concentrations on suspicious localities had to be more and more resorted to, with frequently excellent results as proved by reconnaissance after our further advance''.

GENERAL.

Two great broad facts stand out from a study of these operations.

(1). The amazing staying power, courage and determination of the British soldier, without which nothing else would have been of any avail. The marvellous way in which the men went into battle day after day calls forth the most profound admiration. They faced danger and death with no other thought than to see the task through to which they had put their hands.

(2). The smoothness with which the machinery of that mighty engine, the British army from the front line to the sea, worked at the end of the war. Generally speaking this was due to the efficiency, practical nature and administrative ability of the British race, never so clearly shown as in a great emergency. Actually in the field it was chiefly due to the excellent co-operation of all arms. Contrary to the ideas of some popular writers the staff work had been brought to a very high pitch, fully equal if not superior to that of any other army. British commonsense coupled with long experience had evolved methods suitable to the type of warfare, which had become almost stereotyped. Everyone therefore knew pretty well what was expected of them, the extreme value of co-operation was well understood, and the chief desire of all arms was to work closely with their fellows. This co-operation grows more important as each new war adds fresh inventions and weapons.

The number of tanks available on the Third Army front was small, and, though their intervention had great effect wherever they were employed, the chief responsibility for helping forward the infantry fell on the artillery. Its value as an offensive weapon was demonstrated in every action and without it the infantry could never have made the progress which they did. It is not too much to say that unless an army can be furnished with artillery and ammunition on something like the scale used in these operations, it will only lead to disappointment and disaster to engage in war with a first class power. The difficulty of providing this, especially the ammunition at the beginning of a war is self-evident. But if quick results are desired the effort will have to be made. No doubt numerous and efficient tanks can to some extent take the place of artillery, but it is a hazardous thing to trust too much to so vulnerable an arm.

Attention has been drawn to the enormous importance of the most careful and meticulous reconnaissance of the enemy's position before an attack however slightly the position may have been prepared. The less artillery there is to support the attack the more careful should the reconnaissance be, as there is less chance of every machine gun being dealt with by the barrage. Even with a powerful barrage suspicious places require special attention. This lesson was brought home throughout the war; but the succession of attacks on the Selle are a very good illustration of the great value of careful preparation, even against a hastily prepared position. It is in this question of preliminary reconnaissance that manœuvres fall short of the reality.

There was a good deal of talk of advanced guards, but in point of fact whenever there was serious opposition the army advanced in a continuous line with great depth behind it—in very much the same formation as that in which it held the line. The enemy was never sufficiently distant to form the conventional advanced guard along a road. When possible an advanced guard of a single brigade on the front of a division manœuvred in fighting formation, but it was always on a concerted plan with other divisions operating on the flanks.

The "leap-frog" method of attack was employed on every occasion, and its success amply justified it. This really means that in a deliberate attack every unit is given a definite task in the original plan. The commander of a rear unit knows what is expected of him, and if the unit in front fails to carry out its task, he is on the spot to assist it in getting through and as soon as this is accomplished he is in a position to go on and carry out his own task. If on the other hand the reserve unit is being held ready to act according to circumstances, under the orders of the brigade commander, it is almost certain that delay will occur while information is being sent back, and the opportunity will be missed. A very good instance of this occurred at the attack on Villers-Outreaux on 8th October. The 17th Royal Welsh Fusiliers were held up on the wire of the Masnieres—Beaurevoir line during their night attack. At dawn the 2nd Royal Welsh Fusiliers arrived to mop up the village with the aid of Tanks. The officer commanding saw what had happened, and when the tanks arrived a few minutes later and advanced into the wire, he was able to take immediate advantage of it, capture the German position and then go on to carry out his own task. If he had had to wait till orders arrived from the brigade it is quite certain that the opportunity would have been missed, and the Tanks would have cruised fruitlessly about the German position. At the best, hours would have been taken before the Tanks could be recalled and a concerted attack arranged. In the later battles allowance was often made for failure, and units in rear were ordered to assist those in front of them in carrying out their task, if they had failed, before carrying out their own. Another aspect of the leap-frog system is, that it is the most effective method which has yet been discovered of preserving the momentum of the attack.

As regards zero hour surprise is almost impossible in daytime except in bad weather, on account of aeroplanes. The choice is therefore between "dawn" and "night" attacks. For very large forces night attacks are to be avoided, especially as tanks find it difficult to operate at night. The weight of the advantage is therefore in favour of dawn attacks, and this outweighs the advantage of being able to vary the hour of attack. The best time is an hour before dawn. Infantry then form up unobserved, and shortly after the attack starts they are able to see well. This question of forming up is an important one in open country without trenches, when the enemy possesses a powerful artillery. A large part of the casualties occurred before the attack in most of these battles, and troops less inured to heavy shelling and losses would probably not have been got forward to the attack at all.

Finally these operations show vividly the great value of relentless and methodical hammering on a shaken enemy. The losses of a defeated army in retreat are greater than those of the attacker. Attempts have been made to prove that the German army was not defeated and that the Armistice was brought about by the revolution in Germany. This did not occur till 8th November when the army was in full retreat. No one who had the good fortune to see the closing days of the war can ever doubt that the German army was utterly and absolutely defeated, and that few who were in the field on the beaten side will ever wish to go to war again.

MAP 2.

Issued with the "Journal of the Royal Artillery," Vol. LVIII.   No. 3.

REFERENCE.

Enemy Trenches {
Any trench apparently organised for fire - - -
Other Trenches - - -
(Important ones are shown by thick line. Old or disused by dotted line).

British Trenches - - - -

Wire Entanglement or Other Obstacle

Enemy's Tracks

Buried Pipeline or Cable

Airline - - - -

Supply Dumps	Gun Emplacements	Observation Posts
Ammunition „	Machine Gun „	Listening Posts
Earthworks „	Trench Mortar „	Mine Craters
Dug-outs	A.-A. Gun „	„ Fortified
Huts		Organised Shell Holes

Works reinforced by concrete

Hedge, Fence or Ditch - - -
Ditch with Permanent Water - -

Church   Wind Mill.   Any trig. point.

Conspicuous Points - - -
(Position of point is centre of circle. Dot shows that point is trigonometrically fixed).

Houses - - -   Standing.   Ruined   Shrine +

Railways {
Permanent {
Normal Gauge, Double -
„   „   Single -
Light - -
Temporary {
Trench Tramways
Metre Gauge Railways

NOTE.—The fact that an obstacle is not represented on the map does not necessarily mean that there is none there. It is often impossible to distinguish obstacles or to identify their character. It may be assumed that there are obstacles in front of all fire trenches (shown by thick line).

PROVISIONAL SIGNS.

Blockhouse or Mebu.

Pit dug, not covered - - -	☐
Covered - - - -	☒
Occupied by M.G. - - -	☒▸
Concrete indicated by the letter -	c
Dug-outs - - -	
Known entrances and assumed position shown - -	

INSTRUCTIONS AS TO THE USE OF THE SQUARES.

1. The large rectangles on the map, lettered M, N, O, etc., are divided into squares of 1,000 yards side, which are numbered 1, 2, 3, etc. Each of these squares is sub-divided into four minor squares of 500 yards side. These minor squares are considered as lettered a, b, c, d. (See Square No. 6 in each rectangle).

A point may thus be described as lying within Square B.6, M.5.b, etc.

2. To locate a point within a small square, consider the sides divided into tenths, and define the point by taking so many tenths from W. to E. along Southern side, and so many from S. to N. along Western side; the S.W. corner always being taken as origin, and the distance along the Southern side being always given by the first figure. Thus the point Z would be 63: i.e. 6 divisions East and 3 divisions North from origin.

3. When more accurate definition is wanted (on the 1:20,000 or 1:10,000 scales) use exactly the same method, but divide sides into 100 parts and use four figures instead of two. Thus 0847 denotes 08 parts East and 47 parts North of origin (see point X). Point Y is 6503.

4. Use 0 but not 10; use either two or four figures; do not use fractions (8½, 4¼, etc).

CONTOUR INTERVAL 5 METRES.

The following are the co-ordinates of places mentioned in the text which are indistinguishable on the map:—

AUBENCHEUL	...	{ S.18.b and d. T.13.a and c.
MORTHO WOOD	...	T.1 and 7.
BONABUS FARM	...	S.11.b.
ANGLES CHATEAU	...	{ N.32.d. T.2.b.
ANGLES ORCHARD	...	T.8.a.
MILL WOOD	...	N.30.c.
VILLERS FARM	...	T.20.b.
DEHERIES	...	N.36.d.
ARDISSART FARM	...	N.26.d.
ARDISSART COPSE	...	N.26.b.
MONTECOUVEZ FARM	...	N.31.c.
BONNE ENFANCE FARM	...	M.30.a and b.
HURTEBISE FARM	...	N.20.b.

[To face page 374.

Yards 1000   5 00   0   1000

Metres 1000   500   0   10

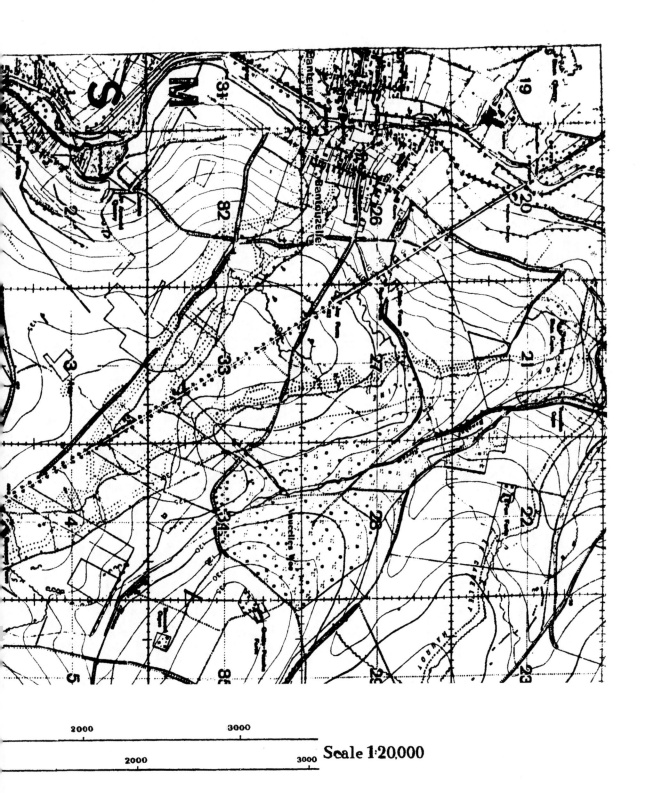

Scale 1:20,000

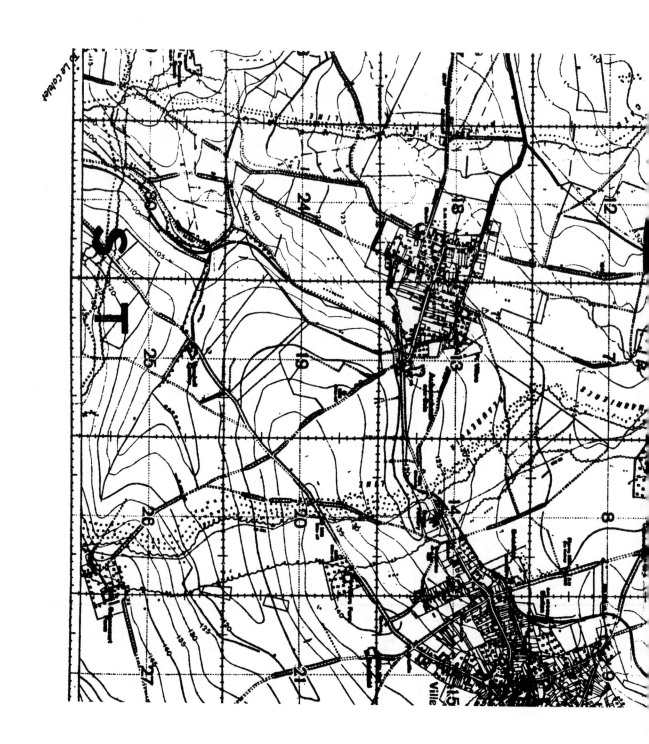

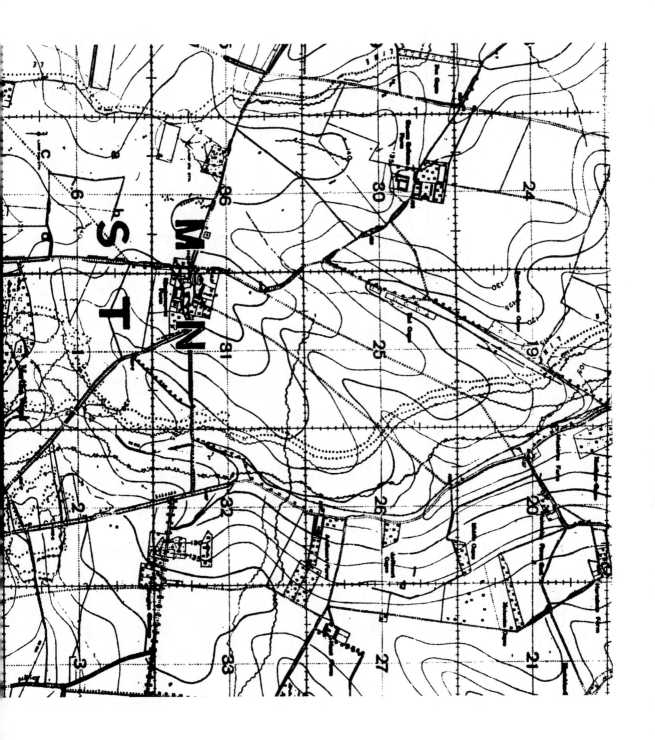

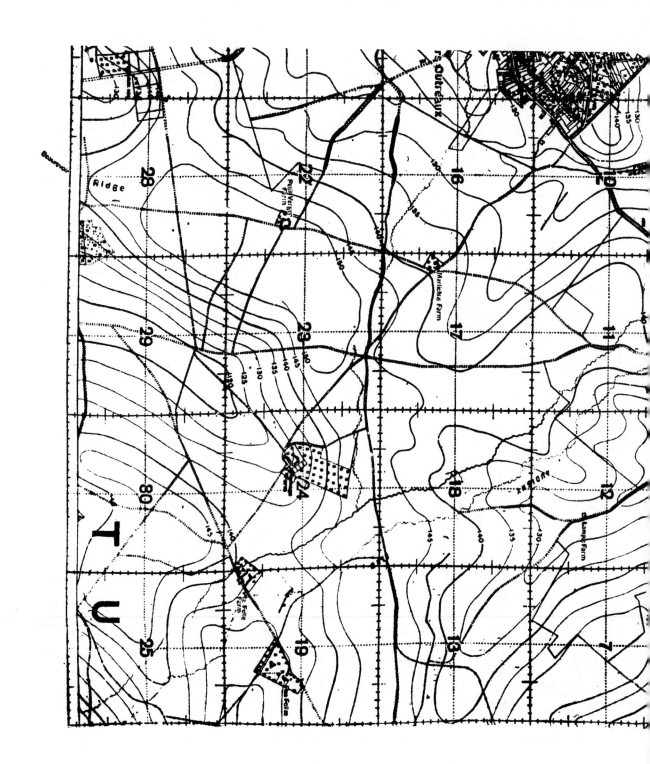

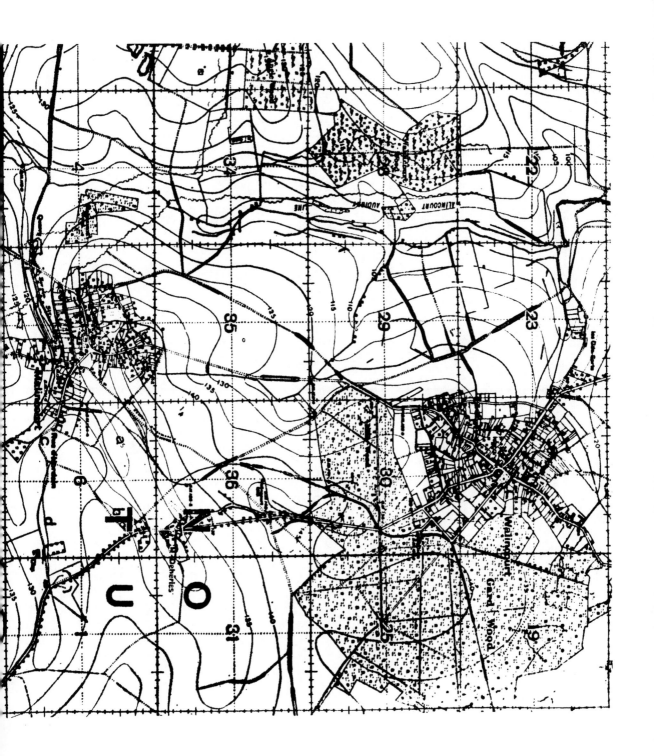

MAP III.

Issued with the "Journal of the Royal Artillery" Vol. LVIII. No. 4.

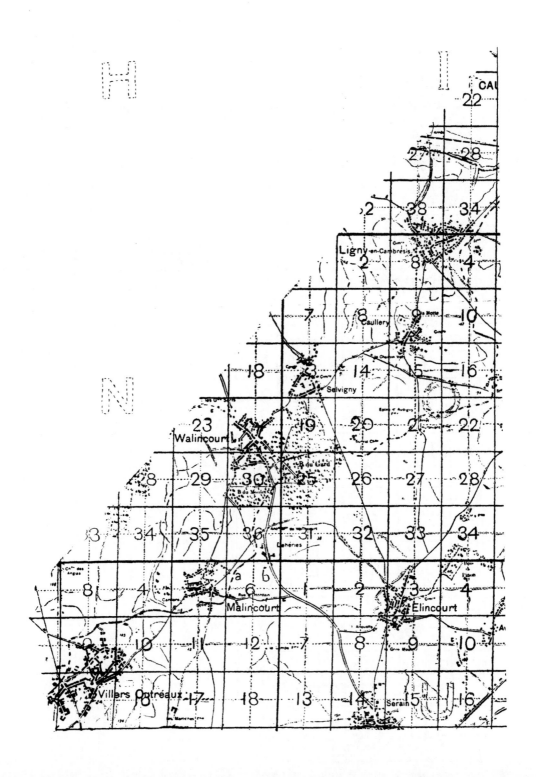

Selle River

a b
6
c d

12   7   8   9   10   11   12

Pt Caudry
13   14   15   16   17   18   13

Beaumont
JDRY   Inchy
23   24   19   20   21   23   24   19
Audencourt

29   30   25   26   27   28   29   30   25

Troisvilles
35   36   31   32   33   34   35   36   81

Tronquoy   le Fayt   Arbre
a   b
5   6   1   2   3   4   5   6   1
c   d

Montigny
11   12   7   8   9   10   11   12   7
Bertry

Reumont
18   18   14   15   16   18   13

Maurois
Clary
8   24   19   20   21   22   23   24   9

Honnechy
29   30   25   26   27   28   29   30   2F

35   36   8   82   83   84   35

a   b
5   6   1   2   3   4
Maretz

11   12   8   9

17   18   13   14

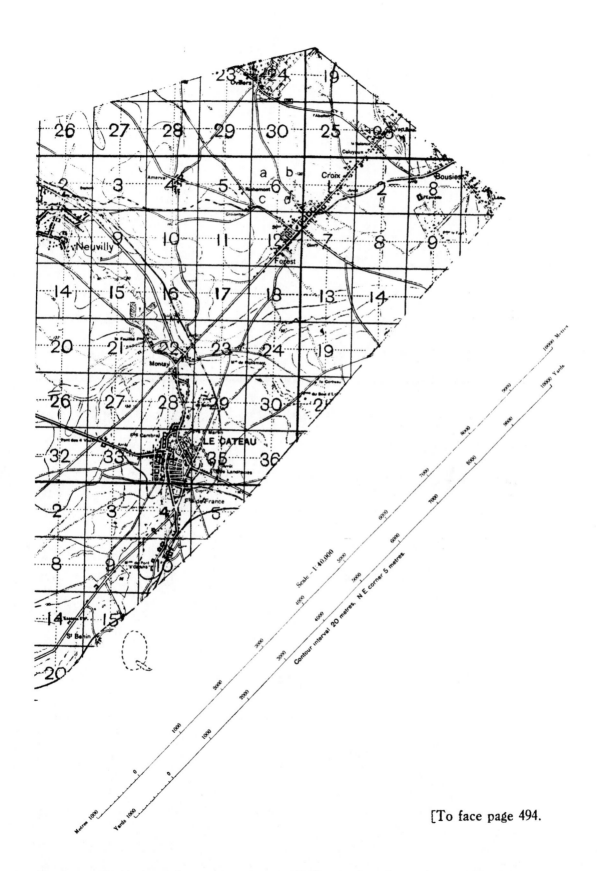

Scale ~ 1:40,000

Contour interval 20 metres, N E corner 5 metres.

[To face page 494.

MAP V.

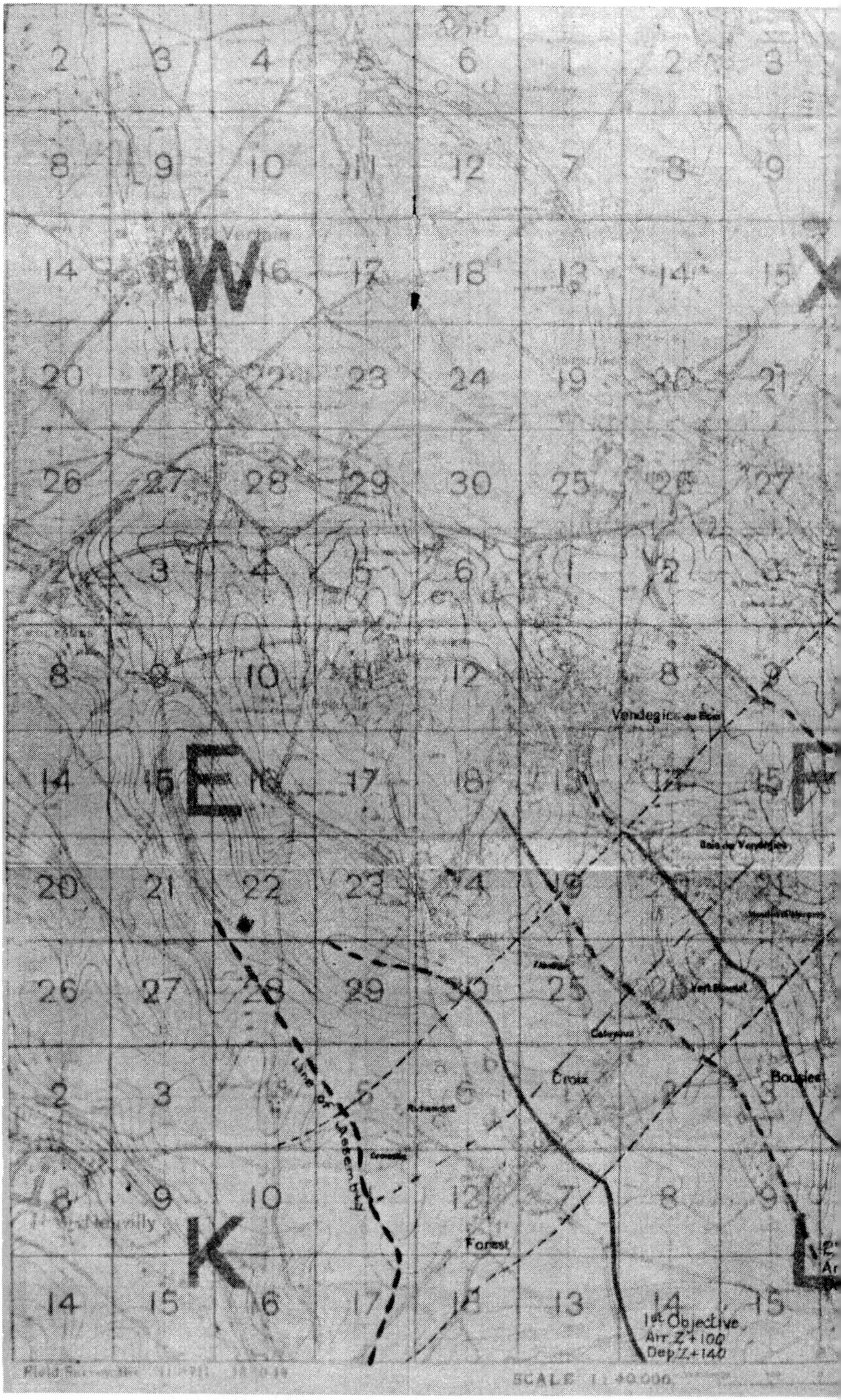
W
X
E
F
K
L
Vendegies-au-Bois
Croix
Bousies
Forest
Line of Assembly
1st Objective
Arr. Z+100
Dep. Z+140
SCALE 1:40,000

[To face page 68.

MAP VI.

Issued with the "Journal of the Royal Artillery", Vol. LIX.   No. 2.

(It is to be noted that this map is made up from four French maps which do not quite coincide).

[To face page 196.

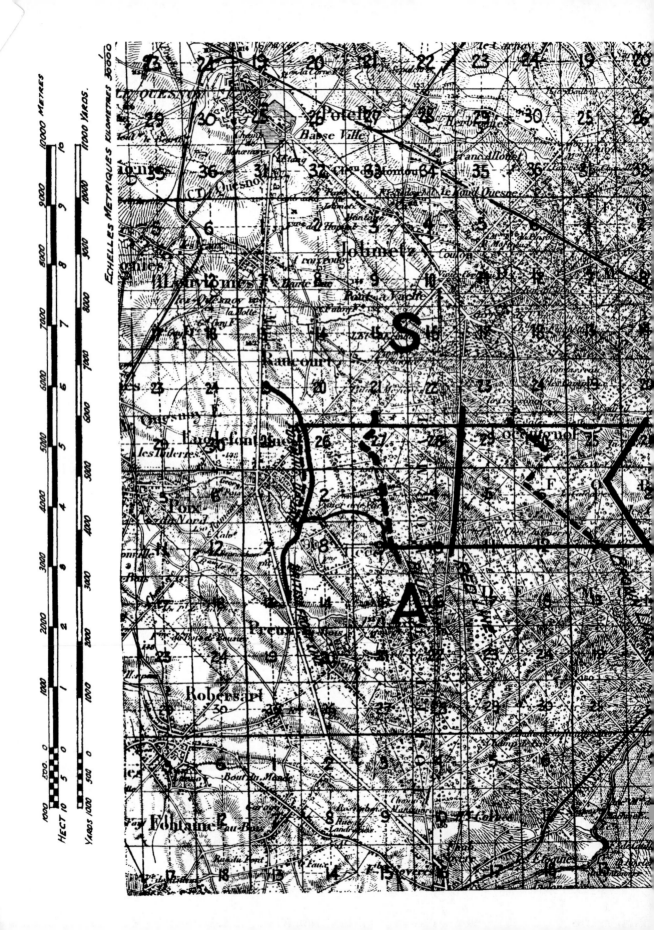

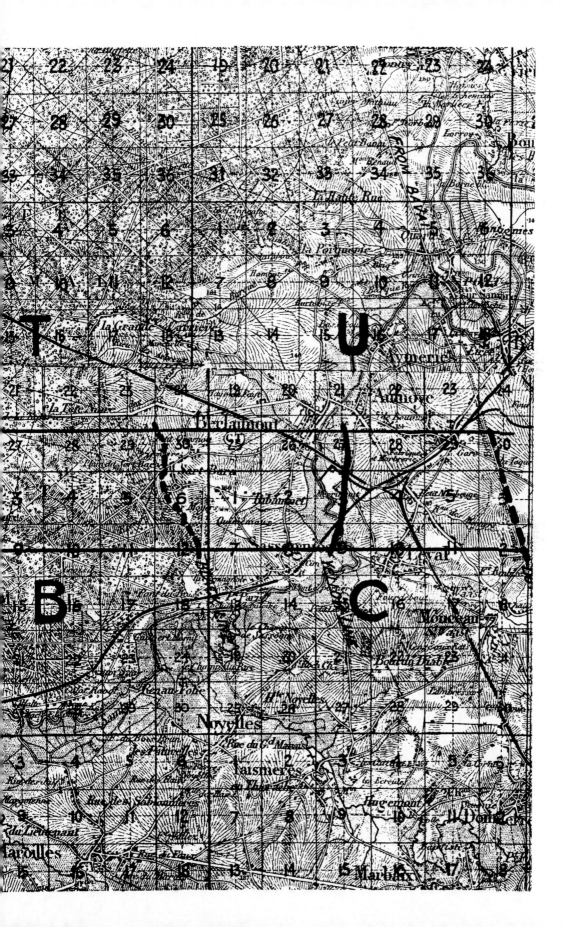

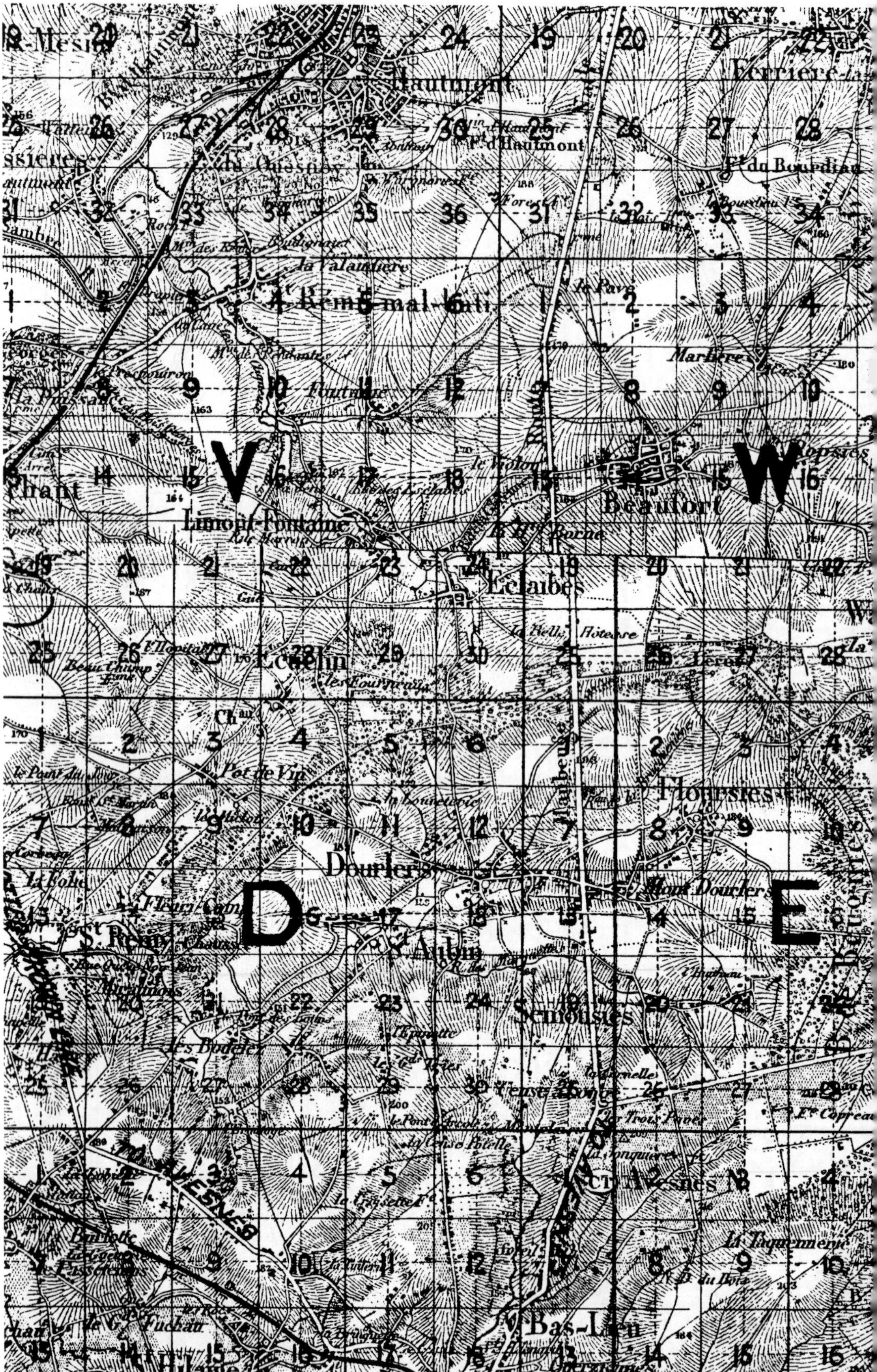

Hautmont
F.t d'Hautmont
Ferrière
Beaufort
Limont-Fontaine
Eclaibes
Ecuélin
Pot de Vin
Floursies
Dourlers
Mont Dourlers
S.t Aubin
S.t Remy Chaussée
Semousies
Bas-Lieu
V
W
D
E

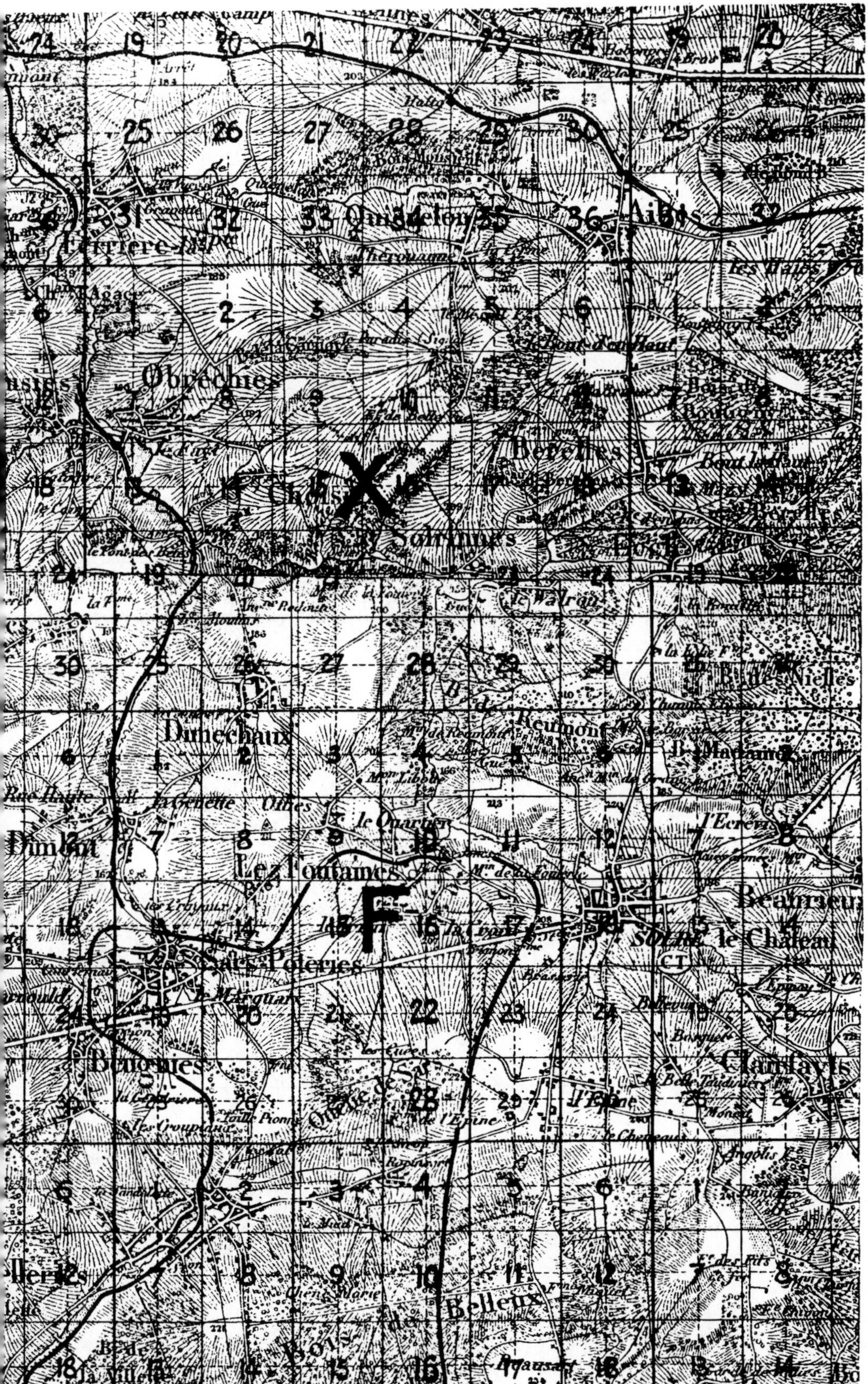
Obrechies
Berelles
X
Dimechaux
Lez Fontaines
F
Sars Poteries
Beugnies
Belleux
le Château
Clairfayts
Aibes
Thérouanne
le Quartier
B. des Nielles

Issued with the "Journal of the Royal Artillery", Vol. LIX. No. 2.

[To face page 196.

MAP VII.

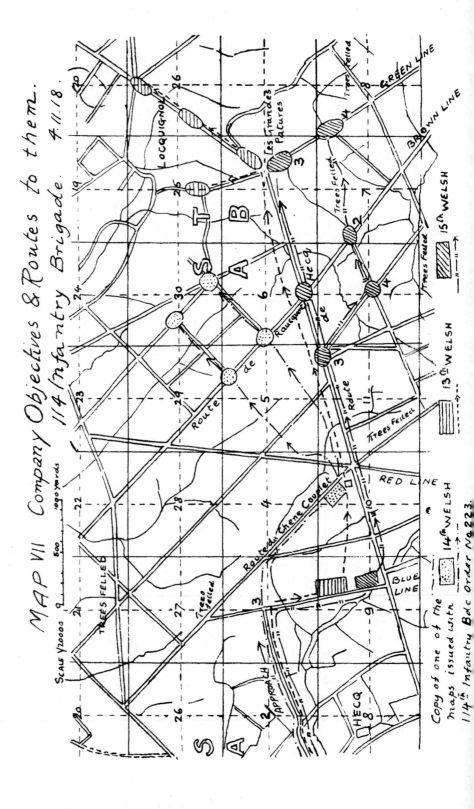

MAP VII. Company Objectives & Routes to them.
114 Infantry Brigade. 4.11.18.